Stained Glass Ceilings

Stained Glass Ceilings

*How Evangelicals Do Gender
and Practice Power*

LISA WEAVER SWARTZ

RUTGERS UNIVERSITY PRESS
NEW BRUNSWICK, CAMDEN, AND NEWARK,
NEW JERSEY, AND LONDON

Library of Congress Cataloging-in-Publication Data

Names: Weaver Swartz, Lisa, author.
Title: Stained glass ceilings : how evangelicals do gender and practice
    power / Lisa Weaver Swartz.
Description: New Brunswick : Rutgers University Press, [2023] | Includes
    bibliographical references and index.
Identifiers: LCCN 2022005278 | ISBN 9781978819993 (paperback) |
    ISBN 9781978820005 (cloth) | ISBN 9781978820012 (epub) |
    ISBN 9781978820036 (pdf)
Subjects: LCSH: Southern Baptist Theological Seminary. | Asbury Theological
    Seminary. | Evangelicalism—United States. | Christian leadership. |
    Leadership—Religious aspects—Christianity. | Sex role—Religious aspects—
    Christianity.
Classification: LCC BR1642.U5 W425 2023 | DDC 261.8—dc23/eng/20220622
LC record available at https://lccn.loc.gov/2022005278

A British Cataloging-in-Publication record for this book is available from the British Library.

References to internet websites (URLs) were accurate at the time of writing. Neither the author nor Rutgers University Press is responsible for URLs that may have expired or changed since the manuscript was prepared.

♾ The paper used in this publication meets the requirements of the American National Standard for Information Sciences—Permanence of Paper for Printed Library Materials, ANSI Z39.48-1992.

www.rutgersuniversitypress.org

Manufactured in the United States of America

For my children. May you each nurture your own prophetic imaginations grounded in faith and sustained in community.

Contents

Stained Glass Ceilings

Introduction

When I arrived in the lobby of the Galt House Hotel in Louisville, Kentucky, I knew immediately that I was in the right place. Men wearing neatly pressed khaki pants stood in small groups talking casually. Many held leather-bound Bibles. Some were accompanied by their wives. Upstairs in a spacious ballroom, two large screens proclaimed, "A BRAVE NEW MOVEMENT: Gospel. Gender. Flourishing," the theme for this year's gathering of the Council on Biblical Manhood and Womanhood (CBMW). I found a seat near the center of the room and watched as the chairs around me slowly filled. By the time CBMW president Owen Strachan, a professor at Southern Baptist Theological Seminary, offered a hearty welcome, the room crackled with energy.[1] A video promotion—titled "The Gospel Project"—followed, featuring an energetic bearded man who exulted in "what God is doing in Christ" through this "grand narrative," this "one story."

The series of TED Talk–style presentations that followed infused the Christian story with gendered significance. Titles included "The Beauty of Differences—on Heaven and on Earth," "Renewing Men: The Gospel Call," and "Renewing Women: The Gospel Call." In keeping with CBMW's belief that only men should teach mixed audiences, even the "Renewing Women" session was taught by a man: CBMW patriarch John Piper. His talk detailed ways in which the differences between men's and women's natures might influence their propensity to sin. Depravity, he instructed, "is given form by nature." While men, according to Piper, can become "ugly, violent, cruel," women can become "manipulative, scheming, doting. Or even more dramatically, depravity may so distort male and female nature as if to exchange the one for the other." The audience listened attentively. Many took notes.

During a break in the program, I heard an eruption of feminine laughter behind me. A small group of women of various ages exchanged warm hugs. One carried a tote bag embellished with the words "True Woman." Though men filled

all of the conference's speaking slots and also composed the majority of attend-
ees, these women did not appear at all troubled by their minority status. Instead,
they formed their own small community in the back of the crowded room. As
I passed the group, I overheard one of them, a woman who appeared to be in
her mid-forties, express sympathy borne from experience for a younger woman
feeling the sickness of early pregnancy. She encouraged her young friend, "But
you look great! Beautiful!" And she did. The expectant mother, like many of the
other young women in the room, dressed stylishly, her trendy striped dress and
burgundy leggings accented by large, dark-framed glasses and long hair, curled
in a classically feminine style.

The conference reconvened with a talk titled "Men and Missions: The Miss-
ing Link." The speaker lamented what he considered to be a crisis in evangelical
mission work: not enough men were stepping up to be missionaries, especially
compared to women. He told the audience that the Southern Baptist Journeymen, a two-year program for young adults, consisted of three times as many
"Journey Girls" as Journeymen. Instead of interpreting this imbalance as a strong
response on the part of women, he mourned men's lack of attention to the mis-
sional call. He also predicted several fallouts. "We're communicating to the
nations that Christianity is a feminized religion," he began, "and men need not
apply." He also noted that in Muslim contexts, women cannot witness to men.
"We're condemning men all around the world to a hell for all eternity without
even a gospel witness," he lamented. His presentation made no further mention
of the 338 "Journey Girls" or the multitude of other Southern Baptist women in
the denomination's rich history of foreign mission work. He concluded, "If
men are not there, then they are not going to hear the gospel."

In the final session, CBMW's conference deviated from its decisively masculine cast. Owen Strachan returned to the stage to introduce a panel of six women.
Hearing from them, he promised, would be an "exciting privilege" for the audience. Complementarianism, he stressed, "is for men *and* women." In case there
was any confusion about the nature of their presentation, long tables draped with
dark fabric replaced the pulpit, and the women situated themselves in chairs
behind them. One of these women, the wife of CBMW's executive director, a man
who was also employed by Southern Seminary's student life office, moderated.
She spoke in a soft southern accent as she introduced each of the other five women
in turn as "a wife and a mom," followed by their other relevant credentials. Each
woman then briefly explained how she tried to live out biblical womanhood. One
described changes in her devotional life as she transitioned from being a wife to
a mother to then a grandmother. Another offered advice for young mothers
desiring to be involved in ministry while still keeping "home their main priority." As the panel ended and the conference concluded, Strachan returned to the
stage to deliver an impassioned plea to spread CBMW's message. To those
struggling with homosexual desire, to those wounded by a fatherless childhood,

to those seeking to change their gender, CBMW offered an all-encompassing solution: the gospel. "If not our gender and sexuality," he asked, "what is the gospel for?"

This gathering's complementarian narration of gender has become deeply influential throughout American evangelicalism. Fused with Reformed theology and cultural embattlement, its language is codified in systematic theology books and institutional statements, promoted by celebrity pastors and their Twitter feeds, and consumed by millions of American evangelicals. Southern Baptist Theological Seminary, located just minutes from Louisville's Galt House Hotel, was both an important consumer and institutional driver of the event.[2] From its campus, which housed CBMW offices and supplied many of the gathering's key actors, the seminary vigorously promotes complementarian ideals of gender differentiation and male headship.[3] In alignment with these prescriptions, only men fill Southern's pulpits, hold theological teaching positions, and enroll in classes on preaching and pastoral ministry. True believers insist that this arrangement, rightly practiced, is the best way to achieve the flourishing that God intends for all humans—both men and women.

––––––

Just over one hour's drive from Louisville, heading east through the rolling hills of Kentucky's bluegrass, Asbury Theological Seminary narrates a very different gendered evangelical story. One typical morning on campus, Rev. Jessica LaGrone, dean of the chapel, assumed her place behind the pulpit with the graceful authority of a pastor shepherding her flock. As was typical for a Wednesday chapel service, the pulpit in Estes Chapel was lowered from its regular position on the stage to the floor just to the right of the platform. The wooden altar, emblazoned with the words, "This Do in Remembrance of Me" and draped with purple vestments indicating the season of Lent, became the focal point. Baskets of bread sat on top. LaGrone's sermon text drew from the biblical story of Jesus feeding the five thousand with five loaves of bread and two fish. In it, she described a beautiful fifth-century mosaic floor in the Byzantine Church of the Multiplication. As she explained the mosaic's depiction of the biblical story, the congregation of students and faculty viewed its image on a screen lowered from the ceiling. The section of the mosaic directly in front of the altar, LaGrone explained, includes a curious feature. There are only four loaves of bread, not five. "Did [the artist] make a mistake?" she asked her audience. The answer, of course, was no. The artist had intentionally positioned the four tiled loaves directly in front of the stone altar from which elements of the Eucharist are still served. "The loaf on the altar itself was the loaf you would break for communion that day. . . . So whenever anyone in front of this altar lifted and blessed and broke the bread, the miracle was still happening. When did the bread run out? It still hasn't. It is being passed today between God's people."

As the sermon drew to a close, LaGrone moved seamlessly from a discursive narrative to an embodied one. Leaving the pulpit, she took her place behind the altar and began the extensive liturgy that always frames the Eucharist at Asbury. "The Lord be with you," she began. "And also with you," the congregation heartily responded. The ceremony that followed was not a thoughtless ritual, tacked onto the end of the service. It was a rich, living enactment of Asbury's collective life. After LaGrone's litany, a team of students—both women and men—rose from the pews to offer bread and juice and prayer. They stationed themselves throughout the sanctuary as the rest of the congregants moved in contemplative lines that led from wooden pews toward the altar. Each person received the elements from a server and physically consumed them before returning to their seats. The chapel resembled a living organism as people moved together in a perfectly choreographed motion to physically participate in the story of Jesus's provision. Just as Jesus provided for all, all were welcomed to the table. Each member—men, women, Americans, Asians, Africans, old and young—was an active participant. All came to the table. All held physical bread in their hands and actively dipped it into a chalice. All had access to Christ's love and forgiveness. The egalitarian imagery of Asbury's Eucharistic celebration was striking. Those who served symbolized equality. Those who partook experienced it. Its message was this: in the house of God and for the people of God, gender does not matter.

But in other ways, gender did matter. As she presided over the service, LaGrone's embodied presence testified to Asbury's open rejection of complementarianism's strictly gendered roles. She delivered her sermon in an audibly feminine voice that matched the subtle femininity of her clothing—a conservative chambray jacket over a tailored white blouse accented with shiny hoop earrings. As she lifted the bread and chalice from the communion table, she displayed neatly manicured fingernails and silver jewelry, details that identified her in this context as a woman, not a man. Likewise, the students who occupied the pews, received the elements, and spilled out the wide chapel doors at the end of the service to embody the community identified themselves as women and men with their clothing, speech, and mannerisms. Gender was palpably present in the stories of their lives, if not in the stories they chronicled with words.

Asbury's construction of gender, then, is strikingly different from Southern's. In contrast with complementarian insistence on male headship, Asbury openly rejects overtly gendered hierarchies. In place of Southern's sharp gender differentiation, the community elevates women as well as men to places of authority and institutional power, including pulpits, faculty rosters, and administrative roles. On the surface, Asbury appears to present compelling counterevidence to W. Bradford Wilcox's assertion that the evangelical subculture is "fundamentally in tension with modernity's embrace of gender equality" (Wilcox 2004, 11). Women enroll at Asbury not in preparation for "women's ministry" but with intentions to pursue ordination, lead congregations, build theology, and speak authoritatively to the Church and society. They preach, invest, and share in the mission of their institution in ways that Southern's women do not. Some within the seminary even proclaim victory over churchly sexism. One administrator wanted to be sure I understood. "Listen carefully," he said. "There are absolutely no barriers to women at Asbury Theological Seminary. Period."

Asbury, however, has struggled to achieve the demographic equity it prescribes. At the time of my research, women composed only 34 percent of the entire student population of just over 1,600—a percentage that had remained virtually unchanged throughout the previous ten years. On faculty, the percentage of women was even lower at less than 16 percent. These patterns mirror the gender inequity within American conservative Protestantism. Examining data from the National Congregations Study, political scientist Ryan Burge pointed out in 2020 that while women's representation in the U.S. Congress had quadrupled between the years 1998 (4.6 percent) and 2020 (23.5 percent), women's gains in church leadership structures had been slim at best. The share of churches led by women between these years rose only slightly, from 10.6 percent in 1998 to 13.5 percent in 2018. Moreover, Burge also noted, women who did hold pastoral positions often found themselves leading congregations that were notably smaller than those led by men. "For women in the pastorate," concluded Burge, "there's been essentially no change . . . the stained-glass ceiling is just as thick and impenetrable as it was two decades ago."[4]

Like stained glass in church windows, this metaphorical stained-glass ceiling contains important stories. Southern's complementarian narrative explicitly blocks women from authoritative roles. As the following chapters demonstrate, its Gospel Story chronicles male headship and female submission as God's divine will. It weaves them into the biblical narrative, throughout a usable institutional history of "Conservative Resurgence," and situates them in the cultural processes of contemporary community life. Asbury's narrative limits women much more subtly. While the seminary's Equality Story narrates gendered differences as peripheral to churchly authority and spiritual life, thereby creating opportunity for women, the story's individualistic genderblindness limits gender equity. Combining theology, culture, rhetoric, and embodied practice, both seminaries narrate powerful institutional stories that center men and limit women's agency.

Evangelicals and Gender: A Brief Cultural History

Historians have situated evangelical gender norms and power dynamics within their contexts. Beth Allison Barr's *The Making of Biblical Womanhood* charts constructions of female submission and male headship as churchly capitulation to the patriarchal structures (2021). Kristin Kobes Du Mez's *Jesus and John Wayne* chronicles what the author calls a "militant masculinity" as it spread across much of the twentieth century, nurtured within white evangelical culture through books like John Eldredge's *Wild at Heart* (2001) and celebrity figures like Mel Gibson, Oliver North, and, of course, John Wayne. Donald Trump, she notes, has become its most recent hero. Kate Bowler's *The Preacher's Wife* (2019) illuminates the "precarious power" that women celebrities have achieved within these evangelical subcultures by accommodating, and in some cases subverting, expectations of feminine nurture and emphasized femininity.

As each of these volumes illustrates, evangelical efforts to reinforce conservative gender norms have intensified throughout the past half century. In the late 1980s, concerned about the threat of feminism—in both secular and Christian forms—a group of evangelical leaders that later became the Council on Biblical Manhood and Womanhood (CBMW) mobilized to shore up male headship. According to CBMW's own history: "Under [John] Piper's leadership, the group drafted a statement outlining what would become the definitive theological articulation of 'complementarianism,' the biblically derived view that men and women are complementary, possessing equal dignity and worth as the image of God, and called to different roles that each glorify him. The group next met . . . before the 1987 meeting of the Evangelical Theological Society. The draft was adopted in meeting and called the Danvers Statement on Biblical Manhood and Womanhood."[5] The Danvers Statement, even as it discounts feminism, also employs the feminist language of equality, a discourse that also emerged within the evangelical subculture during the later decades of the twentieth century (Stacey 1990). The 1990s in fact saw a shift not only in discourse but also in practice. White middle-class evangelical families transitioned from a breadwinner/housewife model toward a dual-earner family arrangement that pushed women into the workplace and reconstructed gendered scripts for Christian men (Gallagher 2003; Wilcox 2004; Bartkowski 2004). Though "soft patriarchs" and "Promise Keepers" clung to a symbolic "male headship" ideal, evangelical marriages began to take a more egalitarian shape in actual practice (Gallagher and Smith 1999).[6]

More vigorous forms of patriarchy, however, persist. The militant masculinity Du Mez illustrates, in fact, remains highly salient in much of the evangelical subculture where it "enshrines patriarchal authority and condones the callous display of power at home and abroad" (Du Mez 2020, 3). Aided by Christian publishing and broadcasting industries, as well as the more recent introduction of social media, this evangelical subculture has centered the middle-class white man as the legitimate bearer of power and authority. This is especially clear among complementarians. Resistant to rapid social change around issues of gender and sexuality, and boosted by the success of the neo-Reformed movement, the men who now lead the complementarian charge have renewed the fight against feminism, homosexuality, gender dysphoria, and softer forms of evangelical patriarchy. Pointing specifically to Southern Seminary's role in this movement, as well as the symbolic value of gender in its evolution, Julie Ingersoll writes, "The inerrancy of the Bible is no longer the central test of orthodoxy at Southern; it has been replaced by opposition to women's ordination and gay rights" (Ingersoll 2003, 59). Led by celebrity pastors and promoted through institutions like Southern Seminary, CBMW, and the Gospel Coalition, complementarianism enjoys widespread visibility among younger evangelicals.

Its message, however, is contested. In 1987, the same year that birthed CBMW, a rival organization called Christians for Biblical Equality (CBE) began publishing *Priscilla Papers*, a journal devoted to theological and biblical scholarship challenging complementarian claims. In the decades since, popular writers and activists like Sarah Bessey, Rachel Held Evans, and the Junia Project's Kate Wallace Nunneley have extended CBE's academic efforts to younger audiences using poetic writing styles and edgier rhetoric. Also building on the academic work of high-profile biblical scholars like Scot McKnight, N. T. Wright, and Ben Witherington, these women—and a coterie of male allies—decry structures of patriarchy and call for the full inclusion of women in church leadership.[7] They have won a substantial following, forged largely through online platforms that bypass older gatekeepers of Christian broadcasting and publishing. In 2013 popular Christian blogger Rachel Held Evans effectively hijacked a major evangelical leadership conference by pointing out on Twitter that only four of the one hundred speakers were women.[8] The conversations that followed focused not on the content of the conference but instead on how to most effectively remedy gender disparities. When she died unexpectedly in 2019, evangelical partisans mourned and decried Evans with an intensity that testified to the breadth of her influence.

The fault lines do not always align with the complementarian-egalitarian divide. In the wake of the #churchtoo scandals that rocked the Southern Baptist Convention, Beth Moore, a phenomenally popular Bible teacher and author of women's Bible study guides, broke ranks with the denomination's masculine leadership. Moore publicly accused key leaders of "misogyny, objectification and astonishing disesteem of women." In an open letter describing some of her disempowering experiences working within the Southern Baptist Convention, Moore wrote, "Scripture was not the reason for the colossal disregard and disrespect of women among many of these men. It was only the excuse. Sin was the reason. Ungodliness."[9] As tensions continued to grow, Owen Strachan provocatively tweeted, "Women do not preach on Sunday to the church. Doing so is functional egalitarianism. We will not capitulate here." Moore took him to task. "Owen," she responded, "I am going to say this with as much respect & as much self-restraint as I can possibly muster. I would be terrified to be a woman you'd approve of. And I would have wasted 40 years of my life encouraging women to come to know and love Jesus through the study of Scripture." She concluded a series of fiery salvos with this tweet:

Above all else, we must search the attitudes & practices of Christ Jesus himself toward women. HE is our Lord. He had women followers! Evangelists!
The point of all sanctification & obedience is toward being conformed to HIS
image. I do not see 1 glimpse of Christ in this sexism. . . . I have loved the SBC &
served it with everything I have had since I was 12 years old helping with
vacation Bible school. Alongside ANY other denomination, I will serve it to
my death if it will have me. And this is how I am serving it right now.[10]

Differences on the question of women's leadership in the church are intensify-
ing divisions in an already-fractured evangelical movement.

The Seminaries

The seminaries profiled in the following chapters represent these two gendered
evangelical traditions. Southern Seminary, with its complementarian stories, is
especially visible within the American religious landscape. One of the largest
theological institutions in the world, Southern is also the most widely known of
the six seminaries serving the Southern Baptist Convention (SBC).[11] Even as the
SBC contends with political polarization and ongoing investigations into pastoral abuse, its leaders and institutions sustain widespread influence. High-profile
leaders and celebrity pastors like John Piper and Southern Seminary's Al Mohler
continue to speak on behalf of evangelicals on matters of culture and politics as
well as faith. They enjoy large followings—especially among evangelicals of neo-
Reformed theological inclinations. In 2015 Southern Seminary itself celebrated
a record enrollment of 3,546 total students, a number that president Mohler called
"a sign of God's good pleasure."[12] While Southern's reputation for rigorous academics and commitment to cultural conservatism make it a popular option for
students from a variety of denominations, the overwhelming majority maintain
close ties to the SBC.

Southern's explicit commitment to male headship accompanies a male-
dominated campus. Men heavily populate most of the seminary's academic
programs. Of the 449 students working toward the seminary's master of divinity
degree when I began my fieldwork, only twenty-seven were women. Of those,
the overwhelming majority chose concentrations like missiology or biblical
counseling rather than Bible and theology.[13] The institution does allow—and
even encourage—women to enroll in all of its academic and ministerial training programs. While these women will not seek ordination or pastoral leadership positions, they prepare to lead and counsel other women in gender-specific
groups and ministries that do not violate the principle of male headship. In
some ways, Southern might be more accurately termed a "hierarchist" or
"hierarchical complementarian" institution. Because the community itself uses
the word "complementarian," however, I employ that term as well.[14] Regardless,

the shape of the institution, its administration, and its student body is irrefutably hierarchical—built around the headship of men.

Asbury's heritage of Wesleyan Methodism has also played an important role in American history (Hatch 1989). Begun as a revival movement in eighteenth-century century England, where its leaders included brothers John and Charles Wesley, for whom it is named, the movement eventually crossed the Atlantic and became a key driver of the Great Awakenings. In the American context it took firm root through the efforts of influential leaders such as Francis Asbury, the seminary's namesake (Wigger 2009). Like most revival movements, Wesleyanism viewed establishment religion with suspicion. In some cases, it sought to elevate marginalized populations such as women and enslaved African Americans (Dayton 1976; Smith 1965). In other cases, Wesleyans accommodated their host culture to justify slavery and middle-class respectability (Mathews 1965). Contemporary Wesleyans at places like Asbury often reach to the past for a usable egalitarian history that narrates how the good news of the gospel in the hands of the faithful can bring about positive social, as well as spiritual, change. Asbury serves the evangelical wing of the United Methodist Church, the Free Methodist Church, the Church of the Nazarene, the Wesleyan Church, and other holiness and pietistic groups. In 2015 the Association of Theological Schools listed Asbury's full-time equivalent enrollment at 1,189, making it North America's fourth largest seminary. By 2020 the institution claimed a growing student body representing forty-four states and forty-one countries.[15]

———

Apart from their theological traditions and approaches to gender, the resemblance between Asbury and Southern is striking. Located in Kentucky, the borderland of the American South, both campuses feature the imposing white pillars and neoclassical design of southern plantations. Moreover, each claims an evangelical identity that emphasizes spiritual conversion, missionary activity, and generally conservative cultural and political leanings. Both also stress the inspiration of the Bible. While their approaches to reading and interpreting its texts differ, as the following chapters demonstrate, both seminaries unapologetically appeal to biblical writings as sacred texts. The Bible, each says, is their full and final authority.

Both also employ official policies on gender as mechanisms of boundary maintenance. Of the two, Southern more overtly positions itself in an embattled posture against broader culture. It marshals its complementarianism against the twin threats of secular liberalism and egalitarian Christianity. Its opposition to these outgroups, coupled with strong institutional growth since the 1990s, fits sociologist Christian Smith's thesis of evangelicalism as "embattled and thriving" (1998). Asbury, meanwhile, employs its egalitarianism as a symbolic boundary against a churchly adversary: Reformed complementarian groups like

Southern. This posture suggests support for sociologist Mark Chaves's contention that policies regarding women's ordination are often heavily motivated by their usefulness as tests for cultural fit in interdenominational alliances (1999). Indeed, when I mentioned my research at Southern to people at Asbury, I quickly learned to expect a visceral response. Typically, their eyes widened with surprise and interest. "Well, *that* will be quite a contrast," many said. One staff member's reaction was particularly memorable. "Wow," she said, shaking her head, "you'll have one foot in heaven and one foot in hell."

Whatever one's assessment of their gender ideologies, these two institutions matter. Graduates of both live and work on six of the world's continents, where they serve as pastors, lead parachurch organizations, teach in theological schools, and direct mission agencies. Their work intersects with the lives of millions who participate in the tens of thousands of Southern Baptist churches and Wesleyan congregations and organizations across the country and around the world. Both Asbury and Southern are also increasingly influential outside their own denominational circles. Albert Mohler, the president of Southern Seminary, regularly produces blog posts and podcasts widely consumed within and outside of Southern Baptist networks. He and many of Southern Seminary's faculty are highly visible in evangelical circles and active in interdenominational networks like the neo-Reformed Gospel Coalition. Likewise, Asbury's resident scholars, including New Testament professors Ben Witherington and Craig Keener, publish extensive research that is utilized by pastors and denominational leaders. Their popular writing, appearing in publications like *Christianity Today*, reaches an even wider audience. Southern and Asbury are two of the most influential evangelical institutions of higher learning in the world.

Seminaries as Gendered Religious Communities

These institutions are not just theological thought leaders. They are also formative social spaces where students from various backgrounds and religious-cultural commitments are molded into agents of tradition, poised to carry the faith into congregations and future generations. This process takes time. A master of divinity (MDiv) degree, the most common path for aspiring pastors, often requires four years or more of study to complete. A PhD takes even longer. In my efforts to connect with one student, I asked if he would be on campus the following week. He responded, "I will be here next week, and all summer and, it seems, forever." As students like this work together toward their academic and vocational goals, they also form a distinct subculture grounded in time and space. Although most also join local congregations, the seminary itself often functions as a primary religious community. Students not only attend classes and chapel services together but also interact with each other over lunchtime

conversations, through on-campus social programming, and in the nearby residential neighborhoods where many of them live side by side as neighbors. Even
as they learn to be church leaders, they also learn to be a community and to function within institutional structures of power. Seminaries, in other words, are
sites of religious formation and "lived religion" (Ammerman 2014; McGuire
2008). To be sure, these institutions produce doctrine, scholarship, and cultural
boundaries. But they also produce people.

While "lived religion" is often mistakenly reduced to questions of individualistic practice, isolated from social life, it does not happen in a vacuum. Religious actors do not act alone, nor do their identities develop in isolation from
their social contexts. As Christian Smith puts it, "Perhaps the most elementary
principle of sociology is that individual human identities are not self-engendered
or formed in isolation, but are always and necessarily constructed through interactions with other humans in the context of relatively stable patterned social
groups. It is by being located in social groups—which themselves have formed
and sustain meaningful collective identities—that one comes to know who one
is, what one should do with one's life, and why" (1998, 90). Even the most individualized lived religious practice cannot be fully understood outside the contexts and communities that facilitate it, nor is its significance irrelevant to
considerations of broader structural realities and institutional power dynamics.
Likewise, individual identity and group identity emerge collectively as groups
defend their boundaries and as individuals grapple with what kind of person they
will be. These are the connections that the following chapters explore. Following the dialectical process of "world-construction" that sociologist Peter Berger
famously describes, this book shows individuals to be both producers and products of their social surroundings (1967). Human actors are shaped by religious
culture even as they live it into existence.

Gender too is lived. Within religious communities like Southern and Asbury,
gendered significance takes shape, just as Candace West and Don Zimmerman's
classic notion of "doing gender" expects, within social interactions (West and
Zimmerman 1987; Ridgeway and Correll 2004). The significance of these interactions also extends to the structures that pattern institutional realities (Fenstermaker and West 2002). Meanwhile, while some scholars have highlighted the
volatility in gender's social construction (Deutsch 2007), others argue that gender
itself is better conceptualized as a structure of social or economic control, difficult to deconstruct (Collins 1990; Hartmann 1979). Collectively, this literature
suggests that gender is, in fact, a complex, multilevel process (Acker 1992; Risman 2004). It is "done," much as religion is "lived," in the often messy realities
of social life where individual performance, relational interaction, structural
frameworks, and cultural norms intertwine. As Julie Ingersoll suggests, "Gender norms, expectations and ideology are always in social process." In religious

spaces, these processes are apparent in moments of conflict, as Ingersoll argues, but they are also at work in ordinary tasks and everyday relationships (2003). Even mundane spaces, I contend, are important sites for the production of gendered culture and for the exercise of power.

This project draws theoretically from Martin Riesebrodt's conceptualization of religion as practice (2010). This includes, first, what Riesebrodt calls "discursive" practices. The words, stories, and metaphors human actors use to communicate about and to superhuman powers serve as vehicles of religious knowledge and mechanisms for its perpetuation and adaptation. Both Asbury and Southern clearly value words. Both take their cues from the written words of the Bible. Both are dedicated to the spoken word of preaching and to the formation of people through conversation and public discourse. Their hallways display Bible verses and inspiring quotes of the Baptist and Wesleyan forebears whose words continue to inform contemporary belief. Though talk is often overlooked as a category of analysis, the use of language is more than simply a byproduct of cultural work. It also serves, in the words of sociologist Robert Wuthnow, "as the means through which values and beliefs acquire sufficient meaning to guide behavior and to provide a template for self-understanding" (2011, 9). As Catholic feminist theologian Elizabeth Johnson argues, "Language doesn't just reflect what we think. It shapes what we think and defines our world" (Johnson 1992, quoted in Katzenstein 1999, 123). Language *is* practice. Its nuances, patterns, and meanings—both explicit and implicit—have much to teach us about religious actors' motivations, choices, and experiences. [16]

Along with discourse, Riesebrodt draws attention to what he calls "behavior modification practices." The same actors who use talk to orient themselves toward the divine also mold their everyday actions toward similar ends. These practices govern personal habits like the consumption of particular foods, the wearing of particular clothing, and rituals of friendship and marriage—all practices that I analyze in the pages that follow. In my treatment of Asbury and Southern, I employ the language of "embodied practice," a slight variation on Riesebrodt's terminology, to emphasize the physicality of these practices and highlight their intersection with material culture. At both seminaries, community rituals and gendered individual scripts powerfully reflect—and shape—deep beliefs about God and the gendered nature of reality. Embodied practices situate belief in the physical body and in the material world.

The following chapters illustrate this process by examining the ways in which students at each seminary are formed into their communities' gendered frameworks. In both cases, I found the communities' most formative practices to be those that tapped the suprarational, appealing to human emotion and offering historically situated meaning through narrative and embodied experience. Highlighting especially the role of storytelling in both discursive and embodied forms, I argue that the sociological notion of "doing gender" in these religious contexts must account for convergences between the physical world and human practices oriented toward the transcendent. Likewise, I emphasize the profound role that gender—and gendered power dynamics—can play in the cultural processes that hold religious communities and identities together.

STUDYING GENDER IN RELIGIOUS COMMUNITIES

If embodied practices matter in religious life, they should also matter in religious research. My analysis draws heavily from my own physical interactions with these two seminaries and their people. The contrast between my experiences at the two campuses illustrates the difference that embodiment can make. At Asbury, I easily fit into the environment. Students generally seemed to be at ease with me from the moment I introduced myself. They explained their theology and outlined their egalitarian positions, clearly expecting me to agree with them. I blended into Asbury's culture physically too. I often worked in the common area of the campus student center, where passersby stopped to introduce themselves and ask if I was a new student.

I experienced Southern in a fundamentally different way. Students—both men and women—were friendly but guarded toward me. Because of my familiarity with the subculture and language of conservative evangelicalism, I was very often able to put them at ease. Nevertheless, they treated me as an outsider, if an empathetic one. Most very clearly expected me to disagree with their beliefs. While they were intrigued with my work, and generally quite eager to talk, they also seemed mystified by me: a married woman fluent in the language of Christian faith and pursuing a scholarly project with feminist overtones. Southern's faculty and administrators, likewise, often appeared to spend our conversations searching for a category to fit me into. As one interview drew to a close, the incredibly poised faculty member I had just spent an hour with learned that I was not only a gender scholar but also the mother of four young children. His composure melted for several awkward seconds as he scrambled to recategorize me. Finally he exclaimed, "That's *glorious!*" His astonishment revealed the extent to which my embodiment of both feminism and maternal nurture challenged his assumptions.

My gender identity simultaneously advantaged and limited me at both institutions. The fact that I am a woman, and that I carry myself with a classically feminine affect, opened doors to spaces like Southern's Seminary Wives Institute and Asbury's Women's Communion services that may have remained closed otherwise. Moreover, the women I interacted with throughout my fieldwork demonstrated vulnerability with me and displayed emotion to an extent that men typically did not. At Asbury especially, women seemed to experience interviews as opportunities to process their experiences—and even their insecurities—with another woman. Conversely, while the men I interviewed sometimes spoke in deeply personal terms, they more often approached the interview as a detached academic exercise. Moreover, I was unable to access the offstage spaces of men's more intimate relationships—men's Bible studies, for example, or Asbury's Band of Brothers accountability groups. Even these inconsistencies and limitations, introduced by my gendered presence, underscore one of this book's most important contentions: gendered standpoint matters profoundly.

The project drew from seventy-six semistructured interviews with students, faculty, and administrators at each school. The majority of these (thirty-two from each seminary) were with students.[17] Most ranged from young college graduates in their twenties to older students in their thirties and forties seeking second careers or wishing to enhance their existing ministries with further education. Many were married, and many brought spouses and young children with them. Most had deep roots in evangelical churches and denominations, and many had attended Christian colleges or participated in evangelical campus ministries on secular campuses. I asked these students a variety of questions about their lives and experiences at seminary, as well as about how their Christian beliefs informed their convictions on the importance of gender, their thoughts on feminism, and their own life choices. The remaining interviews brought me into conversation with faculty or administrators that either students or other faculty identified as having some interest or stake in the school's gender practices. These interviews supplemented ethnographic observations from classrooms, chapel services, and community events, as well as informal interactions with both students and faculty at both campuses beginning in 2013 and extending through 2015. I also analyzed print and online media produced at each school.

My biggest regret is that this book does not represent the experiences of women of color. Aside from a notable presence of international students from around the globe, particularly at Asbury, the embodied legacies of evangelical missionary efforts, both campuses were predominantly white. Moreover, I limited my interview samples to American students, which, given the paucity of American students of color on both campuses, eliminated much of the racial and ethnic diversity in both student bodies. I did interact informally with a few people of color—mostly international students—on both campuses, all of whom patiently explained to me that their perspectives and experiences differed substantially from those of their white American classmates. My analysis in the following chapters can only hint anecdotally at the intersectional challenges they face.

My analytical approach also draws from multiple sources. Aligned with the interpretivist sociological tradition and its call to prioritize the meaning and understanding of social actors themselves, I build this project around the voices of the people who call Southern and Asbury home. I have tried to represent them as fairly as possible while also applying a critical lens. I write not only as a sociologist but as a feminist, informed especially by the standpoint feminism of writers like Dorothy Smith, who calls scholars locate women's everyday experiences within structures of institutional power, and Patricia Hill Collins, who emphasizes the value of human commonalities and solidarities while also recognizing the oppressive structures that limit human flourishing.

Finally, I write as a person of faith. As an Anabaptist, my own religious tradition differs from those represented by the two seminaries I studied. Life circumstances have, however, brought me into close contact with a number of evangelical Christian groups, including both Wesleyan and Baptist communities. This background located me somewhere between emic (insider) and etic (outsider) status within these seminaries. My proximity, in some ways, facilitated critical analysis. I was, for example, already well acquainted with theological debates over women's ordination and had encountered the tropes of godly womanhood while attending an evangelical high school. In other ways, however, my connections to evangelical culture were not so helpful. This was especially the case at Asbury, whose construction of gender I initially expected to match my own more closely than it did. It was only after retreating to a more outsider approach that I was able to identify the community's subtle male-centered processes and their consequences.

The book's central contention is that American evangelical stories buttress constructions of meaning, identity, and power that center men. At Southern, patriarchy takes explicit shape in an all-encompassing narrative of nostalgia and male-centered social order. While many of Southern's women describe an empowering, even freeing, complementarian ecosystem, I find that much of their flourishing is predicated on familial connections to powerful men and on women's willingness to actively prioritize men's interests. Asbury, by contrast, leans on a heavily individualistic discourse of genderblindness, suggesting a strong resistance to patriarchal hierarchies. The community nevertheless struggles to consistently practice egalitarianism in real life. While women celebrate freedom from policies and theologies based on male headship, many find themselves constrained culturally and structurally by the same genderblind egalitarian framework that opens the doors of institutional authority to them. While women in both communities find creative ways to thrive, they often find it necessary to participate in their communities' male centering if they wish to succeed in churchly spaces. Taken together, these two communities' stories—both discursive and embodied—demonstrate the pervasiveness of evangelical patriarchy.

While writing this book, I often recalled Mark Noll's words in the opening paragraph of *The Scandal of the Evangelical Mind*: "This book is an epistle from a wounded lover" (1995). This book is, likewise, a work of both critical scholarship and Christian lament. It draws on a robust conviction, deeply embedded within both the Christian faith and the field of sociology, that humans can—and, in fact, *should*—improve on the status quo, for the sake of a more just, equitable, and peaceful world. I fear that not all of the actors represented in these pages will recognize my motivation as a redemptive one. Nevertheless, I hope that some will accept this book's implicit challenge: to both name and address the limits of their gendered stories as a practice of social holiness.

CHAPTER 1

Male and Female

GENDERED DISCOURSE AT SOUTHERN SEMINARY

We are remembering the past as we are in the present and looking forward to the future. It's something that really, really resonates with me. We're not lost in the past, but we remember those times when we came through hardships in our seminary.   —Alex, Southern Seminary student

Campus hummed with life when I arrived on a crisp October morning to begin my fieldwork. Students clutching books and engaging friends in animated conversation moved purposefully toward the broad doors of the chapel. Others meandered in the opposite direction toward the Honeycutt Campus Center in search of coffee or a place to work. A hub of student activity, this sprawling complex housed not only a small café but also administrative offices, state-of-the-art athletic facilities, and a large dining hall. It also provided a convenient space for me to meet with students and watch the rhythms of campus life. These rhythms, I quickly learned, extended beyond the official seminary curriculum of classroom instruction and research papers. To be sure, the tables in the building's common areas regularly filled with students studying thick textbooks and typing thoughtfully on laptops, but they also hosted mentoring relationships, intimate personal conversations between friends, and brown-bag lunches with spouses and children. Faculty members wearing dark suits and silk ties sometimes passed through the space on their way to the administrative offices and meeting rooms just up the broad, winding staircases in the middle of the building. Mothers pushed strollers and held the hands of toddlers on their way to ballet or play dates at the gym. By the end of my research, I knew the space and its bustling rhythms well.

Southern's vitality draws palpably from the past. Its historic buildings bear the honored names of Southern Baptist patriarchs. Next to the Honeycutt Campus Center, and surrounding an expansive, grassy quad, stand the administrative offices and classrooms of Norton Hall, the James P. Boyce Centennial Library,

Figure 1.1. The Southern Seminary campus. Norton Hall (left) sits across an expansive quad from the James P. Boyce Centennial Library (right). Photo by the author.

and dorm housing in Mullins Hall. Just beyond this cluster of buildings, Alumni Memorial Chapel, a stately structure appointed with tall white pillars and a quintessential white steeple, overlooks Lexington Road and the quiet, leafy streets beyond. Throughout the campus, photographs, architecture, and artwork remind community members of a vibrant past. Yellowed prints of graduating classes, some over a century old, line the walls and stairwell of the library. Even the nameplate identifying a large banquet room in the campus center as Heritage Hall testifies to legacy and tradition. These artifacts illustrate religion's function, articulated by sociologist Danièle Hervieu-Léger as a chain of memory (2000).

In this first of two chapters devoted to Southern Seminary's complementarianism, I examine storytelling as a religious and gendered practice. I show, specifically, how Southern builds students' investment in complementarianism by infusing the biblical narrative with heavily gendered ideals. Students arrive ripe for this socialization. While the seminary's leaders are deeply invested in the theological and cultural commitments of the Southern Baptist Convention, including complementarianism, its students do not always enter seminary quite so committed to this identity—or at least not in the same ways. Many join the community as recent college graduates. Many bring considerable spiritual fervor along with enthusiasm for the neo-Reformed movement and its leaders. But they often come with ecclesiastical identities that are not yet fully defined. In the years that follow each new cohort's arrival, the institution seeks to transform them into Southern Baptist churchmen grounded in denominational identity and invested in the particulars of the seminary's mission, including the advancement of complementarianism. This chapter demonstrates how Southern uses aural, visual, and material storytelling toward these ends.

The community employs two usable histories. The first, a theological "Gospel Story," imbues the biblical narrative of salvation from sin with prescriptions of gender polarization and male headship. A second story of "Conservative Resurgence" reinforces the gendered Gospel Story using Southern's own institutional history. Beginning with the voices of its students, this chapter renarrates Southern's stories, showing how they are "usable" in chronicling the past to prescribe what should be.

THE GOSPEL STORY

I began interviews by asking students about their own lives. I did this partly out of curiosity about their backgrounds and partly in hopes of putting them at ease before I introduced more complex questions. They responded just as I had hoped. Most clearly appreciated my interest and spoke lucidly about their callings. As we transitioned to more difficult questions about theology and gender, this verbal facility continued. When I asked about the significance of the Genesis creation narrative and probed for the particulars of their hermeneutics, they did not strain to remember the theological reasoning they learned in classrooms. Nor did they become defensive or apologetic about articulating beliefs that many of them clearly expected me to disagree with. Instead, they relaxed into their chairs and smiled. They knew exactly what to say.

Invariably, their answers invoked the "gospel." Southern's community broadly employs this vocabulary to signify the Bible's practical application to just about every human situation. Their use of the word differs slightly from its more common meaning. In historic Christian tradition, "gospel" is most often employed as a reference to the ministry, death, burial, and resurrection of Jesus Christ—or to the four New Testament books that outline this biography. Southern's usage, however, extends much further. More than the "good news" proclaimed two thousand years ago, Southern's gospel dictates right living in the contemporary world. Invoking the word imparts authority over nearly any contemporary concern. Calling a particular idea a "gospel belief" infuses it with the weight of God's own call. Upholding a social pattern as a "gospel order" suggests that it has been instituted by God rather than humans. The word functions as a discursive tool that delineates holy from unholy and legitimate from illegitimate. It distinguishes that which aligns with acceptable belief from that which contradicts it. Gospel is nonnegotiable.

By attaching gospel to gender complementarianism, then, Southern students contended that true Christian faith demands gender hierarchy. Alex, a first-semester MDiv student, explained, "We don't think that [women] are lesser beings or that they are less capable of doing great things. But ultimately, we believe what the scriptures have taught us. We believe what the scriptures are saying. We believe what the scriptures are showing us from Genesis until Revelation that just as Christ is the head over his Church, so too is the man head over his wife." Here, Alex argued that complementarian interpretations of the biblical story are universally prescriptive. Male headship, he suggested, was the correct pattern not only in Genesis, but also for the ancient Hebrews, for the early Church in Rome, and for twenty-first-century Americans. So many of Alex's peers articulated this same conviction with confidence and passion. They could have explained these views to me by appealing to neo-Reformed systematic theology. And sometimes they did. But overwhelmingly, these aspiring churchmen explained their community's theology of gender in terms of a beloved *story*.

Gendering Genesis

This Gospel Story begins, as does the Bible itself, in the book of Genesis. Here the narrative opens with a creation account that reinforces God's sovereign attention to order. According to students' narrations of the story, this order takes shape in two normative patterns: gender differentiation and male headship, both of which are embodied by the first human beings. These patterns organize human social life from the first chapters of Genesis, and they extend through the rest of the biblical narrative to the very students who retold this Gospel Story to me over Starbucks coffee in Louisville, Kentucky.

The second chapter of Genesis first prescribes gender difference. God, students explained, created men and women—two distinct kinds of humans—for two distinct roles. Men are leaders; women are followers. Men are providers; women are nurturers. Just as the biblical Adam worked the fields, students reasoned, the Gospel Story calls all men to responsibly lead and provide for their families. Similarly, they continued, it is significant that God gave Eve, not Adam, the biological ability to bear children. Like her, contemporary women are made for the biological and cultural work of mothering. Brad, an advanced student from the West Coast, explained this connection:

> [Adam's] name is tied to his vocation. And what is his vocation? His vocation is to go out into land. It's to bring forth from the land. It's outward focused for the benefit of family. And then you have the name "Eve." It means "the mother of all living." Her name is tied to her vocation, to what her job is. So what is her role? What is her job? It's tied to her identity, which is to bring forth life. Now that doesn't mean that if a woman can't get pregnant then she's not fulfilling her identity, but the idea is nurturing. The idea is mothering— it's motherhood.

Because, Brad and others repeatedly suggested, these differences were instituted at creation (and, therefore, cannot be considered a consequence of sin), they are not to be undone or even downplayed. They should be practiced and celebrated.

Students elevated marriage as an especially important site for this celebration. Their commitment to binary gender differentiation cannot be understood outside the community's sacralization of heterosexual marriage and its rejection of same-sex unions. The Gospel Story's heterosexual Adam and Eve provide a powerfully prescriptive standard for marriage. Following their lead and decades of evangelical "family values" rhetoric, Southern's students upheld heterosexual marriage as a deeply sacred bond, one that is both desirable and necessary (Dowland 2018). Emphasis on Adam and Eve's differentiated roles also reflects students' widespread belief in an essential gender binary, necessarily connected to both biological sex and sexual orientation. Students cited the breakdown in the traditional family and the increasing acceptance of LGBTQ+ individuals in broader society as evidence of humanity's fall into sin. Transgender identities are especially concerning at Southern because they question the essential binary itself. Gay marriage defies the differentiation that Southern assumes to be necessary to make marriage itself work.

For some, this binary makes nearly everything work. Students sometimes extended its significance beyond the marriage relationship, suggesting that the health of society itself was at stake. Reflecting the classically Reformed concern over maintaining God-ordained order in the social world, these complementarians situated marriage as the primary social institution, created by God to ensure human flourishing. Jackson, a tall, confident student who twisted a shiny new wedding band around his finger as we talked, warned that retreat from gender differentiation would damage individuals, families, and broader social institutions: "It's in our DNA that men learn how to be men from men. Women learn how to be women in all of the beautiful crazy good ways that women are women. . . . Those differences are real, and acting like they're not real is first of all ignorant, and also dangerous. So if we act like it doesn't matter, we have confused families, we have confused people, and we have a confused society. And I don't think that God is a god of confusion." According to this paradigm, human flourishing depends on men and women embracing their differences and structuring their lives accordingly. Gospel-ordered lives, and even societies, students like Jackson maintained, must start in the family with traditional gender roles.

Students absorb rhetoric like this in their classrooms and from institutional leaders. Denny Burk, a high-profile faculty member in the seminary's undergraduate wing who became CBMW's president in 2016, regularly writes on gender-related themes. In an article originally published in Southern Seminary's print magazine and reposted online three years later, he warned of dire consequences should society continue its retreat from gender differentiation:

The Bible teaches that gender is something you are before you learn anything. . . .
The union of the first man and the first woman was the most healthy, wholesome, and satisfying union that has ever existed, and it involved a man
leading his wife and a wife following the leadership of her husband. . . . Our
society is confused about gender and sexuality because it has forgotten what it
means to be created in the image of God as male and female. Instead, we have
plunged headlong into the genderless void, not thinking about the consequences for our children and the public good.[1]

Other campus leaders take a more pastoral approach. An MDiv student named
Noah recalled an illustration one professor used to explain gender complementarity: the difference between a paper plate and fine china. This metaphor, he
said with enthusiasm, helped him understand the innate differences between
men and women and, therefore, the reason for their differentiated roles:

There are specific, functional distinctions that sometimes we don't want to
admit because it sounds like we're being condescending. But really, it's just
summarizing what we know in our hearts to be true. There's a reason we don't
send women to war, to fight against men. It's [because] men have testosterone
and bigger muscles, and they are stronger. [Understanding] that just kind of
helped me understand that verse and [my professor's] emphasis on the fact that
women are like fine china. They should be protected and valued and prized
and cherished. . . . This is not about looking down on women. It's about prais-
ing them for who they are and appreciating the way God has made them.

Classroom instruction reinforced Noah's assumptions about the social world in
a way that seemed to advance, rather than diminish, the value of women.

Southern's women also learn to value—and defend—gender differentiation.
While men like Noah and Jackson dominate classrooms and offices during the
day, the seminary sets aside space on Thursday nights for an auxiliary program
called the Seminary Wives Institute (SWI). This program is designed to prepare
women for the expectations they will face as their husbands become pastors and
they become pastors' wives. While not mandatory, SWI, which the seminary
heavily subsidizes for couples already stretched financially by the costs of seminary, is quite popular. Male faculty members teach several courses on theology
and church history, but the wives of seminary professors provide most of the
instruction. The curriculum emphasizes practical topics like "Biblical Parenting," "Women in the Home, Church, and Community," "The Ministry of Hospitality," and other themes relevant to the roles of wives and mothers. Even the
required text for a class on mentoring, a book titled *Spiritual Mothering*, reinforced the gendered order of the Gospel Story by emphasizing maternal nurture
as women's essence (Hunt 1993).

Sacralization of this gendered "gospel order" has given rise to a community of people who generally believe themselves to be two categorically different kinds of beings. Men assume that women live lives, nurture spirituality, and wrestle demons in a realm so foreign that men can hardly be expected to relate. "I think women are to be teachers over women," one man emphasized, then added with a laugh, "which is a wonderful thing that they can do that I will never be able to do." Another affirmed the importance of women ministering to each other for similar reasons:

LWS: How do you think are the best ways for women to use their gifts in churches?

MARCUS: Teaching, as we said earlier, is a huge one. Women's ministry in general is a place that is, in my opinion, is lacking in church. The picture is of a man at the top of the leadership. It's difficult because men relate to people in general differently than women relate to people, and so it's difficult for a man, or I would almost say impossible, for a man to do women's ministry.

Men like Marcus might value women. They might even admire women's abilities and spiritual maturity, but they also see women as so different from themselves that to minister to them might be next to "impossible." The Gospel Story narrates this polarization as God's own design, a legacy of the differences between men and women initiated at creation. It is fueled by fears of a genderless void. The Church, narrators of the Gospel Story say, must uphold essential differences between men and women.

If gender differentiation is necessary, it is not sufficient. According to student narrations of the Gospel Story, faithful adherence to God's created order also requires maintenance of a hierarchy that Southern's complementarians more typically call "headship." Grounding this conviction theologically, Alex invoked the Holy Trinity as a model. Although the Father, Son, and Holy Spirit are all equal in value, he explained, each assumes a fixed role. More importantly, he argued, the Son and the Holy Spirit are subordinate to the Father, who is the head—just as wives are to be subordinate to husbands: "You have three persons. They are all equally God. They are all equal in power. They are all equal in knowledge. They are all equal in their infinite character. But . . . the Son and the Spirit are willingly submitting to the father . . . a willingness to say, 'you have been ordained for this, you are my head.' So as the Father is head over the Son and the Son is head over the church, so too is the man head over his wife." Paradoxically, Alex fluidly intertwined the language of male headship with assertions of equality, suggesting that, for him, the two are not contradictory.[2]

Yet Adam, the man, took clear priority in Alex's narration. Drawing on the chronology recorded in Genesis, Alex emphasized that God created Adam first, only later forming Eve from the man's rib to be a "helper" or "helpmeet" for him. Alex emphasized Adam's need for companionship, painting Eve as a divine afterthought, a gift to Adam: "[God] created Adam, and Adam was there naming the animals and none of these things is a good suitor for him. He's not pleased. There's nothing that complements him. He sees that the monkeys have male and female, and he's just alone. And God ends up saying that it is not good for man to be alone. And so He creates a woman that would complement him, that would be a part of him, and be connected with him and be there to help him." In Alex's telling, Man needed companionship, so God gave him Woman.

With narrations like this, the Gospel Story's opening chapters promote what author Charlotte Perkins Gilman referred to as androcentrism. This term refers to the situating of culture and history around the masculine perspective (1911). In an androcentric context, to be Man is to be human. To be Woman is to be other; it is a deviation from the norm. As Simone de Beauvoir wrote, "Humanity is male and man defines woman not in herself but as relative to him; she is not regarded as an autonomous being" (1953). As a result of androcentrism in broader Western culture, men have produced most of the art that is funded, celebrated, and remembered. Men have constructed policy and laws, designing them, whether by intention or default, primarily to suit their own needs. Alex's narration of the biblical creation account reflects a churchly version of this same pattern. Theology too has been constructed largely by men's minds and publicly preached from the standpoint of men's experience. In contrast to Gilman, de Beauvoir, and many feminist scholars after them who have used the word negatively, exposing society's inattention to women's voices and needs, Southern celebrates androcentrism. Almost without exception, the faculty, administrators, and students I spoke with articulated the belief that God's intention is to elevate men in at least some realms of life. This belief allowed Alex to celebrate his community's male-centered hierarchies without guilt. It is, he and his classmates learn, simply the pattern that God ordained for the sake of order and stability.

I witnessed a stark display of Christian androcentrism at CBMW's conference in Louisville. The men who shared the pulpit throughout the day gave overtly androcentric performances, speaking authoritatively about everything from missions to complementarian history to female sinfulness to the emotional depravity of hip-hop culture. The women's panel that concluded the conference appeared to break from this pattern, giving women a rare opportunity to publicly voice their perspectives. The participants, all confident and well spoken, shared articulately from their own experiences. They especially emphasized the importance of a robust devotional life. One offered special advice and encouragement to young mothers struggling to find time for daily Bible reading. Several acknowledged the difficulty of submitting to imperfect husbands and suggested ways for women to support each other. Much of their discourse, however, reinforced rather than offset the event's male centering. One panelist spoke at length about the importance of wifely submission, what she called "the 'S' word of Christianity." Each then took a turn describing how she showed respect for her husband. One of the panelists addressed an intriguing question about single women—the one category of women who, presumably, could operate outside familial male headship. "My first encouragement to women who are single," she said, "is to pray boldly for men. Ask God to help men stand up . . . to receive the challenge." Encouraging men for leadership is, she explained, the "first and primary challenge for single women." While the women on this panel did allude to some of their own experiences and challenges, when given the opportunity to speak into the male-dominated churchly world, their words continued to uphold, rather than question, its androcentrism.

Seminary students learn to defend androcentrism in the same place they learn to value gender differentiation: the classroom. One student, Brad, explained that both he and his wife enrolled as students at Southern. He confessed his struggle with the propriety of this arrangement, given his commitment to male headship. One professor's lectures, however, helped him to understand how, even in pursuit of her own vocation, his wife could fulfill her supportive role and leave his headship intact: "I'm taking this from my Old Testament professor here. He's very smart. He portrays foolishness as a woman, the damn folly. But then he personifies wisdom also as a woman. Seek this kind of woman, not the foolish woman. Seek wisdom. So yes, definitely, my wife can bring me honor by being a great worker in the workforce. That's completely fine." Brad, however, viewed his labor as fundamentally different from his wife's. While his career served the purpose of building the Church and supporting his family financially, his wife's career functioned as a supplement to his own goals. Her work honored his.

Other students emphasized their professors' stories more than their theological arguments. These students especially praised a required course called "Leadership in Family Ministry." The course, they explained, attended mostly to the roles of women and men in family life. More than one student mentioned that the class drew heavily on the professor's personal anecdotes about his own family. One student jokingly called the class "Storytime with Dr. Sperling." Another described how the stories helped him understand what male headship looks like in practice: "I think the oldest daughter does a lot of maintaining of the environment, especially for the younger kids, but she is also not primarily the one held responsible. Whenever Dr. Sperling gets home, if something went bad, the first thing he does is call in his son and says, 'You're the oldest man here, you're responsible, tell me what happened.' So [the kids have] slightly different roles." The Gospel Story itself is powerful, but when real-life stories come from the mouths of professors who have won students' admiration, they carry additional weight. Personal anecdotes concretize abstract ideals of differentiation and headship. Together, these stories tie the biblical past to the present, offering a glimpse of social life ordered as it should be.

But perfectly ordered ideals sometimes collapse. As the Gospel Story moves through biblical history, Eve succumbs to temptation and eats the forbidden fruit. Adam soon follows. According to the Gospel Story, this disobedience not only separated humanity from God but also disrupted God's gendered order. Man and woman no longer naturally flourished in the differentiated roles they were created to fill. Instead, they began to resist. Man shirked his duty as a strong, masculine leader-provider. Woman resented her supplementary role as "help-meet" and began to contend for power that did not belong to her. Students emphasized the gendered nature of the Fall in Genesis 3. Eve's sin, they suggested, was twofold. She sinned first by defying God's command not to eat the fruit and second by failing to submit to her husband's authority. Likewise, Adam's sin indicated his failure to act as his wife's "head" or protector. Renee explained: "[Men] are responsible. Just like Adam, in the garden, was called upon first, and God said, 'Adam, what have you done?' He didn't go to Eve first, even though Eve sinned first. He said, 'Adam, you were the husband, you were supposed to care for her, you were supposed to protect her, and you didn't do it. Why didn't you do it?' And then [Adam] blamed the wife." Tori shared a similar interpretation, connecting it to the complementarian insistence on male-only church leadership:

> Eve is the one that sinned first. That's something that Paul brings up. She was the one that first fell. Adam fell after her, and [Paul] uses that paradigm to talk about how the man is the one that was supposed to protect his wife, and the man is the one that's supposed to lead the way. God gave Adam the rule, the command to not eat of the fruit of the garden, and he was supposed to have stopped whatever was going on there and he didn't. . . . So I think a man leading the church—and especially men leading men—is more in line with the paradigm that is set in creation.

While both Tori and Renee mentioned that Eve sinned first, neither censured her. The blame belonged to Adam. In this, Southern's Gospel Story represents a marked reversal of the belief, common in earlier Christian eras, that Eve—along with her female descendants—was more sinful than Adam. Instead, while the Gospel Story's Eve remains culpable for her failings, she is perhaps less guilty than Adam, who failed to protect her from sin in the first place.

The story of the Fall also helps men and women grapple with difficulties in contemporary gender relations. Gospel Story devotees may truly believe that its principles are God's design for human flourishing, but few deny the difficulty in upholding them. "This is a Genesis 3 world," said one administrator. "Life is difficult. Marriage is not easy." Katherine, a student in the biblical counseling program, similarly relied on the language of sin and the Fall to interpret her own inadequacies as a submissive wife:

I think that ultimately the conflict and the separation between humans' relationship with God is a separation between man and woman and all human relationships. There's conflict and there's difficulty and there's sin and there's wrongdoing. The Curse talks about how Eve will have pain in childbearing and . . . the wife will want to overrule the husband and to conflict against the husband. There will be conflict in that relationship. I totally know from personal experience, it is within me to want to say, "No, you're doing it wrong," all the time. But I think that I have to respect what the Lord has set. There's going to be sin. My husband's going to fail as a leader. He's going to fail because of sin. He's going to do things that are not right, and he's going to offend me and there's gonna be conflict. And I'm going to offend him and I'm not going to follow him in the way that I should. So there's tension and it's not just an easy relationship.

Struggles like these, students maintained, are to be expected. Human impulses to subvert both male headship and gender differentiation are strong. The Fall, they believe, opened the door to such temptations, so the faithful must always be on guard.

Katherine, Tori, and Renee are all women. This may be coincidental. On the other hand, the fact that their words stood out to me among all of my Southern interviews as the most articulate in describing the Fall and its consequences may suggest that women, more than men, resonate most deeply with this particular episode of the Gospel Story. While male students like Alex and Noah more fluidly drew celebrations of difference and male headship from the creation account, these women seemed more compelled by the theme of struggle. Perhaps they sensed the paradoxical double advantage that the Gospel Story offers men. I heard a popular mantra recited fluidly and repeatedly: equal value, different roles. This formula allows men to denounce misogyny, and even claim the language of equality and human flourishing, while still owning headship authority in both marriage and church life. Tori, Renee, and Katherine did not explicitly disagree, but they seemed less enthusiastic. They, more than men, seemed to feel the weight of the "Genesis 3 world."

Gendering the Good News

Pervasive use of the word "gospel" notwithstanding, Jesus's life and ministry are much less relevant than the creation account to Southern's gendered narrative. Nor did students often cite his death and resurrection. Instead, they described Jesus's primary contribution to the story in terms of his relationship with the Church, illustrated metaphorically by New Testament authors as Christ's "bride." Noah, a confident third-year student, cited the relationship between Christ and the Church as the express purpose behind male headship: "I don't think [God] created that distinction [male headship] arbitrarily as if to say, 'I like men bet-ter, so I'm going to make them leaders and I dislike women so I'm going to make them submit.' I think He's trying to show us that Christ came to sacrificially love the church. [God] created this marriage relationship for men and women where women are going to mirror the church and husbands are going to mirror Christ. This whole marriage thing mirrors the Gospel and points back to what Christ has done for the church." While the assumption of gender hierarchy is always pre-sent, this metaphor nuances the nature of marital headship. Distancing them-selves from non-Christian patriarchy, students argued that a complementarian man must follow Jesus's example of love and kindness. Like the Soft Patriarchs and Promise Keepers of the 1990s, he must engage emotionally with his wife and respect her work in the domestic realm (Wilcox 2004; Bartkowski 2004). "There's just a respect for a woman," said Melody, an SWI student, clarifying the differ-ence between complementarianism and worldly patriarchal systems. "A respect for her ideas, a respect for that [feminine] role and how important it is. I feel like in a patriarchal system, you don't [necessarily] have that respect. You don't have that willingness to see why [a woman's] role is valuable."

Of course, complementarianism extends beyond marriage. The remainder of the Gospel Story grafts ideals of gender differentiation and male headship into the organization of the Church itself. Men not only work the fields as bread-winners for their families but also formulate doctrine and make organizational decisions in their churches. They preach and interpret and proclaim the Gospel. Women support these endeavors by providing behind-the-scenes labor for churches through hospitality, administrative support, and secondary leadership that does not place them in positions of authority over men. Key to this chapter in the story are the letters the Apostle Paul wrote to the young New Testament churches. In these letters Paul prescribes specific qualifications for church lead-ership: "The saying is trustworthy: If anyone aspires to the office of overseer, he desires a noble task. Therefore, an overseer must be above reproach, the husband of one wife, sober-minded, self-controlled, respectable, hospitable, able to teach, not a drunkard, not violent but gentle, not quarrelsome, not a lover of money. He must manage his own household well, with all dignity keeping his children submissive, for if someone does not know how to manage his own household, how will he care for God's church?" (1 Timothy 3:1–5 ESV). Because this list employs masculine language, Southern's complementarians conclude that Paul intended that only men fill these authoritative roles. Paul also instructs his readers not to allow women to speak in church. Rather, he says, they should learn at home from their husbands: "Let a woman learn quietly with all sub-missiveness. I do not permit a woman to teach or to exercise authority over a man; rather, she is to remain quiet. For Adam was formed first, then Eve; and Adam was not deceived, but the woman was deceived and became a transgres-sor. Yet she will be saved through childbearing—if they continue in faith and love and holiness, with self-control" (1 Timothy 2:11–15 ESV). These instructions, students insisted, are not limited to first-century churches. Because Paul appeals to Genesis, underscoring the relevance of the original created order, they are universal and timeless.

Not all biblical women, of course, fit this pattern. Deborah, for example, acted as a judge and prophet in the Old Testament (Judges 4:4). The New Testament book of Romans names Phoebe as a deacon (Romans 16:1). Priscilla, whom the Apostle Paul calls a "fellow worker in Christ," provided theological correction to Apollos, a visiting teacher, in the book of Acts (Acts 18:24–26). The Gospel Story neither denounces nor ignores these women. It simply assumes that they worked in cooperation with the principles of gender polarization and male headship. In fact, students enjoyed telling me stories of biblical women who appear to push the limits of complementarian doctrine. Characters like Deborah and Phoebe fill an important role in the Gospel Story: they provide evidence that complementarianism holds plenty of space for women to thrive, even lead, so long as they follow the rules. Michael, a lifelong Southern Baptist dressed in a blue blazer, khaki pants, and dark tie for his interview, complained that complementarians are often misunderstood as being antiwomen:

> Paul is very acquainted with and relies a lot on certain women, Phoebe being one of them. [She] delivers the letter to the Roman church for him, and a lot of people say she had a church in her house. [She was] probably a deaconess at the church and, you know, responsible for serving the love feast or the Lord's supper or whatever they would've called it. So Paul invests a lot of importance in the role of women in the church. Deborah, Priscilla, Dorcas. The list can go on and on. Also, the Gospels themselves [tell] the importance of Mary Magdalene and Martha. They are the first witnesses to the resurrection. . . . I don't think it's fair for modern critics of the New Testament or of evangelical beliefs on this to look and say, "Well, the Bible is a chauvinistic book." I don't think that they're giving a fair ear to the New Testament or to [complementarian] evangelicals.

Here, Michael acknowledges that biblical women exercised churchly agency, that the book of Romans identifies Phoebe as a deacon or minister. But he chronicles these women's agency in complementarian terms. He explicitly frames Phoebe's actions, for example, in terms of hospitality, an appropriately domestic activity for a daughter of Eve. Steven employed a slightly different argument, imagining that God must have used women in times of desperation when male leaders failed to exercise leadership:

> If God has said, "Here's the standard of what I want: I've created man first in my own image, and woman out of the man." That's already a specific gender role that's to be fulfilled. And who am I to question that? Who am I to really

say, "That's not okay, God"? I believe that there are times in which women are put in leadership by God. Deborah is an example in the Old Testament, where there's lack of men in leadership. And if God wants to do that, that's all on him. You know, I'm not going to argue with that. But, for the most part, if it's within our power I think we should be obeying God's picture hand and foot without question.

Even when Deborah leads a nation and commands an army—or Paul names Junia among the apostles—these students of the Gospel Story do not imagine that these biblical episodes were out of step with the generalized principle of male headship.

The efficacy of the Gospel Story lies in its fusion of gendered ideals and orthodox Christianity. The language of "gospel" facilitates this connection, but it is the discursive work of storytelling that makes it stick. For the men—and women—of Southern Seminary, male headship and gender polarization have become virtually indistinguishable from the good news of God's love for the world. Gender complementarianism stands on a high theological plane alongside God's sovereign authority and the incarnation of Jesus, and it is every bit as salient in the twenty-first century as it was in the book of Genesis. This is Southern's gendered gospel.

THE CONSERVATIVE RESURGENCE AS USABLE HISTORY

Southern also tells its own story of creation, fall, and redemption. The community's memory of its own history extends the Gospel Story's construction of male headship beyond the ancient pages of scripture, through the recent Southern Baptist past, and into the present. While some institutional histories languish in dusty volumes on rarely visited library shelves, Southern's account of Conservative Resurgence enjoys a prominent place in the community's imagination. Chronicled in material culture and everyday language as well as official discourse, this usable history buttresses male-centered power structures, legitimates the current leaders, and encourages a collective identity of embattlement.

Recovering a Vision

I began my fieldwork at Southern at a particularly opportune time. One of my first campus visits coincided with Heritage Week, a series of events held each fall to celebrate the institution's legacy. This year was special. It marked R. Albert Mohler Jr.'s twentieth anniversary as president of Southern Baptist Theological Seminary. Among the festivities, one Thursday morning chapel service premiered a twenty-five-minute documentary titled *Recovering a Vision*. As the chapel lights dimmed, the congregation turned its collective eyes to large projection screens on either side of the spacious sanctuary. The film recounted events that surrounded Mohler's ascension to the presidency, framing them within the institution's full history. Students listened with rapt attention as a segment titled "A Confessional Foundation" chronicled Southern's earliest days, beginning in 1859. In this golden era, the seminary was little more than an idyllic vision of a few faithful men who valued the authority of the Bible and the august tradition of the Southern Baptist Convention. The audience in Alumni Chapel already knew the names James P. Boyce, Basil Manly Jr., John A. Broadus, and William Williams, all of which grace the nameplates of campus buildings.

They were also acquainted with these founders' greatest contribution: a document called the Abstract of Principles. "From the beginning," the narrator declared as sepia-toned portraits filled the large screens, "Boyce insisted that the school needed a confession of faith to define its theological commitments and to set boundaries of acceptable belief for the faculty." The result: the Abstract of Principles, a rigorous confessional statement outlining basic Christian doctrines like the triune nature of God, the necessity of repentance from sin, and the availability of justification through Jesus Christ, as well as specifics of Reformed theology like divine election and the perseverance of the saints. Southern's leadership continues to revere the abstract as a near-sacred text, second only to the Bible in its authority. Every faculty member, agreeing to teach within its parameters, must add their signature. The documentary paired a grandiose orchestral soundtrack with its description of the Abstract of Principles' origins, reminding the chapel audience of an age when leaders were strong, when theology was conservative, when culture was ordered the way God intended.

But liberalism infiltrated. Following the musical score's dramatic modulation to a minor key, the documentary moved into a second segment, titled "A Departure." Its narrator gravely reminded his audience that despite the founders' best efforts, the winds of culture blew the seminary into a dark age. "By the 1960s," he lamented, "Southern Seminary's faculty was thoroughly and decidedly liberal." In the succeeding decades, Southern did indeed become widely renowned for its progressive stance on civil rights, its flexible ecclesiology and theology, and its welcome to women seeking churchly and scholarly credentials. Liberalism, it seemed, had triumphed.

Conservatives, however, remained within the Southern Baptist Convention (SBC). Feeling increasingly embattled against cultural and theological liberalism, they executed a decisive takeover of the convention, much to the dismay of many moderates for whom the SBC had always been home (Ammerman 1990; Cothen 1993). Despite this swift conservative victory in the denominational hierarchy, battles over the SBC's seminaries extended into the 1990s. Moderates hoped to retain Southern Seminary, but the denomination's right guard persisted. The seminary's official institutional history describes a decisive April 1990 meeting of the board of trustees: "Students, faculty, and the moderate trustees feared that conservatives might achieve a majority at the meeting and begin to impose their vision on the seminary in warp and woof. Conservatives feared that moderate trustees would somehow block their majority. When trustees gathered on campus, some 300 students wearing matching 'Maintain the Vision' shirts crowded into the meeting room. When the students were asked to leave during executive sessions, trustees could hear them outside as they prayed and sang hymns, keeping vigil in protest of the conservative threat to the school's moderate character" (Wills 2009, 484). This was the context—an institution wracked by controversy—into which a thirty-four-year-old Al Mohler stepped as the seminary's new president in 1993.

He quickly consolidated control. Mohler's first goal, the documentary suggested, was to restore unity. But that unity was conservative, and it came at a price to the community's moderates. Professor Molly Marshall was one of the first to pay. Most of the moderates who walked the seminary's halls before and during the takeover generally remain nameless in popular memory. Marshall, however, is widely remembered. In an interview, one student mentioned a professor's use of her story in a classroom setting, illustrating the dark days of the liberal 1990s. "She was a professor of theology here at the seminary," he explained, "and during the time of theological liberalism. . . . I guess when Al Mohler came in, he said, 'We need to get rid of the theological liberalism that's going on, because it's taking away from the authority of scriptures.' Which is absolutely true." Another student explained the episode in greater detail, introducing the question of women's leadership: "One of [Mohler's] earliest controversies . . . which kind of defined his taking over . . . was the ousting of Molly Marshall. She was a teacher of theology, a faculty member. I think she was the Chair of the Theology department. I'm not quite sure. [She was] very outspoken and, I wouldn't call her feminist, but very outspoken for women in pastoral roles. . . . When it was found out she was teaching some less than orthodox things, even about the nature of God, she was removed." Even *Recovering a Vision* displayed a photograph of her speaking intently into a microphone, as the narrator described her infamous run-in with Mohler. This run-in, of course, ended in her departure. Although Marshall herself had signed the Abstract of Principles and insisted that her teachings lay inside its bounds, Mohler disagreed. Instead of facing formal institutional charges, Marshall chose to resign her position. Her exit sent shock waves through the community, heightening the already heated controversy.

Marshall may not have lost her job because she was a woman, but questions of gender lay very near the surface. Mohler's commitment to male-centered leadership quickly emerged as a key point of contention. The Abstract of Principles did not require this restriction, many faculty and students objected, but Mohler insisted on it as a marker of theological orthodoxy. Marshall was not the only casualty. When a search committee recommended David Sherwood of Gordon College for a job in the Carver School of Church Social Work, Dianna Garland, the school's dean, was happy to present what she thought was the perfect

Figure 1.2. *Recovering a Vision* includes this image of Molly Marshall as an illustration of the internal opposition Al Mohler faced as Southern's new president. Mohler, the accompanying narration explains, "charged professor Molly Marshall with teaching contrary to the Abstract of Principles, which she herself signed." Digital frame enlargement from *Recovering a Vision*, https://vimeo.com/76963904.

candidate for Mohler. Sherwood was a reputable scholar with strong conservative credentials. Mohler, however, was unconvinced. After meeting with the new president, Sherwood was asked to produce written clarification of his views on four issues outside the content of the Abstract of Principles: homosexuality, abortion, women's ordination, and the exclusivity of the gospel as the means of salvation. In his response, Sherwood, citing scripture, affirmed his support for women's ordination (Wills 2009). Mohler refused to hire him. When she heard of Sherwood's rejection, Garland organized a protest. Her challenge to Mohler's leadership quickly ended in her resignation, one that many considered forced.

Garland's departure incited an outcry that culminated in "Dark Wednesday." In a faculty meeting that day, one of the new conservative faculty members, Tim Weber, called for flexibility on the issue of women's ordination. If the seminary wanted to maintain its place as a mainstream evangelical institution, he urged, neutrality on the issue was imperative. Despite a no-confidence vote from his faculty, Mohler forged ahead. He was convinced that uniform conservatism, powerfully symbolized by the issue of male headship, would rescue the institution from its leftward drift. One by one, other faculty members who both affirmed the Abstract of Principles and supported women in church leadership disappeared from the faculty roster. *Recovering a Vision* narrated these dramatic times through the voices of several high-profile Southern Baptist dignitaries. Each took his turn recalling the dark days when Mohler faced heartbreaking resistance from a largely recalcitrant community. Danny Akin remembered angry students refusing to shake Mohler's hand at graduation. Gregory Thornbury described students carrying caskets and protest signs around the campus lawn. Jimmy Scroggins shared Mohler's response when asked if he really expected to be able to "turn this ship around." Scroggins looked mournfully toward the camera. "I'll never forget," he remembered, "[Mohler] looked at me and he said, 'Jimmy, I'm either going to turn this ship around, or I'm going to sink it.'" Mohler stood his ground.

And he stayed standing. The departure of moderate faculty and the arrival of conservative hires tipped the balance in his favor. Within three years, said the documentary as the soundtrack swelled with major chords again, the new president enjoyed an overwhelming vote of confidence from his faculty. In the film's penultimate segment, titled "A Miracle of God," Southern Baptist statesman Richard Land described Mohler as "the man who was used by God to lead Southern Seminary back to its roots and to provide an example for other seminaries on how to go back to what Southern Baptists want and need for their seminaries to be." The now-disgraced Paige Patterson, a key architect of the Resurgence, added, "One of the miracles of the conservative movement, to me, was how quickly Dr. Mohler was able to take Southern Seminary and put it into the evangelical fold." A tearfully grateful Russell Moore, the seminary's former dean and senior vice president, glowed with admiration for Mohler as he juxtaposed the horrors of the transition with subsequent prosperity: "To walk in every time . . . and see that place filled with people, to know how it was like when I first came there, and would go into the cafeteria and everyone's sitting around telling Mohler jokes and predicting the end of the seminary. To walk in now and see Heritage Hall, which didn't even exist then, packed out with students who have this sort of zeal and buy into the vision. It never failed to move me to see that." Moore concluded, "Al was born to be president of Southern Seminary. It's the most natural thing. It was destined to happen. And he will be a titanic president of Southern Seminary until the day that he dies." The message of the documentary—and the community's Heritage Week celebration—was clear: Al Mohler was Southern's savior.

The plaudits continue. Less than two years after Mohler's inauguration, a 1994 issue of *Time* magazine named the thirty-five-year-old president as one of fifty people under the age of forty poised to shape America's future. Two years later, *Christianity Today* also numbered Mohler among fifty influential young evangelical leaders. With a gift of nearly three million dollars and the blessing of Billy Graham himself, Mohler began work on the Billy Graham School of Evangelism, Missions, and Church Growth. Today the atmosphere on campus remains spirited. A new generation of faculty boasts impressive conservative credentials. Students delve enthusiastically into coursework and community life, eager to equip themselves for battle against liberalism in a new era. Southern's story, still animated by the past, has reached a new chapter.

The Story in the Walls

Material and visual culture molds campus into a living monument to this past. Hanging on the wall of the student center, an antique, sepia-toned print of a previous administration building displayed the words "Old School" in a bold, contemporary font. Across from it, another canvas featured an old photograph of suit-clad men in a Greek classroom. Even the name of Founders coffee shop, where I often purchased sandwiches between meetings and watched students come and go as I recorded field notes, elicited memories of days gone by. To get to Founders, I passed Edgars, a small boutique store named in honor of former president E. Y. (Edgar) Mullins. His portrait hung on the wall behind a cash register camouflaged in an antique writing desk. The photograph portrayed a serious-looking gentleman with a well-trimmed white beard, wool suit, and watch chain draped from his vest pocket. In a more casual photo hanging on the opposite wall, Mullins enjoyed a golf outing with two friends in an era when gentlemen sported stylish hats and tucked in their shirts, even while engaging in athletic activities. Images like these, lining the spaces students inhabit every day, help keep a nostalgic version of history alive.

Across campus, Alumni Chapel tells its own stories. When two advanced PhD students guided me on a campus tour, they pointed reverently to the southwest corner of the building where the Abstract of Principles is said to be cemented into the cornerstone. As students exited the service where *Recovering a Vision* was screened, many no doubt considered that the building, constructed more than six decades ago, has witnessed many of the key chapters in the Conservative Resurgence narrative. It has seen liberalism's rise, Molly Marshall's apostasy,

Figure 1.3. Antique photos displayed in Founders coffee shop during my fieldwork highlight the continued salience of history. One is labeled "Old School" (left), while another says, "Timeless Truth" (right). Photos by the author.

Figure 1.4. Edgar Y. Mullins. This portrait hung behind the cash register at Edgar's during my fieldwork. Author unknown. From the Boyce Digital Library, Southern Baptist Theological Seminary.

and Al Mohler's decisive leadership. When I returned on a later visit to take photos of the empty sanctuary, I was startled by my own hesitation to ascend the steps that lead to the podium. To those aware of its past, even stones and steps reverberate with the power of history.

Although the Honeycutt Student Center wasn't completed until 1997, well after the Resurgence, it too chronicles the story. Just inside one of the building's main

Figure 1.5. Mullins and partners playing golf. Photographer unknown. From the Boyce Digital Library, Southern Baptist Theological Seminary.

Figure 1.6. Interior of Southern's Alumni Chapel. Photo by the author.

entrances, a large glass display case featured three segments: "Truth," "Legacy," and "Vision." Under bold navy-blue letters spelling the word "Truth," three plaques displayed the Abstract of Principles. Below, a wooden lectern held a large, fragile-looking book containing the signatures of faculty members who have signed the document throughout the years. As my tour guides led me past

Figure 1.7. Display case just inside one of the main entrances to the Honeycutt Student Center. Photo by the author.

Figure 1.8. The Duke K. McCall Sesquicentennial Pavilion. Photo by the author.

the display, one mentioned that he believed the book had been left open to the page containing Molly Marshall's signature. He paused to check while I examined the rest of the display. These artifacts, carefully situated in a well-traveled spot, reinforce to students like him the particulars of Southern's story. As these students pass the display on their way to Founders coffee shop or to a workout at the gym, both just a few feet away, they remember that truth—understood as the opposite of liberal heresy—is the foundation of the seminary's legacy and vision. Those who oppose it cannot remain within its walls. Southern's holy trinity of Truth, Legacy, and Vision also embeds the Duke K. McCall Sesquicentennial Pavilion. On each of my visits to campus, the pavilion's dark stone wall greeted me with these words. The three headings accompany smaller quotes from the founders and their heirs including James P. Boyce and Basil Manly Jr. as well as Al Mohler. The story is literally written into the walls.

A USABLE PAST

Southern Seminary's stories are sociologically interesting because they are usable. The narrative of the seminary's creation, fall, and redemption has escaped the fate of many institutional histories, confined to a sleepy existence in dusty library archives. Instead, it animates the campus. Its specifics, grounded in history and divine authority itself, dictate the way things *ought* to be. Hearing and seeing these stories over and over again, etches them into students' consciousnesses. As one student explained, "Simply because seminary has passed it over my mind so many times, I think my mind, my thinking about these things, has taken on the shape of scripture to a small degree. That's why I think the way that I do." As they take ownership of these stories and their gendered prescriptions, students transform into Southern Baptist churchmen, cut from the same cloth as the venerated leaders of Southern's past. These stories, then, are useful as tools of identity construction. They both define what it means to be "in" and identify what—and who—is "out."

Who's In: Individual Formation

The tight coupling of Southern's stories enhances their salience. The Gospel Story and the story of the Conservative Resurgence are less two discrete narratives than they are extensions of each other. When one is referenced, the other is always implied. Alex, the eager first-year student who enthusiastically detailed the gendered principles of the creation account, drank in the narratives of his new community. He even wrote himself into their chapters. I interviewed Alex only hours after we had both attended the chapel screening of *Recovering a Vision*. He glowed as he described the film: "*We are remembering the past as we are in the present and looking forward to the future* [emphasis added]. It's something that really, really resonates with me. We're not lost in the past, but we remember those times when we came through hardships in our seminary. Or where we still battle hardships now and remember that it is God who works all these things for good." Following the film's verbal narration, Alex situated God as the primary agent in the story, working on behalf of the resurgence. Alex also repeatedly employed the word "we," positioning himself as a part of the institution's own story—the Conservative Resurgence—and, by extension, the narrative of God's own work in the world—the Gospel Story. The stories have become so tightly woven that it is unnecessary to distinguish where one ends and the other begins. Alex's facility in citing them signified his fit within the community.

Most of the men I interviewed displayed similar enthusiasm for these stories. Like Alex, they envisioned themselves as actors in an ongoing Resurgence, heirs of the founders and protégés of Mohler. As they inhabit the same physical spaces the Conservative Resurgence story describes, walking the same halls and sitting in the same pews, they can imagine *being there*. These narrative ties, enhanced by material culture, contribute to identity. They offer meaning and a sense of belonging. Moreover, the ongoing embattlement implicit within the story lends purpose to students' unfolding journeys. They see the battles of the 1990s as a fight for *their* institution, and they feel a burden to continue the fight.

But not all students experience the stories this way. While men dominate the campus, the women who also inhabit its spaces sometimes described them in different ways. For example, several of the women students I interviewed also recalled Dr. Sperling's Leadership in Family Ministry course as well as his propensity for classroom storytelling. Maya, a biblical counseling student, remembered that "he used a lot of stories, which is helpful, but I'm also not a man. . . . I'm really glad these men are sitting in his class, but in helping me understand more about [my own life] it wasn't applicable." Katherine voiced similar complaints: "That's a great class, if you're a man, because it's very oriented at the pastor, making sure that he's giving adequate attention to his family. It seems sometimes that it ignores a woman." Personal anecdotes like these, as well as the broader narratives that they support, center men. Women like Katherine and Maya must filter the stories to find resonance for their own lives. Not surprisingly, these two women also expressed limited enthusiasm for Southern's gendered identity frameworks. While both Katherine and Maya considered themselves to be complementarians, they also nuanced their beliefs against mainstream complementarian teachings. Katherine admitted chafing under classroom prescriptions for godly manhood and womanhood. "I probably wouldn't say I'm in line with [them] a hundred percent," she confessed. While women students do not compose enough of my sample for generalized conclusions, anecdotal evidence like this suggests that the stories told in Southern's male-dominated classrooms are likely most formative for men.

Who's Out: Boundary Maintenance

Southern's cultural identity work does not end with its own members. Stories also contribute to the sharp boundaries the institution maintains against outsiders. By associating "gospel" with culturally conservative, theologically Reformed commitments, the stories collectively promote embattlement against a host of cultural and theological "others." Along with secular liberals and feminists, non-Reformed Arminians, mainline Protestants, egalitarian evangelicals, and many global Christians lay outside Southern's carefully guarded borders. They allow little room for diversity or disagreement because "gospel" is always the final word. Even in a host context as hospitable to Christian institutions as the United States, Southern's community successfully nurtures the embattled posture of an underdog, extending Christian Smith's thesis that American evangelicals are at once "embattled and thriving" (Smith 1998).

Two decades after the Conservative Resurgence, gender egalitarianism remains a symbolic foe. It is also a conveniently tangible one. The conservative warriors of the resurgence battled over far more than gender, but an enemy as nebulous as "liberalism" can be difficult combat. It is much easier to attack the visible practice of allowing women in pulpits. Southern's usable history sustains embattlement through this imagery. Rather than downplaying the ousting of Molly Marshall as an aberration, the Conservative Resurgence story emphasizes the episode, transforming it, and her, to represent a persistent liberal threat. Marshall provides liberalism with a name, even a feminine face. While students do not seem to harbor animosity against Marshall as a person, they do condemn the liberalism that she symbolizes.

Gendered symbolism also remains crucial in network alliances beyond Southern's own walls. The powerful Gospel Coalition relies heavily on complementarian language to distinguish insiders from outsiders.[3] It is no accident that the group's rhetoric bears such striking resemblance to Southern's. Mohler is a member of the Gospel Coalition's council, where he and other leaders from Southern work closely with representatives from other complementarian bodies such as the Presbyterian Church of America. Embattlement over gender, which at Southern goes hand in hand with questions about human sexuality, also facilitates more surprising alliances. Just prior to my fieldwork, Mohler delivered an address on religious liberty at Brigham Young University, an institution of the Church of Jesus Christ of Latter-day Saints, which most evangelicals, including Southern Baptists, do not even recognize as Christian. Mohler readily acknowledged this, but he nonetheless extended a hand of friendship: "You know who I am and what I believe. I know who you are and what you believe. It has been my great privilege to know friendship and share conversation with leaders of the LDS church. . . . We do not enjoy such friendship and constructive conversation *in spite* of our theological differences, but *in light* of them. This does not eliminate the possibility of conversation. To the contrary, this kind of convictional difference at the deepest level makes for the most important kind of conversation. This is why I am so thankful for your gracious invitation."[4] The talk explored common interests in religious liberty—specifically in light of the groups' shared rejection of same-sex marriage. Later, when I interviewed Mohler in his office, he explained the visit to me, reiterating, "[Mormons] are way beyond our confession. We do not recognize them as Christian, but on issues of family structure and many deep moral convictions there's commonality there."

Conflation of gender egalitarianism with liberalism also produces surprising enemies. Curious how far these bonds of commonality extended, I asked Mohler to expand on the idea. Could he, I wondered, imagine a similarly congenial relationship with egalitarian Christian groups who would, presumably, have far more in common with Baptist belief? Mohler seemed confused. "I'd like to know what those groups would be," he responded. In keeping with his own definition of confessional traditions, which he had articulated earlier in the conversation, I suggested two egalitarian groups that I knew to be theologically defined: evangelical Wesleyans and segments of the Christian Reformed Church. Mohler had little to say about either of these. Reluctantly acknowledging what he called "concentric circles of affinity," he nonetheless added, "I think those relationships are going to be quite strained, more so than even in the past as we go into the future." "Why is that?" I pressed. "Because," he answered, "I think the hermeneutic involved in egalitarianism is going to have a great deal of difficulty withstanding some of the other cultural pressures." For Mohler, fears that an egalitarian reading of the Bible would lead to an interpretive slippery slope seem to have stymied alliance with egalitarian Christians, even other evangelicals.[5]

Southern's stories erect clear boundaries. More than practical advice to individual men and women on how to conduct their lives, gender polarization and male headship delineate the borders of Southern's group identity. Within these borders is an orderly package of hierarchical gender ideals, neo-Reformed theology, and orthodox Christian belief. These elements, and the stories that sustain them, are so tightly coupled that rejection of any component would signal rejection of the whole—and likely result in social sanctions. Molly Marshall and Diana Garland serve as cautionary tales. Casualties of a theological and cultural battle, their violations of institutional borders resulted in expulsion. Their battles symbolize a much larger war that continues. Even in victory, Southern's true believers remain embattled.

Who Tells the Stories: The Right to Power

Southern's stories dictate who holds power. The SBC's conservative shift in the 1980s and 1990s was itself a struggle for the power to define Southern Baptist identity. Likewise, Southern's own battle over women's ordination was a dispute over churchly power: who has the right to authoritatively interpret biblical teaching and proclaim it from the pulpit. In both cases, conservative white men won decisively. Today, almost uniformly, masculine voices govern public discourse. Men, not women, preach sermons, make administrative decisions, and interpret the meaning of biblical texts. They frame everything from sermon content to syllabi wording around their own experiences and points of view. The institution's usable history legitimates their authority. The Gospel Story's imperative of male headship situates it as a masculine right. The Conservative Resurgence story casts the seminary's founders as rightful guardians of group identity and forges connections between these revered founders and the powerful men who currently walk Southern's halls. They are conservatives all, driven by common conviction, and embattled against all who stand against it. In a persistent cycle of entitlement, Southern's stories legitimate the authority of conservative male leaders, who in turn continue to tell, and control, the stories themselves.

This cycle marginalizes not only women but also people of color. A more complete story of Southern's history, extended beyond its Conservative Resurgence versions, also includes a deep legacy of racism. All four of its venerated founders—James P. Boyce, John Broadus, Basil Manly Jr., and William Williams—were slave owners. Two of them, Boyce and Broadus, served in the Confederate Army in a war fought largely over southern states' rights to retain the practice of race-based chattel slavery. Southern has begun to reckon with its racialized history, but not all African Americans are satisfied.[6] As white America began awakening to the scope of racially motivated violence in 2020, a number of Black Southern Baptists, including pastor Dwight McKissic, openly pled with Mohler to remove the slaveholders' names from campus buildings.[7] Former Southern student Kyle Howard turned to Twitter to make his case. "Statues have not been erected," he wrote, "but the buildings at SBTS and the name of the undergrad school itself, are monuments. As a black student at Boyce College and later SBTS, I walked those halls constantly encountering monuments to confederates/White supremacists. . . . I have to see the faces of slave masters every time I walk down the halls as someone would have them on their shirt, or maybe their coffee mug."[8] Among my own field research photos, captured several years before this tweet, is an image of a display in Southern's bookstore. In the picture, a bobblehead of Mohler sits beside ceramic mugs bearing portraits of Williams and Boyce. Howard's tweet was not hyperbole. When Mohler declined to remove these founders' names from campus buildings, he continued to narratively center white lives.[9] The near complete absence of people of color from my interview sample at Southern points painfully to the extent of these narrative inequalities. Not all men, then, reap the full rewards of Southern's androcentric stories.

Insider voices continue to serve as the stories' narrators. In 2009, faculty member Gregory Wills released an official institutional history, a 546-page tome titled *Southern Baptist Theological Seminary, 1859–2009*. While the book does

Figure 1.9. A display in the campus bookstore during my fieldwork included a bobble-head depiction of Al Mohler alongside mugs featuring portraits of founders James P. Boyce and William Williams. Photo by the author.

include the perspectives of moderates ousted in the 1990s, Wills writes from the inside. Like *Recovering a Vision*, his record of Southern's hundred-fifty-year history chronicles a tale of orthodox conservatism, consecrated by the founders, lost to liberalism, and recovered by Al Mohler himself. The book's final paragraphs bring the story full circle, returning the reader to the story's beginning: "Mohler's deep and genuine appreciation for Boyce shaped his vision. . . . He viewed his role first as a steward administering the seminary on behalf of the founders, donors, and above all the churches of the Southern Baptist Convention. He aspired to fidelity to the founders' commitment to evangelical orthodoxy, to Baptist principles and practices, and to denominational trust. Everything from general vision to specific policy had to rest on that foundation" (Wills 2009, 546). Read in the context of the Conservative Resurgence and Mohler's insistence on hiring only men who rejected the ordination of women, which Wills describes in detail, assertions like this conflate "evangelical orthodoxy" with commitments to male headship. They also build unquestioning support for Mohler's continued authority. One student, particularly eager to help me understand Southern's story, encouraged me to read Wills's book. When our interview ended, he insisted that I follow him down the hall to the campus bookstore to see its display of the books. This is a story of which the community is acutely aware and intensely proud.

More than twenty years after the Conservative Resurgence, Mohler remains the heart of the seminary. He regularly devotes time to questions of gender and sexuality on his popular blog and on the podcast he produces from an on-campus studio. Each time Mohler affirms male headship from the pulpit or denounces cultural acceptance of transgender identity on his blog, students remember the battles of the 1990s. These battles, along with their victors' right to power, live on through the community's stories.

THE OTHER STORIES

Despite its ubiquity and scope, the Gospel Story is, in fact, a recent invention. In times past, Southern Baptists, even those who occupied the authoritative spaces of Southern's administration wing, told a very different version of the biblical story. Only a few decades ago, Southern Seminary housed moderate Southern Baptists like Frank Stagg. "No one," said a colleague, "has ever taken the New Testament more seriously than Frank Stagg, who spent his entire life wrestling with it, paying the price in sweat and hours in an unrelenting quest to hear the message expressed in a language no longer spoken and directed toward a cultural context so foreign to the modern reader" (Tolbert 1984, 2). Stagg's biblical story shared many chapters with the Gospel Story: creation by an almighty and triune God, the fall of humanity into sin, redemption in Jesus Christ. Stagg also insisted on the Bible's applicability to modern life. In contrast to the Gospel Story's stress on creational order, however, Stagg's hermeneutical emphasis on Jesus led to radically different conclusions about gender differences and God's work in the human world. Jesus, he insisted, "opened the door wide for women" (Flowers 2012, 62). Along with his wife Evelyn, Stagg authored a book titled *Women in the World of Jesus* (1978). He also broke with widespread evangelical support for the first Gulf War and urged Baptists to consider Christian pacifism.[10] Stagg read the same Bible but interpreted it through a different lens. Both the creation account and Paul's epistles, which chronologically followed Christ, must be read, he insisted, through the lens of Jesus, not the other way around. These emphases—the centrality of Jesus, his interactions with women, and the cultural barriers he lifted—are noticeably absent from the Gospel Story that Southern students now narrate. In Jesus's place, Paul and creational order take de facto primacy.

This disparity is, in part, what made the battles of the 1980s and 1990s so heated. Both conservatives and moderates fervently affirmed the Bible's teachings as true and authoritative. But the two sides disagreed vehemently about what those teachings were (Ammerman 1990). They did not dispute the Bible. They disputed who had the authority to narrate its message. Standing on the seminary's lawn after losing her post in Southern's theology department, Molly Marshall told a crowd of over five hundred students and faculty that the message Mohler and his new conservative guard preached was "not the Gospel, but another gospel" (Wills 2009, 539). She pled with the community not to allow the

Gospel Story—an interpretation that consecrated gender polarization and centered men—to hijack the broader notion of Gospel. Others agreed, but the Gospel Story and its narrators won.

Among the casualties are the stories of other women. The Conservative Resurgence story remembers Diana Garland for her conflict with Mohler over David Sherwood's faculty appointment. But Garland also helped to build Southern's Carver School of Social Work, which carried the rich heritage of the Woman's Missionary Union Training School. Mohler's arrival, however, spelled the end of that project. Explaining that "the culture of social work and the culture of theological education are not congruent," Mohler recommended that Southern's trustees close the school (Wills 2009, 541). In the end, Garland lost both her job and her institutional legacy.[11] *Recovering a Vision* and the seminary's 566-page institutional history acknowledge the Carver School and Garland's contributions to the institution only in reference to the Sherwood incident.

The Carver school's closure left a particular absence. Unlike theology, biblical studies, and even missions, fields that have largely built the ministerial careers of men, social work has long been the province of women.[12] It is, in fact, one of the few vocations to reward feminine nurture with salaries and career opportunities. By dissolving Southern's social work program, Mohler signaled that the new Southern Seminary would invest its resources in male preachers and theologians, not in lay women (or even men) whose Christian service lay beyond churchly control. He has since replaced the school of social work with a "biblical counseling" degree. This program is distinct from counseling departments at other universities in that it does not carry extrainstitutional accreditation and does not provide graduates with licensure. Men often consider the program preparation for their roles as pastors. While the program continues to be popular with women as well, they are typically limited to employment within churches and parachurch organizations headed by men. The shift from social work to biblical counseling stymied women's vocational agency.

The Southern students I interviewed remained largely unaware of their institution's Other Stories. Names like Frank Stagg and Diana Garland have been all but erased from collective memory, not because the institution denies their existence, but because their stories do not align with its identity narrative. The arc of Southern's stories has no room for Southern Baptists whose study of the Bible led them to egalitarian and Arminian—rather than complementarian and Reformed—convictions. These forgotten actors are undeniably Baptist and every bit as much a part of the institution's past as James P. Boyce and E. Y. Mullins, but they are not useful in forming students into a complementarian identity.

This pattern extends to the broader SBC itself. In 2000 the denomination undertook a considerable revision of the Baptist Faith and Message, its official statement of faith. Among many changes, it removed this statement: "The criterion by which the Bible is to be interpreted is Jesus Christ." The revision instead reads, "All scripture is a testimony to Christ, who is himself the focus of divine revelation," a subtle narrowing of Jesus's centrality in Baptist belief. The new version also removed the following: "Baptists are a people who profess a living faith. This faith is rooted and grounded in Jesus Christ who is the same yesterday, and today, and forever. Therefore, the sole authority for faith and practice among Baptists is Jesus Christ whose will is revealed in the Holy Scriptures." Other changes were more explicitly gendered. For example, the new version featured a contracted interpretation of women's place in church life. Longtime Southern Baptist leader Russell Dilday, who was removed from the presidency at Southwestern Baptist Theological Seminary and replaced by Paige Patterson during the SBC's Conservative Resurgence, pointed out that a new statement on the family featured more length and detail than the sections on God, Jesus Christ, the Holy Spirit, and the Scriptures (2001). Dilday also expressed concern that the revision altered the wording of the long-held Baptist doctrine of the priesthood of the believer or "soul competency." The revisers, Dilday wrote, "expressed their mistrust of personal, individual experience, focusing instead on accountability to an approved belief system. This in essence rejects the historical Baptist emphasis of the priesthood of each individual believer (singular), replacing it with a more Reformed doctrine of the priesthood of believers (plural)."[13]

Dilday was right to see these shifts as momentous. Despite their enthusiasm for history and tradition, the Southern students I interviewed, in training to become the next generation of Southern Baptist leaders, seemed indeed to have sidelined traditional Baptist commitments. No one on Southern's campus used the language of soul competency or the priesthood of the believer in interviews, even when arguing for women's "equality in value" with men. The overwhelming majority of the students I spoke with, however, affirmed the importance of gospel order: strong male leadership in the Church and the role of the husband as spiritual head of his wife. Some even framed the marriage relationship with the language of priesthood. Jackson and Doug explained:

JACKSON: I would say that godly manhood involves a sense of the priesthood, the believer being aware of God's leadership and the biblical distinctives that he would have for particularly family.

DOUG: One of the metaphors that we have for husband and father, one of the pictures that we have in scriptures is the priest. So just as Christ is the final priest of the church, the husband is to a small extent the Xerox copy of Christ's role to the family. . . . I think the priest's role is to say, just as Christ absorbs the wrath of God, if there's a conflict between us, it's my job to eat it as the priest and say it's gone, we're okay. You know what I mean?

It seems that the priesthood of the believer has largely been replaced with the priesthood of the husband and of the authoritative churchman who guards conservative orthodoxy.

Stories are not static. They are pliable and usable. They are made. As this chapter's brief history illustrates, the Gospel Story may be pervasive at Southern Seminary, but it is not a fixed reality. It is a newly constructed narrative, and it is contested. What cannot be contested, however, is its great pedagogical success. While my conversations with students and even some faculty suggested varying degrees of commitment to complementarian expectations, not a single student questioned the basic prescriptions of gender differentiation and male headship. Almost without exception, they articulated these principles, and their biblical grounding, with ease and enthusiasm. Even more importantly, no one questioned the men whose authority the stories uphold, at least not while physically situated on campus. The single exception to this posture of deference only reluctantly voiced misgivings about Mohler's uncontested power—and only after insisting that we move our conversation to a remote location on campus where we were less likely to be seen, much less overheard.

The form of Southern's stories facilitates their usability. The Gospel Story and Conservative Resurgence share thick and intricate ties. Together, they tightly couple history with theology and gendered practice with biblical truth, effectively sacralizing male-centered power. The result is a single metanarrative, spanning the entirety of human history and held together by heavily gendered notions of order. The authoritative story offers identity to individual community members who find purpose in its principles. There is indeed power, even *agency*, in story.

These stories work so well, in fact, that they often take on a life of their own. One administrator, rolling his eyes, explained that some students become overzealous in their complementarian enthusiasm. "We call them cage stagers," he said. "It's the joke amongst professors. [The students] are young and they learn just enough theology where you need to build a cage around them so they don't hurt anybody." He went on, "They get excited about all sorts of aspects of the theology, and they just want to live it out to the nth degree. They're not abusive. That's not what I'm communicating, they're just overzealous. . . . They're just uptight about it, and I just say, 'Alright look, you are supposed to lead your home, but just relax about it.'"

Indeed, zealous—and even not so zealous—articulations of gendered discourse leave casualties. While women do appear in Southern's narratives, they play only supporting roles in stories propelled by masculine leads. Or, like Molly Marshall and Diana Garland, they surface as Jezebels, antagonists expelled for their liberal deviance. Similar dynamics play out in contemporary practice. Women participate in the life of the community, but largely from behind the scenes. Their identities are formed and informed by the principles the stories contain, but their voices have nearly disappeared from Southern's pulpits, boardrooms, and administrative offices, rendering them all but silent on decisions about programming and hiring, and—importantly in an era of #churchtoo—pronouncements about church discipline and accountability. Mostly, women's voices echo the stories that men tell. If a woman wishes to question the stories or deviate from their principles, she is reminded of Molly Marshall's fate.

To be sure, women have long found creative paths to empowerment within restrictive religious frameworks (Mahmood 2005; Chong 2008; Griffith 2000; Bowler 2019). Indeed, despite their overtly patriarchal constructions, Southern's stories promise both religious agency and opportunity to women who obey complementarian rules. As chapter 2 will show, some women, though not all of them, are able to realize these rewards.

CHAPTER 2

Beard Oil and Fine China

EMBODIED PRACTICE AT SOUTHERN SEMINARY

My wife is a phenomenal cook, and some of these young women have not had the opportunity to really learn. She teaches a pie crust class that draws all kinds of people, of all ages. She has the mirrored table and all, and it's kind of like Southern Living. —Albert Mohler, president of Southern Seminary

Al Mohler, despite his reputation for machine-like efficiency, was running late. Apologizing for the delay, his receptionist offered me a bottle of water and introduced me to a young intern named Collin. He greeted me with a shy smile as we both realized that we had met during an earlier stage of my research. Collin seemed happy to see me, and we talked for a few minutes about his summer job and plans for the upcoming academic year. A few moments later, Mohler emerged from one of the office suite's two wings. Even on a stifling hot summer day in Kentucky, the president wore an elegant dark suit and red bow tie. He welcomed me—and, to my surprise, Collin—through the wide glass doors that led into his office. The office's most striking feature was a massive wooden desk. The desk, an exact replica of the Resolute Desk that sits in the Oval Office, displayed a collection of expensive fountain pens used for personal correspondence. The room surrounding it was meticulously arranged with books, photographs, richly polished wooden furniture, and a grandfather clock. Mohler settled into a leather wing-backed chair and indicated a spot for me on a nearby couch. Collin quietly took a seat near the door.

As our conversation began, I asked about the institution's approach to student formation. Mohler explained, "We are just as committed as we have ever been to a classical model of theological education, but at the same time for all kinds of healthy reasons we are deeply involved in what sociologists would call lived religion as a project. The distinctions that might have been present a generation ago between theory and practice or theology and the spiritual life have largely disappeared." I nodded, impressed that he employed the vocabulary of "lived religion," terminology from my own discipline. "What does that mean in practical terms," I asked, "especially for gender ideals?" He continued,

> Students who come here are buying into an entire project, a way of life. In other words, they're not just making a decision about theological education, they're making a decision about the kind of person they are and the kind of person they want to be. . . . Gender issues, sexuality issues, theological issues, biblical authority issues—theological distinctives that were once something you listed in a catalog—are now the substance of every day conversation. I would say that we try to model it, we live it out publicly, we talk about it all the time, we try to provide support structures, constant experiences. We obviously make this a total priority when hiring faculty. The curriculum has been constantly revised and is under constant revision in order to respond to that very challenge.

Mohler, in other words, is committed to not only telling stories but living them. To be sure, the seminary articulates its complementarianism in theological language, as chapter 1 described. But Southern devotes as much effort to embodying its gendered stories as it does to narrating them with words.

No one embodies the "new" Southern Seminary as visibly as Mohler himself. His office, personal accessories, composure, and even imposing desk powerfully invoke Southern's usable history. Constantly visible on campus despite a rigorous travel schedule, Mohler also maintains a perpetual presence on Twitter, blogs, and podcasts and regularly fills the chapel's pulpit to moderate services and preach sermons. Clad in a suit and iconic bow tie, Southern's esteemed president carries an aura of confidence, respectability, and power. He has become a living symbol of conservative masculine authority, and his presence saturates the campus. Students like Collin hear Southern's stories told in sermons and classroom lectures, but they also see them embodied by Mohler and the faculty members he carefully hires.

As Mohler himself told me in his office, this is by design. Southern conducts holistic student formation. As the following pages illustrate, Mohler and the new conservative guard have constructed a pedagogical experience that attends to students as social, not just spiritual and intellectual, beings. It nurtures both individual identity and group identity, implicitly recognizing gender as an important element in self-presentation and awareness (Chodorow 1978; Messner 1990) and as an accomplishment of contextualized social relationships (West and Zimmerman 1987; Ridgeway 2011; Pyke and Johnson 2003; Ridgeway and Correll 2004). As this chapter demonstrates, Southern also recognizes the implications gendered practices carry for communities and broader social structures (Risman 2004; Collins 1990; Hartmann 1981). The following pages explore the community's thickly gendered codes of Godly Manhood and Godly Womanhood, their symbolic meanings, and the mechanisms that sustain their salience within the community.[1] Specifically, I show how these codes transform everyday choices like food and clothing into symbolic representations of the male headship and gender-differentiated order Southern's identity narratives celebrate. This tight coupling of discursive practice and embodied practice is powerfully formative.

GODLY MANHOOD: DESIGNED FOR DOMINION

Southern's men know what it means to act like men. Their community prescribes specific patterns of masculinity, codified into a set of scripts it enthusiastically refers to as Godly Manhood. My treatment of these scripts as ideal types accentuates their most notable traits, illustrating them through the community's use of material culture as well as students' explanations in interviews. These scripts do not, in other words, exist in perfect form in the real world. No one man embodies them flawlessly. Nevertheless, because the seminary is visibly dominated by men, Godly Manhood governs the institution's ethos and is readily evident even to me, an outsider. Its three scripts—the churchman, the family man, and the manly man—saturate sacred spaces like the chapel and color everyday interactions between community members.

Churchmen

At Southern Seminary, all men are churchmen. While Godly Manhood's expectations apply to all Christian men—not just those pursuing seminary degrees—those who enroll in seminary are, by self-selection, pursuing a more intense form of churchly leadership. The seminary community expects them to become churchmen, living, breathing heirs to the Conservative Resurgence that triumphed over liberalism and feminized pulpits in the 1990s. Strong church leadership has become increasingly important among Southern Baptists. Grady Cothen (1995), Arthur Farnsley (1994), and others have documented a growing denominational emphasis on pastoral authority in the years since the Conservative Resurgence. As the previous chapter also demonstrated, the traditional Southern Baptist stress on each believer's spiritual accountability has given way in recent decades to emphasis on the authority of the inerrant Bible and, especially, of the powerful men who preach it. As President Mohler announced Southern Seminary's new W. A. Criswell Chair of Expository Preaching in the fall of 2013, he declared, "It is very much about the pulpit. . . . The Lord has raised up men in every generation." The gendered order that Southern's stories promote fits comfortably within this movement toward a more hierarchical, leader-driven ecclesiology.

Nowhere is this churchly power showcased more clearly than in Southern Seminary's twice-weekly chapel services. The expansive sanctuary of Alumni Chapel seats twelve hundred worshippers in old wooden pews that groan when audience members collectively stand to sing. Though music was an important part of the services I visited, worship bands and song leaders positioned themselves not on the stage at the front of the chapel but on the floor below. Indeed, Southern's stage is a carefully guarded space. A four-foot wooden partition separates the stage from the choir loft behind it, and the stage itself rises another three feet from the carpeted sanctuary floor. There is flexibility in these surrounding areas, but the polished wooden stage itself is an uncontested domain of masculine authority where only preachers roam. These preachers are carefully selected. Each semester, the seminary's leadership invites speakers, including some of the Southern Baptist world's most prominent voices, to reinforce the community's biblical and institutional narratives from the chapel pulpit. They espouse inerrancy. They perform conservative authority and respectability. They masterfully deliver polished sermons. The men who fill this space are the churchmen whom seminarians sitting in the pews aspire to become. In my visits to Southern Seminary, I never saw a woman address the chapel audience to make an announcement, read scripture, or even stand on the stage that holds the pulpit. Although women filled seats in the pews and participated in the groups that provided music for the services, chapel at Southern Seminary is clearly the domain of men.

These churchmen project a powerful image of Southern Baptist masculinity. Wearing dark suits and light-colored dress shirts, often accented with silk ties, they preach with confident voices. One morning, popular guest speaker David Platt's sermon escalated in volume and emotional intensity as it progressed. He gripped the sides of the pulpit, squared his shoulders, and leaned toward his audience with a piercing gaze as he warned of the dangers ahead should the church neglect to take a stand against "so-called same-sex marriage." With his voice he denounced liberalism, abortion, androgyny, and homosexuality. With his body he performed the powerful script of a conservative, heterosexual churchman.[2]

In another chapel performance, one of Southern's own professors provided a different masculine model. As he took the stage and situated himself comfortably behind the pulpit, this preacher's broad shoulders, white hair, and confident presence gave him the air of authoritative respectability. His deep voice filled the auditorium. "It's a joy to pastor a church called 'Buck Run,'" he said in a soft southern drawl. "It is the manliest church name in the state of Kentucky. And at Buck Run . . . we put conceal and carry permits in the new members packets. It's a little bit of a different culture there. I can't promise you that no nut will ever come in the church and shoot me one day when I'm preaching, but I can pretty well promise he will not get out alive. Our big concern is crossfire. So it's a very special place."[3] The words were spoken tongue in cheek, but this celebration of gun culture did not seem to be out of place in the chapel. Students all around the sanctuary chuckled. Some laughed out loud. If anyone questioned the implicit

approval of violent masculinity in these introductory remarks, they were outnumbered by those for whom conceal and carry seemed a legitimate expression
of Godly Manhood.

Though he carries a different, more refined, demeanor, Al Mohler most powerfully embodies churchman masculinity. He presents a striking example of
what Max Weber termed "charismatic authority" (Weber 1956). To be sure,
Mohler's leadership relies on more than his personal charisma. It was, in fact,
through highly bureaucratic maneuvering that the architects of Conservative
Resurgence placed him in a position of power in the first place. But over time
the community has come to uphold Mohler as a compelling leader who has
earned his right to authority. His construction of the past animates Southern's
historical understanding. His vision of the future inspires. While the community does not understand him to have divine powers himself, it certainly views
him as an exceptional person whose authority comes from God.

Mohler and Southern's other churchmen give flesh to the community's discursive stories. With their suits and commanding postures and deep voices, these
men set themselves apart from women who enter the chapel as spectators and
backup singers. Their embattled postures and authoritative voices, vivid performances of what Martin Riesebrodt calls "behavior regulation practices," urge
continued vigilance against liberal encroachment. They reinforce the notions
that true Southern Baptists are conservative and that godly leadership is masculine. Aspiring churchmen within the student body are eager to emulate their
examples. Occasionally a student is invited to deliver a scripture reading, prayer,
or announcement in chapel, but these opportunities to stand on the formidable
stage are rare. More often, students rehearse the churchman script in more subtle ways. They carry stacks of scholarly books through campus and devote stu-
dious attention to their studies of theology and doctrine. They invest in their
preaching classes and meet with each other in the campus center to debate cultural and theological issues. These practices all communicate ambition toward
the type of commanding leadership that the chapel stage symbolizes.

As Riesebrodt anticipates, these embodied practices are powerful. They reinforce the consolidation of churchly power into the hands of trained, creden-
tialed, churchmen. The priesthood of the believer has become a priesthood of a
certain kind of believer: the respectable, classically masculine, seminary-trained,
Southern Baptist man. When students graduate, they take this expectation with
them—along with their hefty ESV Study Bibles, their knowledge of Hebrew, and
their polished homiletics skills. Southern's own community practice encourages
an almost unquestioning deference to the authority of seasoned churchmen.

Family Men

Godly Men lead more than churches. They also exercise headship as husbands
of wives and fathers of children. Southern engages nuclear family life with the

same public intentionality as it does matters of church polity, extending the Godly Man's authority into his private life. Here too Mohler provides a powerfully prescriptive symbolism. Just as the president's churchly performances set the bar for the public churchman script, his familial life provides a highly visible model for domestic life. As we talked in his office, Mohler stressed the importance of marriage, particularly his own. His description of his wife Mary's involvement in his own work illustrates the porous boundaries between a Godly Man's public and private worlds.

MOHLER: It would be very difficult for a single man to do this job.

LWS: Why is that?

MOHLER: Because he could not model many things that we talked about here . . . such as what it would mean to be a good husband. How to balance the responsibilities of being a husband and leader in many other areas of life.

LWS: How have you been able to exemplify that?

MOHLER: My wife travels with me when she can. At every major event my wife is there and happily there, participating and intellectually engaged, relationally engaged. . . . It would be difficult for someone to do the kind of job I do and to have a family and wife that were distant from the campus and not engaged. My wife directs the Seminary Wives Institute as a volunteer and runs an entire program for seminary wives. . . . She loves students, and she spends a great deal of her time especially with faculty wives; with the wives of our donors and with the wives of our students and female students; just encouraging them and helping them. I mean my wife . . . I'm afraid this is going to sound trite and almost play into a stereotype—but my wife is a phenomenal cook, and some of these young women have not had the opportunity to really learn. She teaches a pie crust class that draws all kinds of people, of all ages. She has the mirrored table and all, and it's kind of like *Southern Living*. That's just something she gives and they know who she is. They know how to get in touch with her. We're a part of the local church here. I'm a teaching pastor of a local church here. I've been here for twenty years in that capacity. This is my twenty-second year beginning at the seminary, so they've seen our children grow up. In the Christmas card that the institution sends out every Christmas that so many of our friends and supporters of the seminary put up on their refrigerators and use to remember to pray for us, they can watch our kids grow up from being babies to my daughter's wedding last year. There's an enormous credibility that comes because they know who we are, where we live.

Mohler's credibility as a leader, he suggests here, is closely tied to his embodied headship of his own family. His wife's support and even her own participation in his public ministry are crucial to the job he does and the authority he sustains.

The connection is not lost on students. When I asked men to explain what Godly Manhood meant to them, several prefaced their lengthy answers with brief comments about commitment to Jesus and the practice of spiritual disciplines. But they quickly moved, unprompted, to explanations of headship in marriage. This was often more than hypothetical. Even though many of the students I interviewed had only recently graduated from college, many were already married, engaged to be married, or seriously dating. As their secular counterparts wait longer and longer to walk the aisle, Southern students defy the trend of delayed marriage. One professor told me proudly that even students in the school's undergraduate programs are eager to settle into married life: "I've been invited to five or six weddings in the last year. A student just asked me to perform a wedding in the fall, actually. These are all college students. At the seminary you expect it. . . . I think it's pushing against the new narrative where you get married when you're thirty—or, if you're in Manhattan or Lincoln Park you get married when you're thirty-eight, you know? So [this institution is] encouraging guys to just step up and take a wife." Southern encourages men to "step up and take a wife" because to be a Godly Man is, largely, to be the head of a wife and family.

Most family men expect to provide financially for their wives and children. By assuming economic responsibility for families, they identify with the Gospel Story's Adam who worked the ground of Eden. The implications of this expectation, however, present a practical dilemma for men, including most seminary students, who do not bring home large paychecks, especially when their wives' jobs do provide salaries. Katherine explained, however, that this need not present a problem. Her own income, she reasoned, could facilitate rather than compromise her husband's headship:

> My husband is accountable for the financial wellbeing of our home and making sure that, you know, our budget is where it needs to be. . . . He keeps track of finances, but I'm a participant in it. So I work, and I bring in income as well. He says, "This is how much we have to use at the grocery store." Like, "Will you help me make sure that we do that?" I'm the one who makes the grocery list. I may say, "No, we can't get that. It's outside of the budget." But he is held responsible for where we're at financially and for the provision.

Charlie and his wife had a similar arrangement. A sturdy southerner with several years of seminary education under his belt, Charlie had given a great deal of thought to his role as a family man. While he affirmed the importance of a husband's role as provider, Charlie also explained that, in order to meet the financial demands of raising a family during his seminary enrollment, his wife currently worked full-time while he took classes, and both parents juggled child care duties. Aware that this description suggested a de facto egalitarian arrangement, Charlie clarified,

I have the burden of knowing what's going on with the household. I'll give you a story to illustrate. [My wife] was in the elevator with some of her coworkers and they were talking about paychecks and stuff. She said, "I don't even know how much I make." And they're like, "What?!" And she said, "My husband takes care of all that." And then they got closer to the bottom and they asked, "Didn't you bring an umbrella today?" She's like, "No, my husband didn't tell me I needed it." So even though she's going to work, there was still a headship there.

Charlie admitted feeling guilty for the extra burden his wife carried but insisted that he nonetheless retained responsibility. He was the head of the family.

As Charlie's elevator story illustrates, a family man's headship requires far more than financial provision. Wives may exercise agency within marriage, students often assured me, but they are ultimately accountable to their husbands' vision. I asked Kevin, a recent graduate of a conservative Christian university in the South, if Godly Manhood was different from Godly Womanhood. "Yes," he responded immediately. "I would say one of the primary differences is that the man leads and the woman responds and helps in that leading. While the man leads and is carrying out a vision, the woman is the one who responds and helps with her gifts and talents in carrying that out." Eric, a newlywed, concurred, illustrating from his own experience, "[my wife and I] were very cautious about how we interacted spiritually in the dating process. Even in making decisions, whether that was asking her on a date or establishing some kind of relationship, she willingly let me do that and would be like, 'Hey man, I'm going to let you do this. I expect you to as a man. Here's a way you can lead even though you're not my spiritual supervisor,' you know? 'You can already be a leader in [the relationship].' And so she was—she is—an enabler to me, which is really helpful." As each of these men recognized, the family man embodies headship not only through financial earning but through relational rhythms.

In other words, Godly Manhood is social. Charlie explained, "I don't become a man apart from loving my wife, being a part of a church, being a part of creation, and being a father. Those things are integral to it." Expounding on this point, Charlie even framed his relationship with his dog as an opportunity to exercise male headship.

[This] doesn't mean that I plant the food that my family needs or hunt the food that my family needs. It means supporting my family through other activities, providing for those under me. . . . I think even the fact that I have a dog that does what I tell him to do—for the most part—and he's *my* dog. I mean, even my wife and kids can't get him to do everything I can get him to do, you know? If I come in the room or into the yard, he's gonna obey me, no matter what anybody else is saying. Even in this broken and fallen world, I'm exercising dominion by training that animal.

Within the Gospel Story's nonnegotiable gendered order, the family man can affirm gender differentiation and male headship in a host of ways. Everything from paychecks to umbrellas to pets has the potential to become a sacred prop, illustrating the order of the universe as God intended.

Learning to embody this order is an ongoing—and sometimes confusing—process. As I sat in the student center writing field notes one afternoon, I overheard one young man seeking a friend's advice. Leaning against the wall next to the table where I worked, he described his wife's anxiety over a series of recent email exchanges at her job. Her stress, he told his friend, was serious enough that it caused her to be apprehensive, even after work hours. As her husband, anxious to lead as a Godly Man in their relationship, he wanted to view the emails himself, but she resisted. "She said she doesn't want me to solve her problems for her," he explained uncomfortably. Then he wondered aloud, "Should I insist that she show me the messages? I know she's a professional and all," he said, exasperated, "but I'm supposed to be her protector." Male headship might be nonnegotiable, but it can be difficult to implement in everyday life.

Godly Manhood's own parameters intensify these complexities. As important as authoritative headship is to the construct, the Gospel Story's reminder to "love your wife as Christ loved the Church" also cautions men against callous authoritarianism. Along with leadership in decision making and breadwinning, students of Godly Manhood expect to provide attentive, relational care for their families. Charlie appealed to the Gospel Story's imagery of the Church as the bride of Christ: "For husbands, it looks like laying down your life for your wife as Christ lay down His life for the Church. It looks like, first off, me being willing to ask the question, 'What's best for [my wife] right now? In this situation, what's best for her?' Not, 'What's best for me?' And that's everywhere from in the marriage bed to what we're having for supper." While nurture remains a far more salient expectation for women, the family man script allows—and perhaps even requires—men like Charlie to engage in relational caregiving without bringing their manhood into question.[4]

Not every man at Southern, however, is a husband. Troy, a recent graduate of a more progressive Christian college, pointed out the dissonance this can create for the many students who, like him, remain unmarried. "Whether the single people want to admit it or not, they're deeply lonely and rather broken over the fact that they're single. Most single people that I know don't like [being single]. Even friends that I have, when you first get to know them they say, 'It's great. It's wonderful. I can do my own thing.' Once you get down beneath all that stuff, you understand that they're looking. They're searching. They're wishing that they could just find somebody." Single men often practice the family man script by imagining their future wives. They consider the roles they will someday take in marriage and, as Troy suggests, actively search for a spouse. What married men achieve relationally, they pursue aspirationally: public mastery of a private script. In either case, successful practice of the family man script demonstrates a man's ability to exercise headship and communicates his fit in the community. Whatever else it might be, marriage to a woman is a Godly Man's most potent articulation of his heterosexuality and assent to conservative cultural norms. It is little wonder that Southern's single men are so often eager, even desperate, to find wives.

Manly Men

Southern is nothing if it is not serious. During my fieldwork, light posts alongside the campus's sidewalks displayed graphic banners, each proclaiming this seriousness. "We are serious," one declared, "about theology." Another read, "We are serious about missions." A promotional graphic I spotted online that same semester featured an icon of Godly masculinity: a bearded man clutching a large book and staring intently into the camera along with the caption, "We are serious about the Gospel." Many of the students I interviewed were attracted to Southern because of this sense of seriousness. When I asked Henry, who had embraced evangelical Christian faith as an adult, why Southern's messages about Godly Manhood were significant, he emphasized the Bible's own authority:

> Ultimately, I would say that [these messages] are important because they are scriptural. If the Bible means anything to us, then we ought to be listening, reading, and dwelling on what it says. . . . Like I said, I grew up [in another Christian tradition], and I stepped away from the faith for about, I don't know, maybe six years or so. Then I came to Christ, and I told myself, "If I'm gonna do this." Forgive my language but "I'm not gonna half-ass it." I really want to know more and more and more. So it's a slow process, but I'm not just gonna pick and choose from the Bible. So I guess to answer your question, it's biblical and if that's what I believe, then that's what I am called to adhere to.

Being a Godly Man meant taking his faith—and his Bible—seriously.

Men like Henry were serious about being students, and they were serious about being men. They poured themselves into their Old Testament assignments in the library and filled the coffee shop with spirited conversations about systematic theology and spiritual disciplines. These men were not just pastors in training. They were literate, intellectually curious students of ideas, eager to find masculine identity in their vocation as gentlemen-scholars. In interviews, men frowned critically at their peers in broader culture who shirked responsibility and floated through life without clear direction. Some blamed feminism and lazy men for eroding the value of initiative, hard work, and responsibility. In protest against a feminized culture that they believed asks too little of men, these students approached their studies and their faith with fervor. Manly men, they held, work hard and get things done.

Southern's manly men also attend, often in earnest, to the details of personal grooming. The iconic image of the Southern Baptist pastor in a conservative suit

Figure 2.1. A banner outside Norton Hall features faculty member Owen Strachan. Photo by the author.

and tie with fastidiously cropped hair persists, especially among faculty. One PhD student remembered a professor explaining the importance of pastoral clothing styles: "He talked about how he would never go outside the house without wearing khakis—like if he was going to the supermarket—because he was protecting the image of being a pastor. He's like, 'What if I ran into one of my church members at the supermarket and he saw me wearing jeans and a T-shirt? What would he think of me? He would associate that with something that doesn't promote the image of a pastor or leader.'" While the particulars of this pastor's self-imposed dress code do not appear to be ubiquitous (the jeans-wearing student who told this story, for example, recounted it with a slight eyeroll), the community does place a high priority on personal grooming. Southern's leadership has long recognized that students may not have the fashion sensibilities—let alone the bank accounts—to accommodate this priority. For students in residence during my fieldwork, Edgar's store was there to help. Conveniently located just across the main hallway from Founders coffee shop, Edgar's stocked numerous personal accessories for the manly man. Just inside the front entrance, a selection of dark suits hung in neat lines, ready to be sent away for tailoring. An antique table in the middle of the room displayed an array of colorful neckties meticulously arranged by shade. In the far corner, glass bottles of beard oil surrounded a porcelain sink. The store's walls were lined with displays of notecards, pocketknives, and expensive-looking cuff links emblazoned with the emblem of Mohler's twentieth anniversary as the seminary's president. In

Figure 2.2. Entrance to Edgar's. Photo by the author.

Figure 2.3. A display inside Edgar's. Photo by the author.

recognition of the president's preference for fountain pens, Edgar's also carried an impressive collection of high-quality pens and bottles of richly colored ink. On one of my visits, the store advertised a sale: 20 percent off all bow ties, another favorite of Mohler's. Accouterments like these offer opportunities for both seasoned and novice manly men to rehearse their masculinity.

The men who shop at Edgar's, and places like it, are Southern's company men. Even if they do not always wear suits, they dress impeccably, always aware of self-presentation. During my fieldwork on campus, leather satchels were almost as common as the ubiquitous ESV Study Bibles, and several of my informed consent forms were signed with the ink of a heavy fountain pen. Nostalgic fashion choices like these facilitate physical connection with the institution's usable past. Edgar's customers can imagine themselves as heirs to the men who drafted the Abstract of Principles and sat behind closed boardroom doors strategizing the conservative takeover in the 1990s. By manipulating a bow tie into the perfect shape or uncapping a fountain pen, today's seminarians participate in that history, and they anticipate a future in which they will serve as guardians of Southern's institutional legacy.

But these company men no longer hold a monopoly on Godly Manhood. Other students, equally serious about their masculinity, follow a different version of the script. They take their cues from a genre of Christian literature popularized by John Eldredge, author of a book called *Wild at Heart* (2001), which celebrates the untamable masculine spirit and its thirst for adventure. Those who follow this updated model are looser, in some ways, than their bow-tied, clean-shaven colleagues. They wear Converse sneakers and Ray-Ban sunglasses instead of fine leather shoes and silk ties. They carry backpacks and Trader Joe's water bottles instead of leather satchels and coffee mugs. Many cultivate full, but always neatly groomed, beards.

They also eat meat. While busy students who live in and around suburban Louisville generally do not kill their food themselves, they can nonetheless identify with the masculine image of a hunter through their dietary choices. Founders, the student center's coffee shop, offers a menu of sandwiches and salads along with requisite coffee and pastries. As I pursued the café's menu board, the "He-Man Grinder" sandwich stood out among its lunch offerings. Intrigued by the name, I asked the young woman at the cash register about it after placing my order for a more feminine Caesar salad. She laughed awkwardly, as though she was a little embarrassed and a little surprised that the answer wasn't obvious to me. "It's just because of all the meat," she replied. The connection was certainly obvious to a chapel speaker who employed the consumption of meat as a sermon illustration: "Let's talk about joy," he began. "So if we're going to talk about joy, this week in my life I gotta talk about Brazilian steakhouse. Anyone ever been to a Brazilian steakhouse? They're amazing. . . . They have this beautiful salad bar. I mean it's got bowls of *bacon* and *cheese*. It's wonderful. But they should put a sign above it that says, 'Distraction' because for the main event, they'll bring out 15 choice cuts of meat on skewers to your table, and they'll slice it off for you. One by one. It is glorious. Glorious."[5] In addition to its intended purpose as a call for churchly focus on the work of the Holy Spirit, the Brazilian steakhouse illustration also facilitated this preacher's rhetorical and physical display of serious manhood. The celebration of carnivorousness bolstered his own masculine presence: a hybrid of wild-at-heart ruggedness and company man gentility. His dark hair was cut in a short, almost military style, accented by a full, dark beard. He wore a stylishly tailored dark suit accessorized with a deep red tie and spoke loudly and confidently as he paced the stage, extending his spatial reach. Projections like this one reinforce the imperative of serious masculinity. Choices between the company man's well-groomed style and the bacon-loving, wild-at-heart image offer an aspiring Godly Man the opportunity to exercise masculine agency—as long as he is serious about it.

Manly seriousness also affirms gender differentiation. In a gospel-infused version of what psychologist Sandra Lipsitz Bem describes as "gender polarization," Southern's manly men distinguish themselves from women in everything from fashion to literature to their lunches. Bem writes, "It is thus not simply that women and men are seen to be different but that this male-female difference is superimposed on so many aspects of the social world that a cultural connection is thereby forged between sex and virtually every other aspect of human experience" (1993, 2). The gendered ordering of the Gospel Story suggests that this is exactly what God intended. The serious student of manly manhood distances himself from effeminate bodily practices and androgynous clothing styles. He carefully avoids anything—body jewelry, fingernail polish, long hair—that might smack of effeminacy. These things not only suggest an overly casual attitude toward personal grooming, a deviation from manly seriousness in itself, but might also connote lax gender and sexual norms. Not all Godly Men look the same. Some choose fine leather shoes, while others opt for sneakers. Some prefer cleanly shaven faces, while others cultivate neatly trimmed beards. But all of Southern's men measure these personal choices against idealized standards of manly manhood. On this the company man and the wild-at-heart man agree: Godly Men must present themselves like *men*. The two unite in shared embattlement against secular and liberal culture and androgyny. They might roll their eyes at each other, but both reinforce the masculine code.

In addition to liberalism's evils, Godly Men also embattle themselves against another foe: hypermasculinity. Because the Gospel Story's image of Christ and the Church has introduced nurture into the codes of manhood, acts of service and even domestic labor can substitute for more traditional masculinity signifiers. Brad explained:

The idea of courage, the idea of adventure, I think is tied to maleness. But I think it can be expressed in more ways than just riding a Harley or skydiving, or hunting, or something stupid like that. It can be expressed in sport, or it can be expressed in doing the dishes for your wife. It could be more masculine and more "man" of me to do the dishes than to go ride a Harley. So yeah, I'm gonna rebel against that. If a man comes to me and says, "Yeah, I feel like a man, I rode a Harley all week." Well, how's your marriage doing? "Aw, man, it's suffering." You're not a man. Man up. Serve your wife.

Men like Brad need not step outside of their manly man script when performing Christlike love for their wives as the family man script dictates. Instead, they reframe these acts as embattled opposition against an inferior form of masculinity.

In this constant negotiation over masculine legitimacy, nostalgia is a favorite tool. When I told the young man behind the Edgar's store counter about my research, he eagerly introduced me to Dr. Ericson, a distinguished gentleman in a brown tweed coat and neatly trimmed beard who was casually browsing the front of the store when I entered. Dr. Ericson was a member of Southern's faculty and eager to answer my questions about the store. I understood the fountain pens and fine stationery, I told him. But, I asked, gesturing to a tall glass case next to an antique dresser, "Why do pastors need knives?" Dr. Ericson chuckled, "They're really more of a thing for men rather than specifically for pastors," he reasoned. After searching a few moments for an explanation, he remembered the small Swiss Army knife in his own pocket. "It's a really handy thing," he said. "Sometimes I use it to trim loose threads from my clothes." He demonstrated by shaving a small piece of fuzz from his tweed suit jacket with a tiny blade dwarfed many times over by the knives in the display case. As if reading my mind, Dr. Ericson pointed out that some of the younger men like to carry the larger knives in their jeans pockets, as he did, occasionally, on walks. "Just because," he said, "you never know. Maybe I'll run into a mean dog or something." As he talked, the value of knives seemed to solidify in his mind. "It's a rite of passage," he continued, "when boys are old enough to use a knife. It's something that dads teach boys, which happens less and less nowadays." He lamented the decline in fatherly investment in their sons. "It's different than it was back then," he said, gesturing to the picture of E. Y. Mullins behind the cash register. "People used to go to baseball games and wear bow ties and gloves. That just doesn't happen anymore," he concluded sadly.

Dr. Ericson's nostalgia illuminates some of Godly Manhood's cultural commitments. His focal point was not the Bible or even church history but an imagined era of America's past. The black-and-white photographs hanging on Edgar's walls and throughout campus draw viewers back to a time when it seemed that Southern Baptist culture dominated—or at least better matched—broader

American culture. Bow ties and gloves worn to the baseball games of yesteryear signify an orderly gender binary, a refreshing prospect for those fearful of cultural feminization and androgynization. Standing on Southern's campus, surrounded by monuments to this well-ordered past, men like Dr. Ericson reminisce about a time when men knew what it meant to be hardworking providers, responsible for their families and protective of their wives. The knives in Edgar's glass display case were less practical necessities than symbolic constructions of this nostalgia. Like fountain pens and silk ties, they provided students with the opportunity to materially join the battle against a culture that no longer valued traditional masculinity.

But nostalgia is rarely as innocent as it seems. Symbolic or not, knives carry overtones of the violent and domineering traits that define what gender theorist R. W. Connell has termed hegemonic masculinity (1987). Much of Southern's Godly Manhood script, in fact, reflects this construct, including its heteronormativity, its expectations of masculine dominance over women, and its elevation of idealized standards impossible for any man to live up to. The seminary context does, to be sure, moderate the more expressly violent and destructive of these tendencies. Nevertheless, its patterns are hard to miss. From pocketknives to He-Man sandwiches to jokes about conceal-and-carry permits, Southern's nostalgic manly manhood script sustains a subtle but powerful form of the militant masculinity that has long characterized white evangelical spaces (Du Mez 2020).

Hank and Dr. Mohler: Case Studies in Godly Manhood

In a special feature of *Towers*, Southern's campus magazine, a smiling model named Hank demonstrates Godly Manhood's scripts. The full-page photograph shows Hank surrounded by objects labeled to ensure that the reader knows why they are relevant. Though cheeky, the graphic nods to the seriousness behind the masculine codes of churchman, family man, and manly man.

First, Hank's scholarly accessories reflect his ambitions as a churchman. The ESV Study Bible, which the caption points out is the choice of the "especially devout," signifies his devotion to the pulpit, where churchmen preach and interpret the Word of God. Hank carries other books too, including one titled *Godly Young Man* and another called *Preaching the Word: Revelation*. Together with the Bible, these affirm Hank's aspirations to follow in the footsteps of celebrated churchmen like his professors. The fact that these books are distributed by Crossway Books, the Southern Baptist publishing house that also operates the campus bookstore, establishes that Hank will take a neo-Reformed, Southern Baptist path in his journey toward leadership.

Second, Hank's clothing and personal effects show him to be a manly man: serious, scholarly, and certainly not feminine or lazy. He is intentional even in the choice of his smallest personal accessories. While not in a position to own a replica of the Resolute Desk as Mohler does, Hank carries fine leather accessories

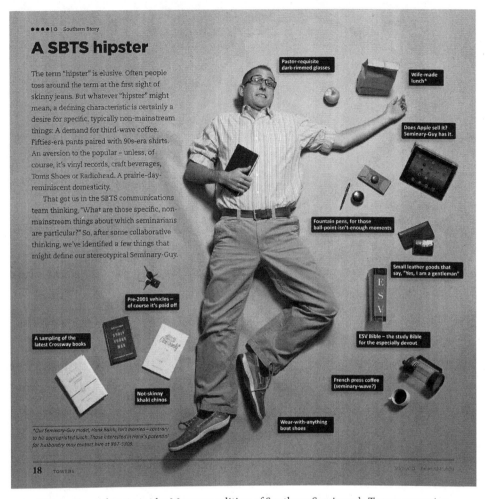

●●●● | ○   Southern Story

A SBTS hipster

The term "hipster" is elusive. Often people toss around the term at the first sight of skinny jeans. But whatever "hipster" might mean, a defining characteristic is certainly a desire for specific, typically non-mainstream things: A demand for third-wave coffee. Fifties-era pants paired with 90s-era shirts. An aversion to the popular – unless, of course, it's vinyl records, craft beverages, Toms Shoes or Radiohead. A prairie-day-reminiscent domesticity.

That got us in the SBTS communications team thinking, "What are those specific, non-mainstream things about which seminarians are particular?" So, after some collaborative thinking, we've identified a few things that might define our stereotypical Seminary-Guy.

Pastor-requisite dark-rimmed glasses

Wife-made lunch*

Does Apple sell it? Seminary-Guy has it.

Fountain pens, for those ball-point-isn't-enough moments

Small leather goods that say, "Yes, I am a gentleman"

Pre-2001 vehicles – of course it's paid off

A sampling of the latest Crossway books

ESV Bible – the study Bible for the especially devout

French press coffee (seminary-wave?)

Not-skinny khaki chinos

Wear-with-anything boat shoes

*Our Seminary-Guy model, Hank Balch, isn't married – contrary to his appropriated lunch. Those interested in Hank's potential for husbandry may contact him at 867-5309.

18   TOWERS

Figure 2.4. A feature in the May 2012 edition of Southern Seminary's *Towers* magazine illustrates students' common use of material culture to construct identity. https://sbts-wordpress-uploads.s3.amazonaws.com/equip/uploads/2017/01/Towers-2012-May_web.pdf.

communicating that he is "a gentleman." The title of the article itself, "An SBTS Hipster," hints at embattlement. "Whatever 'hipster' might mean," says the article, "a defining characteristic is certainly a desire for specific, typically non-mainstream things: a demand for third-wave coffee. Fifties-era pants paired with 90s-era shirts. An aversion to the popular—unless, of course, it is vinyl records, craft beverages, Toms Shoes, or Radiohead. A prairie-day-reminiscent domesticity." But Southern's codes do not match all facets of the hipster style. The article describes Hank's pants as "not-skinny khaki chinos," in defiance of more trendy styles that might border on effeminacy. A step down from the traditional churchman's suit and tie, these chinos also illustrate the flexibility in Godly Manhood's physical codes. While Hank's conventional style identifies him as a company man, the feature could easily have taken a wild-at-heart form too. But Hank's slightly bookish boat shoes and lack of facial hair serve as a subtle reminder that the company men still hold institutional power.

Finally, Hank demonstrates his commitment to becoming a family man. Among his Godly Manhood accoutrements is a "wife-made lunch" in a brown paper bag. This lunch signifies the importance of marriage and the intertwining of Godly Manhood with Godly Womanhood. Like the rest of the feature, the lunch is in good fun and, I am confident, resulted in hearty chuckles from the publication's intended readership, but the asterisk and its corresponding footnote underscore the seriousness behind the extended joke: "Our Seminary-Guy model, Hank Balch, isn't married—contrary to his appropriated lunch. Those interested in Hank's potential for husbandry may contact him at 867-5309." Hank's quest for Godly Manhood will indeed not be complete until he finds a wife and adds "family man" to his list of credentials.

———

While no individual—even the Hank prototype—perfectly embodies all of Godly Manhood's ideal typical scripts, Al Mohler comes remarkably close. It would be difficult to overemphasize the reverence that Mohler garners within his campus community. At some institutions, administrators are little known by those who walk the halls and enact the rhythms of daily institutional life. This is not the case at Southern. Here, no one is more visible than the president. One man who had spent several years as a student on Southern's campus told a story illustrating the far reach of Mohler's authority. "I overheard this myself [when] I was outside on the lawn. There was a young seminary wife with two toddlers, and [one of them] was climbing on the trees. . . . She said, 'Johnny, get off those trees. Those are Dr. Mohler's trees. He'll be upset if you break one of the branches.'" Southern's president animates anthropologist Clifford Geertz's contention that symbols, vehicles for meaning, both reflect and shape reality around them (1973). Indeed, Mohler's own history and persona inform the script of a churchman. His marriage informs the role of a family man. His style of self-presentation informs the seriousness of the manly man. The president does not create Godly Manhood; its codes exist outside of his person. And his example is certainly not the only mechanism by which it is perpetuated. But on Southern's campus, as Geertz would anticipate, Mohler's embodied presence both symbolically reflects and actively constructs the ideal that everyday patterns of campus life constantly affirm and reaffirm.

Mohler's carefully hired faculty members are also embodied symbols. The institution, Mohler told me, does its best to appoint men who will go beyond merely upholding the institution's confession of faith:

> MOHLER: Our model of confessionalism here is not [about hiring] people who can agree to sign the confession. We're looking for people who are eager to teach in an institution for which this is the confession of faith. . . . So we're looking for a total buy-in, and that has led to some particular hiring decisions. In other words there are people who intellectually, theologically, convictionally would fit an institution like this except for our larger expectations about living here as a part of the community, about being accessible to students. We're looking for a buy-in from the entire family that this is a life project which they want to be a part of.
>
> LWS: And the complementarian perspective that I've heard articulated here, how big of a part of the criteria is that?
>
> MOHLER: It's a huge part. Now I don't want to exaggerate that. It's not a huge part because that's where we begin in terms of the body of divinity. It's not a huge part in that that's where we begin a conversation. It's a huge part because in this particular sociological and cultural context, this is something that stands out in rather remarkable contrast from the society at large. . . . It's talked about because, number one, we had to clarify those issues here painfully.

It is not enough for faculty to teach within the boundaries of the institution's stories. They must devote themselves (and their families) fully to the cause.

GODLY WOMANHOOD: CREATED TO FOLLOW

Godly men are not alone on Southern's campus. They might dominate classrooms, intellectual discussions, and administrative offices, but as the Gospel Story teaches, men are complemented by women. In addition to the women who enroll in coursework themselves, many more join the community because of their husbands' enrollment or employment rather than their own. While their official connections to the seminary are secondary, these women play important roles within Southern's mostly masculine milieu. They do not "head" their families. They do not preach or anticipate pastoral authority. They do not grow beards. But they too pursue godliness.

I met one of these women late on a Thursday afternoon. The day had been long for both of us. I had packed more interviews than usual into my day, and Cristiana had just finished a full day of work at her off-campus job. I was relieved to find her friendly and engaging as we chatted in comfortable window seats overlooking the campus. She didn't spend much time here, Cristiana told me. Her husband took classes during the day while she worked and came only for

Thursday night Seminary Wives Institute (SWI) sessions. Cristiana talked enthusiastically about the women she met at SWI and others who were a part of her congregation. She described her admiration for an older woman, married to the man who led their church small group:

> They kind of do it together. She's awesome. They have four kids and she runs her house, takes care of their kids, and works out all the time. She does all kinds of crafts. She helps [the kids] with school stuff, and she is just always serving in the church. She's over [the children's ministries], and she opens her home. She has us there every couple of weeks, and she's just great. She really is serving, and she really makes an honest effort. You know that she's in the Word. She talks about it. She loves it. It's just a great thing to see.

Cristina's admiration for this woman illustrates the three scripts of Godly Womanhood as it is constructed at Southern Seminary: disciplined spirituality as women of the Word, submission to husbands as supportive wives, and care for those around them as motherly nurturers.

Women of the Word

Like men, Southern's women also expressed deep devotion to the Bible. Nevertheless, they also displayed varying levels of enthusiasm for the Gospel Story's gendered prescriptions. Some of these women had been a part of complementarianism all their lives and did not question its ideals. Others came to embrace Godly Womanhood after considerable struggle. Heather, for example, told me,

> [The Bible] is very clear when it says that a leader is a husband of one wife, so I just think it leaves you with no wiggle room. That's pretty clear! Which was hard for my feminine self because I could get easily offended. There could be a place of like, "Well, what's wrong with me?" Or "I'm just as good." . . . [But] He has chosen this in His infinite wisdom, and His thoughts are high above my thoughts, and His ways are high above my ways. So there must be a greater purpose for our greater good if this is the order He has established.

Heather, like so many others, employed the language of order. She framed it in terms of a passage from the book of Isaiah: "For my thoughts are not your thoughts, neither are your ways my ways, declares the Lord" (Isaiah 55:8 ESV). As Heather's comment illustrates, feelings and experiences should not trump the inerrant Word and the ordered roles it dictates.

For Godly Women, commitment to the Bible is more personal than public. While Godly Men demonstrate their love for scripture through preaching and public teaching, Godly Women mark it with personal devotional practices, especially Bible study. For women like Renee, being "in the Word" promises a close relationship with God Himself. A single woman in her first year of full-time study at Southern, she was still struggling to hone her understanding of Godly

Womanhood when I met with her. Unlike other women who eagerly answered my questions about Godly Womanhood, Renee sighed deeply and paused while my question hung in the air for several heavy seconds. "I'm trying to just formulate it," she said finally, sighing again before continuing. "I think that for me, following the Lord is the biggest thing. Having a strong relationship with Him. . . . He is my father. He is my Lord. And I'm going to do what He asks me to do and learn the Word. Being in the Word is really big for me, because that's how I hear from Him, so I know what to do." The pulpit may be off-limits to women like Renee, but men hold no monopoly on biblical literacy. Time spent "in the Word" often yields a wealth of biblical knowledge and spiritual maturity. For single women, knowledge of God as revealed in Scripture helps to compensate for the fact that they are not (yet) mothers or wives. For those who are, encounters with the Word provide confidence and stamina for their demanding roles.

Husbands generally acknowledged and admired the spiritual maturity they saw in their wives. One man, a PhD student, freely admitted, "My wife is probably more godly than I am. I don't have any doubt of that." Another PhD student grounded his appreciation for women's spirituality in his understanding of the Genesis creation story, reiterating the importance of order: "When I say that I believe that the Bible teaches that men are to occupy the office of elder, bishop, and pastor, I don't mean that women have nothing to add to a man's understanding of spirituality. Going back to Genesis 1:26 and 27, I think the complementarity between men and women is very helpful. The fact that my wife has strengths where I am weak and I have [strengths] where she is weak. I think that there's a beautiful harmony that comes together in the biblically ordered church, biblically ordered home." Men almost universally assumed, however, that women's gifts and spiritual insights belonged in their homes and in circles of female relationships, not in broader churchly conversations.

Submissive Wives

But time in the Word is just the beginning. As elemental as this spiritual discipline might be, it is, as one woman pointed out, the "lowest common denominator." Godly Womanhood also emerges in human relationships. The quintessential Godly Woman is also a supportive wife to the Godly Man. Because Godly Women take their cues from the Gospel Story's description of Eve as a "helpmeet," they draw their goals and callings from their husbands. Just as Eve was created to help Adam, a Godly Woman is called to support her husband by creating a warm home environment and by joyfully submitting to his leadership. In my interviews with seminary wives—women whose paths more or less reflected this idealized script—I noticed that their struggles to identify vocational callings were often far less pronounced than other students', both women and men. Most knew before they even began that domesticity was their primary responsibility, and they were often eager to meet its challenges.

Marriage to a Godly Man does offer opportunities for agency. While submission is of paramount importance, students assured me, Godly Women do not expect to be doormats. As long as a woman does not defy her husband's authority, she is free (at least to some degree) to speak her mind and even to disagree with him. Identity as a woman of the Word gives a wife spiritual credentials to speak, even prophetically at times, to her husband. She may even participate in his churchly leadership, so long as she upholds his authority. Because wives' advice and spiritual insight "help" their husbands, this religious agency becomes a part of submission, a behavioral affirmation of the Gospel Story's gendered order.

SWI offers students of Godly Womanhood space to intellectually explore these parameters. Throughout the curriculum, which includes courses on topics like Baptist beliefs, discipleship, prayer, and hospitality, they learn that much of Godly Womanhood is about celebrating Godly Manhood. In one class session, the teacher, a middle-aged faculty wife named Becky, shared from her experience as the wife of a pastor. "What does it mean to respect our husbands?" she asked the class rhetorically. "We need to think that our husband is just the greatest thing. He is just the greatest. . . . Admire his manly qualities and submit to his authority." Becky encouraged her young students to praise their husbands in public and find out what communicates respect to them. She illustrated with a personal anecdote. When she was a young wife, Becky told the class, she often concluded her housekeeping tasks by parking the vacuum cleaner beside its cord. She soon learned that her husband preferred the cord to be wound up and was bothered by the fact that she didn't prioritize his preference. Becky eventually came to see this bit of extra work as an opportunity to show him respect. "It's not that we're a doormat," Becky carefully clarified. "You can be the life of the party." Outgoing and flamboyant personalities are fine, as long as husbands know that "no matter how excited we get, we're still going to submit to him."

For married women, submission can also involve prioritizing their husbands' sexual preferences. In a class session on "Intimacy," Becky encouraged her young students to pay careful attention to their husbands' sexual needs and desires. "Be a servant," she urged. "YOU need to know what your husband's needs are because you are the only one who can meet those needs. And you should feel very special about that." Becky also encouraged the women to communicate their own sexual desires, carefully clarifying that their needs and preferences too were important. But even this suggestion was framed in the context of male sexuality. "Most men want to know that they're good lovers," she told the class. "They want to know how to please us."

The emphasis on marriage complicates matters for women who do not have husbands. When single women explained Godly Womanhood to me, they often referenced hypothetical marriages or future husbands. Renee and Tori, both enrolled in theological programs of study, illustrate the assumption that if a

Godly Woman is not a wife, she should be preparing to fill that role. "I think," Tori began, "that [being a single woman] means that . . . she's called to submit to the Lord first and foremost." Nevertheless, she concluded by centering even her conception of Godly (single) Womanhood in terms of male headship: "I think [a Godly Woman] needs to be developing within herself a willingness to submit to a man and looking for a man that would lead her." Like Tori, Renee had given careful consideration to Godly Womanhood, even before enrolling in seminary. It was important to her, as a single woman, that godliness not depend on marriage, but her answer nonetheless heavily prioritized the marriage relationship. "I think that as a woman, you have to learn different responsibilities. You need to learn how to be a good [wife]—if you're planning on getting married. Some people aren't, but I would love to get married one day. So how do I be a godly wife? How do I submit to my husband? How do I meet his needs? Whereas the husband is called to lay down his life for me, you know? I think that that's a different responsibility than I have." For Godly Women, even more than for Godly Men, marriage is the context in which one's role in the ongoing Gospel Story can be enacted with the most clarity. Without a husband, to whom will she be a "helpmeet"?

Lacking the marital attachments that the Gospel Story celebrates, single women often find themselves in unscripted social spaces. In interviews, these women often described their on-campus interactions with men as awkward and fraught with sexual tension. When Maya introduced herself to classmates, for example, she noticed that they quickly found ways to communicate their marital status: "When I ask 'Where are you from?' they'll say, 'Oh, me and my wife. . . .' It's like they're always going to drop that. I'm like, 'Okay! I'm not trying to date you!'" Maya also noticed that some of her classmates avoided interacting with her. "I could be in the library or down in [the coffee shop] at this big table, all by myself, in a little corner, all these chairs open and everything else is full. And then some man will come in and see [me] and be like 'Oh, there's nowhere to sit.' And I'm at this huge table!" Renee, one of the few women MDiv students I interviewed, shared an awkward moment of her own. The memory of her first day in a New Testament classroom illustrates how difficult complementarian social dynamics can be: "It was a big lecture hall. There were a hundred or a hundred fifty people, and there were only three girls in this class. I walked in and I was like, 'Where do I sit? It's all men. Am I going to sit beside somebody who's married and they're going to think that I'm being inappropriate? Or am I going to sit beside a guy who like, you know. . . .' It's kind of intimidating to know how to handle yourself as the minority when you're not used to it." Both Maya and Renee were confident, likable, and articulate. They loved studying at Southern. They spoke passionately about their enthusiasm for the Bible and their commitment to the Church. Had they been men, their classmates would almost certainly have recognized them immediately as peers and potential leaders. But the imperative of gendered order interrupted this recognition. Instead, men most easily saw these women as potential wives—or, perhaps, as Renee worried, potential seductresses. In consequence, Renee, easily one of the most impressive students I met at Southern, found herself unnerved, intimidated, and unsure how to uphold the importance of order in an unscripted space.

Men occasionally recognize—and even resist—some of these consequences. Gregory, a first-year student, assessed his own observations of Southern's gendered relational patterns:

> GREGORY: Sometimes there will be male students who are very awkward towards female students—because of a concern to make very clear that they're not acting inappropriately. And they may also have an unhelpful view of their own calling to the pastorate. They may view a female student as a second-class citizen because she's not going to pastor. Especially married men interacting with female students. For example, a friend of mine, she introduced herself to the guy next to her in class and he went, "Married."
>
> LWS: He held up his hand to show the ring?
>
> GREGORY: Yeah. It was like, "There's no reason to be nice to me or interact with me" or something.

This reluctant conversation partner was likely eager to enact—and to be seen enacting—Godly Manhood. Embodying its scripts in public shows that a man belongs. Other relationships or collaborations with women would be suspect, in part, as they might detract from the sacred marriage bond or, presumably, open the door to adultery.

I experienced some of this fear of impropriety as I interviewed faculty and administrators in their offices. In one case, a secretary was stationed just outside an office, and the door was intentionally left ajar. In another, an intern sat in on the meeting. One professor, whose office sat in a quiet hallway without these safeguards, paused for a long, painfully awkward moment after I entered his office before deciding to leave the door open, even though it was fitted with a large window. His indecisiveness suggested that he was not accustomed to having women in his office. In contrast, a more experienced professor, also careful to leave the door half open when he welcomed me to his office, invited me to take a seat that was also in full view of a large window. After a few preliminary questions, however, he seemed to grow uncomfortable. After pausing for a moment, he sighed and decisively stood to close the door before returning to our conversation with a much less guarded posture. He had, apparently, determined me to be less of a threat than potential eavesdroppers. All of these examples serve as important reminders that the orderliness of Southern's gendered scripts belies the complexities of social life. Unmarried women, whose singleness places them on the margins of Godly Womanhood's expectations, feel these complexities especially acutely.

Motherly Nurturers

While single women search for their place in the community, Southern's young wives often become mothers. Godly Men might act as the spiritual heads of their homes, but Godly Women oversee the domestic rhythms of family life. This expectation reflects a legacy left by church women of the early twentieth century who, as the influence of the powerful women's missionary auxiliaries of the previous century waned, found their legitimacy and churchly agency relocated in the practice of homemaking (Bowler 2019, 33–37). Following in their footsteps, Southern's Godly Women consider their own vocations and ministries to be oriented primarily around the domestic—rather than the public or churchly—sphere. They may sometimes seek paid employment, but in most cases only once a mother has established a firm commitment to her identity as "wife and mom" does she in good conscience pursue a career. The idealized Godly Woman constructs a warm, loving home where her husband can find reprieve from the challenges of public work and ministry. She also provides physical and emotional care—and sometimes homeschool education—for their children, guarding them from the dangers of secular society.

Campus architecture and programming has made public this private domesticity. I often noticed young women confidently pushing strollers and shepherding toddlers through the halls of Honeycutt Student Center, on their way to children's ballet lessons and "Mommy and Me" classes. A spacious play area next to the pool greeted them with toy trains, play food, comfortable couches, and a video gaming station. In addition to providing regular child care and family health clinic services, Southern's Student Life office also includes a "Women at Southern" branch. Its staff designs evening programs that bring women together to build relationships while they decorate pumpkins, construct care packages for missions, or learn about hospitality and spiritual discipline.[6] Women students are included as well, but they are easily outnumbered in Southern's community by the wives.

The seminary also hosts family festivals on its expansive lawn. One of these festivals occurred on a day when my own family accompanied me to Louisville. My children's faces lit up when they spotted the enormous inflatable toys on the lawn, the cookie-decorating station, and the craft centers. They fit easily into the crowd of young children eagerly running from one attraction to another, freeing their parents to relax and catch up with friends on folding chairs in front of the library. One young mother, wearing a T-shirt with the words "I Love My Husband" emblazoned on the front, hurried past us chasing a straying toddler. These events simultaneously provide a break from the rigors of academic life and function as a stage on which both men and women demonstrate mastery of their familial roles. The women who participate both celebrate and reinforce the scripts of Godly Womanhood. Even if wives have no official affiliation with

Figure 2.5. A campus family festival on April 17, 2014. Photo by the author.

the institution themselves, they are valued members of the community, embodying the feminine half of the Gospel Story's gendered order.

The seminary's labor structure also reflects expectations of motherly nurture. While the wives who bring toddlers to the pool are mothers in a literal sense, other women fill motherly roles within the institution. Given the focus on feminine domesticity, I was initially surprised to see so many women walking the halls of the student center, working in the library, and managing office desks. The women who staffed the front offices on campus often introduced themselves to me as wives of students. As they answer phones, keep schedules, and plan events, these women provide a version of motherly nurture through their supportive labor. Even the women who enroll in academic degree programs reinforce the script. While women's presence in PhD and ministerial training programs is thin, the school's "biblical counseling" program is very popular with women, particularly single women who do not yet have families of their own to nurture. Graduates understand the parameters of the degree and do not expect to provide counseling for men. Instead, they prepare to nurture other women through personal counseling and mentoring relationships.

Women also nurture each other in less formal arrangements. The women-centered spaces of SWI facilitate deep relational bonding and emotional caregiving. In one class session, I listened as one of the younger women in the room hesitantly asked for advice about how to connect sexually with an emotionally distant husband. I could hear the anxiety in her voice melt away as others rushed to reassure her. They understood and would be there for her in the days and months ahead. Another recounted feelings of desperation when, in her husband's first year of seminary, she stayed at home with their kids for the first time and felt a painful disconnect from her husband and the outside world. Around the room others nodded that yes, they too felt isolated from their husbands. They too felt worn down from too much parenting and too little adult interaction. By the end of the class hour, women had both offered and received practical advice, kind words, and prayer. They had constructed a warm relational space that augmented official lecture material with wisdom borne of their own experience and facilitated by human connection. They had cried together and laughed together, offering solidarity and promises to email each other with ideas and resources. When the class concluded, no one seemed eager to leave.

Mrs. Mohler: A Case Study in Godly Womanhood

What Al Mohler does for the codes of Godly Manhood, his wife Mary does for Godly Womanhood. Mrs. Mohler, as she is referred to on campus, provides a compelling portrait of flourishing Godly Womanhood. According to a written tribute titled "The Unseen Ministry of Mary Mohler," which celebrated the Mohlers' twenty-fifth anniversary at the seminary, being Al Mohler's wife is the life she always wanted.[7] In an interview for the article, Southern's first lady described the cultural whiplash she experienced when she tried to connect with the women of the community upon her husband's installation as president in 1993: "There were women who were clearly not interested in being identified as anybody's wife. 'Don't call me a pastor's wife,' was the attitude. 'I'm not going to let them get two for one. My separate role must be recognized and compensated too.' That was all foreign to me." Unlike the other women who inhabited the seminary before the Conservative Resurgence, Mary longed for children and a quiet, domestic life. She was happy to build her identity around her role as a "wife." According to the article, "To be a wife and mom was, of course, always Mary Mohler's dream job, and that commitment to family translated into her support for thousands of other seminary families. As is often the case for wives and mothers, much of her work has been behind the scenes, but its effects are far-reaching, trickling down to future generations, demonstrating what a high calling women truly have." The article includes several photos depicting the graceful poise with which Mrs. Mohler inhabits this calling. One shows her posing in front of a broad white front door ornamented with a flowery fall wreath. Her posture reminds readers of her commitment to home, family, and hospitality. In another photo, Mrs. Mohler smiles broadly from behind a lectern in a full SWI classroom. She is, the article reminds readers, a competent teacher and a wise and capable Woman of the Word. Finally, the last photo shows Mrs. Mohler next to her husband, offering warm handshakes and greetings to a receiving line of guests. She is, of course, a supportive wife.

I first met Mrs. Mohler in the hallway of a classroom building, having arranged to observe SWI's Thursday evening sessions. An assistant assured me that she would arrive soon, but other women were beginning to filter through the hallway and I began to wonder how I would recognize her. I needn't have worried. Moments later, a tall, confident woman greeted me warmly by name and introduced herself. Bright pink heels perfectly matched her manicured fingernails and a sleek iPad cover of the same shade. She carried herself with dignity and a charisma that easily matched her husband's.

Mrs. Mohler executed the scripts of Godly Womanhood flawlessly. Promptly at seven o'clock, she brought the very full classroom to order and opened the floor for prayer requests. She led an eloquent, measured prayer, remembering the requests, the women's husbands, and the women themselves as they supported their spouses during a busy time in the semester. Her words were articulate and graceful, yet comfortable and familiar. They marked her as a Woman of the Word, fluent in the spiritual language of prayer. Mrs. Mohler then proceeded with the course itself, a seminar devoted to the subject of hospitality. An appropriate expression of motherly nurture, Mrs. Mohler framed the subject more in terms of practical domesticity than Christian ethics. The previous week's assignment had been to craft a plan for a child's birthday party including devotionals, themes, and menus. Some of the students misunderstood and had tackled the baking itself. Mrs. Mohler chuckled good naturedly at their mistake before moving on to the evening's main topic: event planning. She outlined several steps: (1) Pray; (2) Brainstorm; (3) Recipe Search; (4) Plan Ahead/Get Organized; (5) Enjoy Yourself; and (6) Keep Good Records. As if anticipating complaints that the material wasn't relevant to their lives as seminary student wives, Mrs. Mohler reminded these young women that there would come a time when their lives would look very different. "When I was sitting where you sit, I had no clue that I'd live in a house with eight sets of china that belong to the seminary. . . . You just don't know where the Lord's going to place you."

A little later in the evening, Mrs. Mohler had an opportunity to demonstrate her role as a supportive wife. Just as she began to talk about preparing for times when party planning might go wrong, her husband Al poked his head into the room and smiled at the class. Mrs. Mohler did not seem at all flustered, explaining to visitors that "he does this sometimes to all the classes." Bantering back and forth for several minutes, the president quipped to his wife, "I just came in to test out her hospitality!" After giving her a warm hug and a lingering kiss, President Mohler left the class to its discussion of recipe selection and baby shower etiquette. With this performative exchange, President and Mrs. Mohler reminded students that human flourishing is indeed possible for men and women who follow the community's gendered scripts.

Classroom experiences like this also reinforce the social nature of Godly Womanhood. Whatever the value of course content, the real significance of SWI rests in the embodied, relational connections it facilitates. Above all, students come to SWI for the opportunities it offers them to interact with faculty wives like Mrs. Mohler. These women, like their students, have struggled to respect imperfect husbands, wrestled with the physical exhaustion of motherhood, and found strength for their journeys in Scripture. Godly Womanhood, with its focus on domesticity, can be isolating, and students eagerly reach out for the solidarity these women offer. "If you want to get girls to something," a staffer from the student activities office told me, "you bring in faculty wives." More than solidarity, though, Mary Mohler and the other faculty wives powerfully symbolize Godly Womanhood. Students in the SWI classrooms I visited dutifully took notes from bulleted outlines printed on pastel-colored paper. Few, however, asked questions or expressed interest in exploring the material more deeply. But when their teachers departed from formal class content to describe their own marriages or illustrate a point with a funny story about a grandchild, students dropped their pencils and devoted their full attentions, sometimes asking questions or sharing stories of their own. Their teachers nodded knowingly and gave these younger women hope. If they had been able to thrive within the codes of Godly Womanhood, surely their students could too.

Gendered Order and Centered Power

Southern's stories and their gendered scripts accomplish more than individual student formation. They shape community life, facilitate collective identity, and reinforce cultural boundaries against outgroups. Above all, gendered order buttresses masculine authority, infusing it with historic—even transcendent—meaning and clothing it in embodied practice. On one end of the Honeycutt Student Center, the spacious Heritage Hall hosts meetings and events throughout the year. Portraits of the seminary's presidents, each dressed as a serious, manly churchman, encircle the room. Mohler's portrait hangs on the wall directly across from James P. Boyce, the seminary's first leader. The narrative of institutional authority these portraits chronicle gives no indication of the women, even dutiful wives like Mary Mohler, who have invested in the seminary's story. This absence does not trouble members of the community. If they notice it at all, insiders might well celebrate the homogeneity as evidence of the institution's faithfulness to conservatism. These portraits remind the room's occupants that Southern's group identity requires the practice of male headship.

The seminary distributes power accordingly. The institution Mohler resurrected from the ashes of liberal apostasy has grown into a thriving haven for conservative, neo-Reformed complementarians. And who better to guard the legacy than its own faithful sons? Southern's 2015–2016 academic catalogue listed the names of sixty faculty members. The list included only one woman, a professor of church music whose presence reminds skeptics that faithful, conservative women sometimes find opportunity within complementarianism. She was, however, overwhelmingly outnumbered by the remaining fifty-nine men, a full twenty-five of whom received degrees from Southern itself. Thirteen others carried credentials from other Southern Baptist institutions, many of which share a similar history of Conservative Resurgence. Women's voices remain all but absent from pulpits, boardrooms, curricular decisions, and workroom discussions about what the Word of God means to the contemporary world. Insiders defend this exclusion as faithful conservative practice. It does not devalue, they say. Centering men in churchly power structures is God's best, not only for men, but also for women.

But simply saying something does not make it true. Repeated claims that women are "equal in value" certainly do not mean that women are, in practice, equally valued by the institution. In fact, the sharp separation of men and women often leaves intellectually gifted, ambitious women with few opportunities. Because they are women, they will not participate in the construction of doctrine or contribute to the intricacies of institutional policy, even if they have interest and competencies in these areas. Moreover, while men, aspiring pastors and theologians, receive intensive mentoring and modeling from faculty, women navigate similar degree programs largely without these benefits. While faculty members might invest in their women students to some degree, given institutional attention to gender differentiation and concerns for propriety, these men are not likely to mentor them. In private devotional times too, women often purchase, consult, and reference books and sermons written by men. Even Southern's most successful Godly Women remain under the watchful eye of the men who lead institutions and control publishing houses, blog platforms, and conference funding. Southern's women have little voice in the scripts and stories that direct their own lives.

Economic benefits are also uneven. While no one is under the illusion that seminary is a path to wealth, graduates do expect to earn respect and salaries as pastors or leaders within parachurch organizations. Women, however, will not be candidates for most of these jobs. Without licensure, even graduates of the "biblical counseling" program will be unlikely to earn enough to support a family. The institution's own economic power is concentrated into the salaries of faculty members and administrators, while their wives carry the significant expectations of nurture—and even teaching—without commensurate pay. Southern's complementarians would quibble with this critique. The Godly Woman, they would argue, should not be burdened by economic realities, but freed from financial worries through her husband's provision. This logic, however, betrays the culturally situated nature of Southern's prescriptions. Godly Manhood and Godly Womanhood bear a striking resemblance to the breadwinner/housewife family model that emerged after World War II, driven by postwar middle-class prosperity and fear of communism. Even in its heyday, writes historian Stephanie Coontz, the single-income, suburban family model was largely unachievable by people of color and families of lower socioeconomic classes (1992). While Southern's complementarians have accommodated somewhat by allowing women into the workforce, their gendered scripts continue to sacralize "traditional" familial roles that are, in fact, not timeless and universal standards—even among Christians.

Instead, these scripts reflect particular cultural contexts. While Godly Manhood's scripts draw deeply from hegemonic masculinity ideals, complementarian notions of domesticized femininity rely heavily on Victorian notions resurrected during the postwar era (Connell 1987; Coontz 1992). They would be unfamiliar in many other historical and geographic contexts—including, for example, historically Black churches that otherwise share much of Southern's theology. Together, these scripts subtly code "godliness" in terms of middle-class white American culture, visibly deviating, for example, from the various constructions of masculinity that Black American men have often assumed as alternatives to white expectations (Majors and Billson 1992).

This is not to suggest that all men at Southern are white. Men of color can, and sometimes do, achieve positions of authority and influence. However, the few who do teach and learn at Southern are also held to the culturally white standards of Godly Manhood. During the 2019 annual meetings of the Southern Baptist Convention, Curtis Woods, a professor of applied theology at Southern Seminary, addressed the assembly, appealing to the denomination to consider critical race theory and the language of intersectionality as helpful analytical lenses through which to understand contemporary racial issues. That a Black man spoke positively and publicly of these lenses, both of which center Black experience, from within the Southern Baptist Convention—a denomination birthed largely by earlier leaders' commitment to the institution of slavery—is remarkable. But even as Woods, a graduate of Southern Seminary, spoke as a Black man, he also appeared in unmistakable Godly Man garb: a tan blazer, horn-rimmed glasses, and striped bow tie. Even this was not enough. In the end, Al Mohler had the final word. "We stand together," Mohler wrote in response, speaking alongside the presidents of the five other Southern Baptist seminaries (all, notably, white men), "in stating that we believe that advocating Critical Race Theory or Intersectionality is incompatible with the Baptist Faith & Message, and that such advocacy has no rightful place within an SBC seminary." He concluded, "I think it speaks loudly to Southern Baptists that we take this stand together." Mohler made no mention of Woods or other Southern Baptists of color who did not "stand together" on the subject, adding only, "We are thankful for our African-American brothers and sisters in the SBC whose voices are so needed and must be honored."[8] Whiteness still permeates Southern's gendered culture—in power dynamics as well as fashion.

While this historical and cultural context might not seem salient to Southern's students, it does not have to be. It is baked into Southern Seminary's tradition. The institution has only recently begun to reckon with its racist past. [9] Cultural patterns of whiteness remain, passed down through generations of

Southern Baptist churchmen (and women) through language patterns, clothing styles, relational practices, and stories. Boyce's name remains emblazoned on the library, and his portrait graces Heritage Hall. Meanwhile, the student body remains heavily white, and women of color were all but absent in both my interview sample and my fieldwork notes. They remain unrepresented in positions of influence and heavily marginalized by a culture that celebrates white men—even slaveholding men.

White men do not, however, hold all of the power. Many of the women I interviewed would feel misrepresented by descriptions of their lives in terms of women's disempowerment and power structures that centers men. Indeed, attention to their experiences suggests that gender polarization can birth surprising gifts. Most importantly, it has created rich subcultural spaces that center women's lives and amplify their voices. These women-oriented spaces facilitate what Dorothy Smith calls women's standpoint, the depth of insight borne of women's experiences (1987). SWI provides Southern's most noteworthy example of this. The institute offers solidarity, collective identity, social support, and a rich, distinctively feminine spirituality, well suited to the lives of the women it serves. It also provides opportunities for leadership and religious agency. I could see the results. The emphasis on submission and caregiving, combined with the more academic goal of becoming women of the Word and nourished by rich relationships, manifested in many of the women I met as a winsome and gracious confidence. Like Mary Mohler, they were thriving, just as Godly Womanhood promised. For such women, complementarianism's benefits are real.

But here there is a catch: not all women are Mary Mohler. Not all seminary wives have personalities, interests, and gifts that equip them for the scripts she so gracefully embodies. Perhaps even more importantly, not all women who are suited to the kind of leadership and authority Mary Mohler exercises will be married to a man like Al Mohler. In fact, not only marriage but marriage to a husband who is himself in a position of power seems to be a de facto prerequisite to a complementarian woman's leadership. The women who teach for SWI, by definition, have this opportunity because their husbands are employed by the seminary. They not only teach about being wives, they teach because they *are* wives who are married to the right men. Similarly, the women managing the various offices I visited during my fieldwork almost always told me that their husbands were students or their fathers were professors. All but one of the women on CBMW's women's panel were, likewise, married to high-profile churchly leaders. Godly Womanhood, with its prioritization on marriage and family, is the only code available to women, regardless of their marital status, competencies, or senses of calling. Complementarian apologists at Southern eagerly affirm that Godly Womanhood can be attained by single as well as married women. In practice, however, its gifts fall to the wives.

It is not surprising, then, that the unmarried women I met at Southern seemed
to struggle most with the community's complementarian expectations. The Gospel Story's sacralization of marriage often leaves these women searching for
both gender identity and spiritual identity. While no less invested in the pursuit
of godliness than their peers, they could claim fewer credentials for the task.
Renee, one of the few single women enrolled in Southern's MDiv program, confessed to me that she had struggled with the complementarian framework for
much of her life: "I always thought that something was wrong with my personality, because I'm very talkative, very outgoing. I'm very opinionated and I have
all these [ideas]. . . . I want to lead things. So how do I do that in a biblical sense?
I always felt like something was wrong with me, like God had created me right
and I just messed it up." Single women, especially those with assertive personalities and intellectual proclivities like Renee, walk a lonely path. They are not
in positions to enact wifely submission or to nurture husbands and children, two
of Godly Womanhood's most important elements. Intersectional losers on these
two important axes, they lack the marital connections that launch other Godly
Women into positions of leadership. These single women often emphasized their
personal devotional practices, the one script of Godly Womanhood that they
could easily rehearse. But even this is difficult. Bible study is a largely personal
discipline, not a performative practice. Even the most dedicated woman of the
Word cannot publicly declare her devotion to the Bible from the pulpit in the same
way that a single churchman can.

Southern's stories reward those who fit and demand much of those who do
not. The inflexibility of their demands is all too real for those on the margins.
Men and women from nonevangelical backgrounds not only must learn to speak
the language of the Gospel Story but also must learn to dress, move, and eat in
ways that accommodate its prescriptions. Some men cannot grow full beards.
Some women will not be mothers. Sexual orientation, a call to celibacy, or a
simple inability to find a suitable partner inhibit heterosexual marriage for
others. Nevertheless, many flourish. As they embody Godly Womanhood and,
especially, Godly Manhood, they become living, breathing actors in the community's narratives, characters with agency to shape future iterations of these
beloved stories. When men purchase bow ties at Edgar's, apply cedarwood-
scented oil to their beards, or sign their names with heavy fountain pens, they
physically identify with E. Y. "Edgar" Mullins, James P. Boyce, and Al Mohler.
When their wives open floral "Godly Womanhood" study guides for their morning devotions or follow Mary Mohler's hospitality advice, they identify with the
promise of her own flourishing. Even as Southern's men and women "do gender"
in the sense that West and Zimmerman (1987) describe, they also "do identity,"
and they "do power."

What students cannot do is ignore these codes. In the face of an overwhelming preponderance of students and faculty who perform the institution's gen-

dered scripts, those who cannot—or will not—are likely to leave the manicured campus feeling disillusioned. Others find peace and cultural salvation by conforming to the clear expectations of androcentric, marriage-centric complementarianism. Southern's embodied realities are as powerful as they are pervasive. Its gendered gospel—told in historical and theological narratives and materially shaped into the warp and woof of embodied community—insists on being both heard and seen.

CHAPTER 3

All One in Christ

GENDERBLIND DISCOURSE AT ASBURY SEMINARY

So God created humankind in his image,
in the image of God he created them;
male and female he created them.
—*Genesis 1:27*

Just a ninety-minute drive from Louisville, through the rolling hills of Kentucky's bluegrass, Asbury Theological Seminary enjoys an outsized presence in the small town of Wilmore, Kentucky. Between the town's two stoplights, on an understated but neatly manicured campus, students learn, work, pray, sing, and live together as they prepare to lead the next generation of Wesleyan evangelicals. On one end of campus, a statue of Francis Asbury, the circuit-riding Wesleyan preacher who popularized John Wesley's teachings in the United States, surveys the sleepy intersection from atop his bronze horse, reminding visitors and longtime community members alike of the institution's heritage.

Asbury's students often reminded me of their counterparts at Southern. Most were earnest, intellectually curious, and likable. I met one of them, Tyler, at a coffee shop just a short walk from the main campus. Over the hum of espresso machines and study groups, Tyler explained that he had left a fulfilling job as an engineer to pursue a call to ministry. Accompanied by his wife Robin and their three young children, he moved to Wilmore to enroll at Asbury. The family was clearly thriving. Tyler, nearing the end of his third year of study, expressed gratitude for what he had learned, the people he had met, and the warm community his family had experienced.

But Tyler did not *sound* like a Southern student. Asbury, he told me, had changed him in many ways, including his views on women in church leadership. Tyler did not initially share the institution's egalitarian positions. He described his time at Asbury as a "journey of trying to figure this out." Though the jour-

Figure 3.1. Asbury Seminary's Estes Chapel sits in front of B. L. Fisher Library. Photo by the author.

ney was not an easy one and voices from his complementarian background remained present, Tyler now believed that women should be allowed to preach:

> Some [of my] influences would say, "Yes, there are definite roles . . . men can be in all ministries, but women can only be in certain ministries." That [way of thinking] has broken down over my time here, and I don't agree with that anymore. Now I'm of the understanding that any ministerial or pastoral role, anything within the Church, which a person is gifted to do, they should be able to do that—regardless of gender. So if a woman is clearly gifted with preaching and they feel called to preach, then why should gender matter? If they're clearly effective in winning people for Christ as an evangelist, why should we hamper what the Spirit has done in that person's life? It not only hampers the work of God, it hinders the work of the Spirit in the world.

Tyler also distanced himself from male headship in marriage. He and Robin built their marriage on principles of mutual submission and shared authority. "I think we really lead together," he told me. "Some people will say, 'Well, how do you make decisions then? Somebody has to be the leader, or you don't make decisions.' I think that's forcing something that's not really there. If two people can't make a decision together, there's just something wrong."

"Why does this matter theologically?" I probed. "Hmm," Tyler puzzled thoughtfully as he paused for a moment before answering. "To me, it starts back

at creation. In the valuation of humanity as God created them—the understanding that there's equality and value and worth that's all coming out of that
understanding of God creating. So when we do things where we judge based on
gender or social or racial issues, we're devaluing something about the way a person is made—and that person is made in the image of God." Asbury's administration would have been proud of Tyler's answer. His words testify to the
community's success at forming him into an evangelical egalitarian grounded
in biblical authority.

They also fit clear discursive patterns. This chapter explores Asbury's discourse, examining the ways that students, like their Southern Baptist counterparts, weave gender ideology into narrative forms that combine history with
theology and prescribe contemporary practices. Similar to Southern's Gospel
Story, Asbury's genderblind "Equality Story" draws heavily from the biblical narrative. In place of Southern's gendered hierarchies and role prescriptions, however, Asbury students' interpretation prioritizes women's access to leadership
positions using an individualistic logic that, paradoxically, also alienates the
community from gendered awareness. Students also leaned on a parallel discourse that I call the "Difference Story," which valorizes an essential binary
realized primarily through marriage. In the end, however, a "Mission Metanarrative" often overshadows the first two stories in community practice. These
three narratives, constructed with the help of distinctly evangelical cultural tools,
facilitate Asbury students' bifurcated rhetoric of public genderblind equality and
privatized difference. Generally unnamed and more loosely constructed than
Southern's, these stories are nonetheless powerfully told and heard.

Public Genderblindness

Most Asbury students enthusiastically supported women in ministry. I learned
right away that this did not mean the gender-specific "women's ministry"
promoted by Southern's complementarians. Instead, Asbury students eagerly
explained that every office of churchly authority should be open to women. They
especially admired the women who modeled this leadership within their own
community. But I wanted to know more. How did students arrive at their beliefs?
What significance did gender itself carry for them? Were gender differences
important in the Church at all?

To answer these questions, students turned to biblical history. Like Southern's Gospel Story, Asbury's gendered narrative coalesces around several key
themes, evidences of what sociologist Ann Swidler calls a cultural toolkit (1986).
As human actors navigate their lives, explains Swidler, they develop a common
set of practices that help them make sense of their social worlds and orient their
behavior within them. Just as humans tend to utilize the home repair or kitchen
tools that they have the most experience with, they also naturally employ famil-

iar words, assumptions, and linguistic patterns. As Asbury students recounted the biblical narrative, they consistently utilized genderblind individualism and anticollectivist unity, cultural tools that uphold Asbury's egalitarian framework as both Christian and antifeminist.

The Equality Story

Asbury's first story shares an opening scene with Southern's Gospel Story, but the two quickly part ways. Like their Southern Baptist counterparts, Asbury students affirmed the importance of the Genesis creation account. Adam and Eve, they agreed, offer a prototype, a precedent applicable to all human relationships that come after them. Instead of interpreting the creation of the first man and woman through the lens of gendered difference, however, these students emphasized that the first humans were both created in God's own image—the *imago Dei*—giving them full and unqualified equality. "The man and the woman are standing side by side as equal creations." Tyler explained. "[They] were meant to reflect a whole image of God." Others pointed to the creation of Eve from Adam's rib, signaling God's intention that man and woman work and live side by side, as equals. This construction solidifies equality as a biblical mandate. It also grounds equality in an individualistic logic: people matter not as members of gendered groups but as individual persons, as bearers of God's image.

Students emphasized the absence of hierarchy in this model. Ethan, a first-year scholarship student already strikingly well versed in the teachings and writings of the early Church fathers, explained, "In looking at the Godhead as the triune life, there is no subordination—at least not for orthodoxy. . . . The first five centuries of the Church and its reflection in theological inquiries have been very formative in how I think. . . . And from that perspective, it becomes problematic if you say that there's any subordination in the Godhead or that there has to be subordination in gender." For Ethan, the very nature of God's being necessarily ascribed equal value to every human being, simply because all bear God's image. Ryan, a winsome first-year student wearing thick, curly hair, a red hooded sweatshirt, and sneakers, agreed. Underscoring the importance of relationships— both divine and human—he explained, "There are relationships there. Without the Son, the Father is not the Father. And without the Father, the Son is not the Son. We were meant to be in relationship." For Ethan, Ryan, and others, the Holy Trinity offers a compelling symbol of this vision. This Trinity, they stressed, is free not only from hierarchy, but also from selfish ambition and discord. Likewise, they said, often with conviction thick in their voices, humans are created to live together in unified community, free from division.

This Edenic imagery fills students' imaginations with visions of full, but differentiated, equality. Students like Ryan and Ethan envision Adam and Eve walking together side by side in perfect, nonhierarchical unity, free from selfishness and struggles for power. They were, students insisted, complete and unquestioned equals. This egalitarian formulation does not deny difference. Students insisted on a meaningful gender binary. They also, like their counterparts at Southern, assumed this binary to be a direct reflection of biological sex. Even as they rejected the idea that these differences should dictate leadership roles, they upheld the value—even necessity—of difference itself. It is, they agreed, important in Christian lives and communities. But, they also urged, Christians ought to practice gender difference in ways that prioritize the kind of harmony and unity modeled in Eden. In other words, they prescribed genderblindness.

Humanity's fall into sin confounded this vision. When Adam and Eve ate the forbidden fruit, Eden's utopian paradise came to a regrettable end. What God intended as a community of equality and unity, students lamented, became one of personal ambition and *dis*unity. While well acquainted with this chapter in the Genesis story, most students were not accustomed to talking about it in gendered terms. When I asked them to explain the gendered effects of the fall, many focused not so much on gender, or even equality, but on a more general loss of unity. Tyler, for example, acknowledged that humanity's fall into sin negatively affected relationships between men and women, but he *de-emphasized* the gendered nature of this break: "They were—they could be—in right relationship both with each other and God prior to the fall. And when the relationship with God experienced a break, that had the consequence of also damaging the horizontal relationship between the man and the woman. And not just the man and the woman but all individuals as they interact. And so that's what we get in Christ re-creating the world in his redemption: the opportunity for this repaired and right relationship again." Tyler emphasized the individual actor, prioritizing individualized choices over collective experiences.

A few deviated from this pattern and included more gendered specificity. Hannah, for example, nodded subtly to the reality of gendered patterns in social practice:

> I think before [the Fall] happened, we were able to have that unity that I was talking about—and we were one, you know, together. There were still differences but those differences served each other. Those differences were played out in a beautiful and loving way and were accepted by each other and were honored instead of exploited. And I think afterwards, exploitation happened and those differences start to make us draw apart from each other. We started to have desires that we didn't have before and we started to think how we can use the other and maybe judge the other for being a certain way, putting down other people and that kind of thing.

Mattie suggested that men and women bore the weight of the fall differently: "I think that [the woman] will desire [the man], but it's a misplaced desire for her husband to rule. God is supposed to be the one that she looks to. And so rather than a partnership where she is expressing the nature of God to [the man], where she's his helper, she's looking for him to lead her and to be her lord . . . and the man in his fallenness is going to totally accept that." Jack, one of only a few to introduce the language of power, said, "I think up until that point it was an equal partnership, but sin brought about this dominating compulsion in men. I'm not sure how that impacted women but . . . it was a power struggle essentially. Both sexes fighting the other for power or dominance in their own way." Analyses like these, however, were unusual, and they lacked consistency. Most often, student storytellers resisted exploring gendered repercussions of the Fall, preferring to frame sin's consequences as a break in unity between human beings who only happen to be men and women.

The remainder of the Old Testament, while not central to Asbury's gendered stories, does sustain them. It contributes passing references to a few remarkable women who served God's purposes as the people of Israel wandered the violent world of the ancient Near East. Students occasionally mentioned the story of Deborah's leadership in the book of Judges, for example, but without the theological nuance and enthusiasm they applied to the story of Eden. Still, Deborah and other Old Testament women anchor the Equality Story in history, underscoring one of its key points: God has always called and used women for leadership. While important evidence of the story's consistency, these episodes carry less import than the biblical stories and characters that follow.

As the narrative pivots away from the ancient stories of the Old Testament toward first-century Palestine, momentum builds. Jesus's life, death, and resurrection represent a critical shift within Asbury students' cosmology. Keeping with the Equality Story's genderblindness, students resisted searching for gendered significance in the story of Jesus. Instead, they appealed to a familiar tool: individual value. Just as students emphasized every individual's possession of the *imago Dei* in their accounts of creation, they also stressed God's gift of salvation for all people, accomplished through Jesus's death and resurrection. Collective human characteristics like gender, along with ethnicity and race, fade in the face of this great leveling.

Students definitively opposed gendered constructions of discipleship. Many grew noticeably uncomfortable when I introduced gendered language into conversations about holiness or Christian living (e.g., "What does it mean to be a godly *woman*?"). Aware of the polarized ideals of "godly manhood" and "godly womanhood" popular at Southern and in broader evangelical circles, most Asbury students rejected them—often forcefully—in favor of a degendered, individualized approach to following Jesus. Kara, a third-year counseling student, explained that while gender difference is important, it has little to do with godliness: "It's mostly about being a godly *person* and if everything centers around God and everything focuses around Him. If your goal in life is just to chase after God, then that shapes your character and makes you look more like God. And then it just happens that you're a woman, so you have your other things that make you a woman." Others concurred. Asked the same question, they framed their answers in ways that prioritized universal human equality. Jack, for example, was unable—or unwilling—to describe how godliness might be different for men or women. He preferred, like Kara, to think in terms of being a "godly person." I asked him to explain what that would look like. "Well, hopefully this isn't too vague of an answer, but the likeness of Christ. And equating oneself with the spirit of Christ and that sort of moral standing and disposition. That sort of holiness. And seeing how that translates into you in your own unique role. Whether you're male or female or whatever culture you find yourself in." Jack wanted me to understand that personhood matters. Gender does not. Like the gift of salvation, Jesus's personal invitation to discipleship overwhelms gendered subcategories.

Nevertheless, some gendered assumptions linger. Lindsey, for example, readily agreed with her peers that godliness itself is not gendered. But when I pressed her to give me an example of a godly woman, her answer followed the script of domesticized femininity. "My pastor's wife would be a good example," Lindsey said. "She lives it out. . . . She has people over to their house every week and prepares dinners and all this kind of stuff. She's really hospitable to the Church and always there, if anybody's sick, to ask, 'Do you guys need anything?' She's just really good at that kind of stuff." As Lindsey demonstrates, even students who adhere to genderblind convictions in theory sometimes revert to deeply gendered assumptions when it comes to the practical realities of social life.

All students agreed on the importance of biblical guidance. They especially invoked New Testament passages celebrating Christian unity. Jeff, a first-year divinity student, paraphrased Paul's letter to the Galatians: "I think it almost goes back to how there's no slave nor free, Greek nor Jew, man nor female. So if we're all identical in Christ—I mean, that's what I really think Galatians 2:20 is all about—we let our own personal identity die so that Christ can take up our lives and live through us. And that includes my masculinity or femininity. That includes whatever I have in my identity, however I identify myself, laying that down and letting Christ live through me." The passage Jeff invokes here is a favorite among students. The language of "all are one in Christ Jesus" powerfully reinforces their genderblind vision for Christian unity. Within this framework, celebrating a gendered identity—or even *having* a gendered identity—would be selfish because it elevates what is shared only by some (gender) over a spiritual identity shared by all. It is a choice, Jeff suggested: self or Jesus.

Many imagine an ideal churchly community where gender differences are present—even acknowledged—but not operative. Barring women categorically from exercising leadership would contradict this ideal. But so would dwelling on their collective experiences and scrutinizing their differences from men. This kind of gendered awareness, students suggested, could foster internal division, violating biblical directives to be "one in Christ Jesus." They expressed fears that investment in collective gender identities might do exactly this. "I think God made us to relate completely and with harmony and respect to one another," Paige explained, but "the Enemy comes in and wants to create differences and point out all the ways that there can be strife between man and woman." Like most of the community, Paige preferred to subordinate collective gendered experiences to the widely agreed-upon goal: unity in Christ. The New Testament story of Jesus, like the story of Creation, thus prescribes a construction of Christian community free of gendered division. While allowing for the presence of difference, it nonetheless serves to diminish more than accentuate gender's salience to Asbury's students.

As the Equality Story forges ahead, the Holy Spirit takes the starring role. The New Testament's accounts of early Church practice are key to the genderblind Equality Story. In the second chapter of the book of Acts, students explained, the Spirit—and consequently the Church, which recognized the Spirit's authority—empowered every member, both men and women, not because of gender but because of their individual gifts. Students spoke fluently about the New Testament women who answered the Spirit's call. Priscilla worked alongside the Apostle Paul and her husband Aquila as a missionary. Phoebe delivered Paul's letter to the church in Rome. Junia, named in this letter, served as an apostle.[1] Collective memory of these women's leadership yielded students' most heartfelt defenses of contemporary gender equality. If the Spirit's call was sufficient reason for women to lead in Christianity's earliest communities, it is enough for the twenty-first century as well.

The Spirit who calls also equips. Students expected potential leaders to demonstrate "gifts," competencies given by the Spirit, evidence of the recipient's calling. While these gifts, they explained, were idiosyncratic—different for each person—nearly everyone resisted the idea that their dispersion had anything to do with gender. As Dillon explained, "I think that a big message of Asbury is that we all bring something different to offer to the body of Christ. We all have different strengths and different abilities. I think that that's a big deal, but I don't think that's gender exclusive necessarily. I don't think that one gender has certain gifts that another gender wouldn't. I think that's just based on the individual. We all have different gifts. I think the overall message that Asbury has on similarities is that we're all united as a priesthood of believers." Ethan too responded viscerally when I asked if men and women should take different roles in church leadership. "No!" he answered definitively. "Not at all?" I pressed. He shook his head, adding firmly, "However God has gifted you is where you should be led and where you should serve." Ethan noticeably reframed the question. Correcting my own collective categories of "men" and "women," he substituted a singular "you," an abstract individual, in his answer. Keith, another first-year student, also pivoted away from collective gendered categories toward individuals, invoking the distinctively Wesleyan conceptualization of "gifts and graces": "I think that Scripture affirms that both men and women can be pastors, in all capacities, depending upon their gifts and their graces. And if a woman has truly experienced a call to ministry, and you have seen fruit in their life that they have the gift to preach, or that they have the gift to lead others or disciple, etc. etc. Then who am I to say no to them?" The Holy Spirit's call is not to be questioned. If an individual exhibits leadership capabilities, gifts of the Spirit, as Keith put it, "Who am I to say no?"

Notably, students did not dismiss gendered categories altogether. Jack, for example, agreed that any position of churchly leadership should be open to women. "In terms of offices and official roles within the church," he said, "I don't think [gender] determines that at all." But, he continued, "I do think that [women] can do so without sacrificing their, whatever this means, their femininity. Because women bring something unique to leadership, because they're, whatever that means." Declining to identify what, specifically, he might expect women to contribute, Jack nonetheless noted the possibility that their leadership would look different from men's. Kara broke from genderblindness even more explicitly. Recognizing the disconnect between the egalitarian ideal of equality and the historic realities of institutional leadership, she admitted, "It's always been the male role to be a pastor." Kara also explained that her own church background had given her numerous experiences with women in pastoral positions. "I honestly think women make better pastors," she confided, "because women are better at talking to people and taking care of people and making sure people are emotionally taken care of." Despite the community's widespread idealization of feminine nurture, which chapter 4 will explore, Kara was the only student at Asbury to make this argument.

Indeed, her classmates overwhelmingly gravitated toward the community's dominant vision of individualistic genderblindness. Although there were exceptions, like Kara, most often students' narrations of the biblical Equality Story examined people not as women or men but as individuals, de-emphasizing any potential differences in their experiences and contributions to the Church. In many students' minds, the key question appeared to be a simple one: should women be allowed to exercise churchly authority, interchangeably with men, or not? As Dillon argued, "I think you're either on one side or the other. I don't think you can ride the fence on that. I think you're either for it or against it." Dillon and most of his colleagues were decidedly "for it." They told a story of gender-blind equality.

"Context, Context, Context": Learning the Equality Story

While Asbury's required curriculum does not include classes devoted to explicitly gendered topics, mandatory coursework often introduces related content. One required class, titled "Vocation of Ministry," covers a variety of themes—

including women in leadership. I observed from the back of the classroom one morning as the professor appealed to the gifts of the Holy Spirit. "Pentecost," the lecture began, "is the third most important day in the church calendar" (presumably behind Christmas and Easter). The Spirit is given entirely to both men and women, the speaker continued, as is salvation in Jesus. "So," the professor paused, looking expectantly at the class, "wouldn't you agree that God's two best gifts are given to both?" The class rewarded the question with nodded agreement. "Who gets to decide who gets what spiritual gift?" their teacher continued. "It's not you. It's not me. It's not [complementarian theologian] Wayne Grudem." The answer, so obvious that no one bothered even to voice it, was the Holy Spirit.

Like Southern, Asbury invests in holistic formation. The process often begins in classrooms like this one, which facilitate social exchanges as well as intellectual work. As students interact with each other, and with their professors, they learn the language of the Equality Story. New Testament faculty members contribute heavily to this work. Students often mentioned these professors as key in their egalitarian development. Sara, for example, admitted that she had been "a little bit confused on the issue, actually, when I came. . . . I had heard so much about the man being the spiritual head of the house growing up that I just took for granted that there's some element of truth to it. I would have said before that both equally share spiritual responsibility. Just in different ways. . . . It wasn't that I had this dogmatic, well thought out viewpoint, it was just like the wallpaper; I just didn't think about it." Sara's New Testament professors, she remembered gratefully, nurtured her toward a more robust understanding. "They can articulate some of those difficult [scripture] passages really well—their meaning from a scholarly point [of view]," she said. "That was fantastic." This faculty includes prominent biblical scholars like Craig Keener, whose books have sold well over half a million copies and earned him widespread recognition as a leader in his field of biblical studies.[2] Keener has consistently and strongly affirmed gender equality and women's leadership, most notably in his 1992 book *Paul, Women, and Wives*. Keener's colleague Ben Witherington likewise highlights, as the title of his first book indicates, *Women in the Ministry of Jesus* (1984). Significantly, both of these men cut their scholarly teeth on questions of women in the New Testament and have been intellectual leaders in the field of egalitarian biblical scholarship for decades.

If students learn anything from these professors, it is this: context matters. In a widely read blog post titled "Why It Is Important to Study the Bible in Context," Keener argues, "Using verses out of context one could 'prove' almost anything about God or justify almost any kind of behavior—as history testifies. But in the Bible, God revealed Himself in His acts in history, through the inspired records of those acts and the inspired wisdom of His servants addressing specific situations" (2013). The Bible is an ancient book, professors like Keener remind their students. Its truths are timeless, but they are also articulated from the perspectives of real human beings who lived in historical and cultural contexts very different from twenty-first-century America. To fully understand the truths that God intended Paul's letters to convey, professors teach, one must understand the cultural, economic, and political realities of Paul's original audiences.

Context also provides a defense against complementarian "clobber verses." Most students, I found, were acutely aware of these New Testament passages, often used by complementarians to prohibit women from exercising leadership over men. Eager to illustrate that proper contextualization reveals their author, the Apostle Paul, to be a great advocate for women, students confidently recited these verses in their interviews. Context, they argued, changes everything. Stephanie, an advanced counseling student, explained, laughing at the irony: "At that point women weren't educated. They really didn't have the ability to receive education, so they were taking up most of the time, during church, asking questions. So that's why [Paul says], 'you should ask your husbands.' They could learn at home first, and then continue [learning]. That makes sense to me, but if you don't have that context then [you might think], 'Yeah, women don't have rights, and obviously they're not as smart as men.'" I also asked Josh, a third-year PhD student who had just articulated an impassioned defense for women in church leadership, how he understood biblical passages that seemed to prohibit this practice. He smiled confidently, clearly enjoying himself. "Context, context, context," he repeated the word firmly and deliberately, leaning back in his chair for emphasis. "All of Paul's letters are *occasional* letters. Written to specific people. Specific times, specific messes. And a lot of people want to take Paul out of his context. So the big debate is 'is Paul a misogynist?' I mean, especially the feminist interpreters are all over Paul about that."

"Is Paul a misogynist?" I inquired.

"NO!" Josh responded forcefully. He continued, "Paul is an ANTI-misogynist! Both Jesus and Paul, in their own day, elevated women to such a height in such a patriarchal, misogynistic society! If you look at Paul in his context, you see how radical he is in how he treats women and the roles he gives them. The same with Jesus. Who does he appear to first when he's raised from the dead? Women. . . . In their context they were both very, very radical." Interpreted properly, Josh maintained, Paul and the faith communities he shepherded *empowered* women. Like his peers, Josh narrated New Testament characters Phoebe, Junia, and Priscilla as striking departures from patriarchal first-century norms, leading within beautifully and radically countercultural churches. Understanding the cultural context of the Bible, students told me over and over, makes all the difference.

Men and women, however, used the notion of context differently. Josh, who championed the primacy of "context, context, context" as a hermeneutical principle, used "context" as more than a word. For him, and for many of the other men I interviewed, it was a mantra. Employing it demonstrated their knowledge and competence as interpreters of the Bible's ancient words. It built their legitimacy as aspiring pastors and scholars and facilitated embattlement against other Christian traditions who read (or misread, as Josh would argue) the same passages without context as a hermeneutical tool. Women valued the primacy of context too, but in more personal ways. Rachel told me that her professor's emphasis on separating "the Bible's culture from the Bible's message" held deep meaning for her, particularly because she had not grown up in an egalitarian church:

> There was a sense in most of my years that we just take the Bible at face value. So if it says women shouldn't talk in church, women shouldn't talk in church. I didn't even go to strictly conservative [churches]. I went to fairly mainstream churches. This is just regular mainstream teaching. So I think that was huge for me to have access to teaching that said, "Whoa. Here's what was going on in that culture. This is what Paul was working with. He was actually liberating women by suggesting that their husbands teach them. By suggesting that they actually *learn*." That was huge for that culture that women should even have the opportunity to learn. So, when he tells them to be quiet, it's, "be quiet until you've had the chance to learn" not, "be quiet forever and this applies to all women forever for the rest of time." It's that simple. When I read it, I thought, "Of course." But for many years I just assumed that that's what the Bible taught and that's what we needed to do. Even though I didn't like it, I had nothing to say about it. I just felt kind of stuck with it.

For Rachel, like the first-century women in question, a culturally specific understanding of Paul's instruction provided practical empowerment. Like many other women at Asbury, Rachel treasured this revelation, both as a student of the Bible and as a woman. When she first enrolled at Asbury, she did not expect to pursue vocational ministry. As her understanding of New Testament context expanded, however, so did the opportunities she saw for her own life and calling. In contrast with Josh's clinical use of the concept, Rachel's felt more personal and sacred than academic and professional. Contextual hermeneutics changed Josh's beliefs, but they changed Rachel's life.

As Rachel's story also illustrates, however, the Equality Story can also be limiting for aspiring churchwomen. Its contextualized readings of biblical texts offer powerful historical precedents of women called and equipped for the work of mission, preaching, and discipleship. They affirm contemporary women's deeply personal convictions that they are, similarly, called to the work of the Church. The same story's genderblind individualism, however, also works against the development of collective identities, even around shared experiences with the story itself. This individualism inhibits the rich solidarity that Southern's women enjoy. Indeed, Rachel's formation was accomplished largely through private academic and devotional practices, not so much in conversation with other women about their own thoughts and experiences. The Equality Story might free

women in some senses, but the personal connections they feel to the newly contextualized New Testament stories remain largely confined to their individualized journeys.

The Equality Story's emphasis on context has other limits as well. Neither men
nor women applied the deep cultural analysis they championed for biblical interpretation to their own context. While Josh gushed with enthusiasm about Paul's
and Jesus's "radical" treatment of women against a first-century social backdrop
that he described as "patriarchal," and "misogynistic," he stopped short of suggesting that twenty-first-century American Christians too might need to subvert cultural patterns to overcome patriarchal barriers of their own day. Nor did
Rachel explicitly critique her own context for unequal systems and cultural
assumptions. Instead, for both men and women, "context" remained largely
limited to the practice of hermeneutics, a tool for understanding the Bible and
releasing women for ministry.

"I Thy True Son": Maintaining Genderblind Unity

The contemporary context does, however, present gendered challenges. Even
Asbury's own community is not fully unified in its egalitarianism. Asbury's identity is a tricky one. While it is self-consciously Wesleyan and egalitarian, it
serves a decidedly evangelical constituency, one that often assumes complementarian ideals. It is conceivable—even likely—that some students enroll at Asbury
without realizing that it is, in fact, egalitarian. While the majority are convinced
egalitarians, a notable minority remains uncertain about—or even dismissive
of—women in positions of religious authority. These nonconformists introduce
the real possibility of conflict, a potential threat to unity. Dissenters do occasionally raise objections in class. When this happens, professors told me, they
generally attempt to gently but firmly rearticulate the institution's position and
move on. While renegade complementarian students may not be excluded from
the community and may, sometimes, even instigate spirited discussions, their
ideas remain decidedly on the margins. Given the range of backgrounds represented in the community, maintaining unity sometimes means agreeing to disagree on questions of women in leadership.

Sometimes even egalitarian students make it difficult for faculty members to
teach egalitarianism. I watched the Vocation of Ministry class closely as its professor promoted explicitly egalitarian readings of scripture, curious if anyone
would object. Midway through the lecture, a middle-aged man near the back of
the classroom frowned, wrote intently in his notebook, and seemed increasingly
agitated. Ah, I thought as I watched him raise his hand, here it comes. But instead
of arguing for male headship, as I expected, the man complained, "I'm confused.
Why are we still talking about this? Didn't we in the United Methodist Church
settle this question a long time ago?" He was not unaware of complementarianism's growing popularity; indeed, one of his classmates had just described leav-

ing another denomination because it denied women leadership positions. But from this man's perspective, the question already had been "settled" in Wesleyan circles by sound theology and definitive policy adjustments, leaving no need for further conversation. Perhaps he too was aware of the inflammatory possibilities that haunt conversations about gender. Perhaps he felt that broaching the subject at all legitimized the possibility that women could be excluded from ministry. Or perhaps he was simply eager to move along to other content that seemed to him less tangential to the practical demands of vocational ministry. Regardless, this story illustrates how difficult it can be to initiate conversations about gender at Asbury. Resistance can come from both sides.

In a coauthored 2018 book, Sue Russell, professor of mission and contextual studies, suggests a strategy for resolving these fraught conversations. The book, titled *Relationshift: Changing the Conversation about Men and Women in the Church*, breaks from genderblindness to acknowledge women's collective experience in unequal societies, recognizing, for example, that women globally are more vulnerable to violence and are often dismissed by the Church. Following the narrative of the Equality Story, the book contrasts these injustices with Eden's equitable utopia. "In the beginning," the opening chapter reads, "God was community, and He created us—man and woman—to be communal, to be in relationship . . . there is a constancy of giving, receiving, affecting, and being affected—mutuality" (Russell and Roese 2018, 24). Human society, Russell suggests, has fallen far from this ideal of mutuality.

Nevertheless, the book argues forcefully against considering women as a collective. Russell shares parts of her own story, recalling her frustration when a complementarian church refused to allow her to teach a Sunday School class. "I was excluded," she writes, "not because of who I was as a person but because I belonged to the category 'women.' It is easier to exclude people based on their category than to exclude individuals we know" (2018, 7). Elevating categories like "women," this logic implies, cannot be the solution because categories are, in fact, part the problem. The remainder of the book accordingly advocates only individualized, relational solutions for the gendered inequalities that, the authors recognize, persist within the Church. As their title suggests, they promote reframing conversations about gender in terms of individual "brother-and-sister relationships" that do not seek to change existing social arrangements. "We are called," the book urges, "to relate to each other according to our overarching identity of 'in Christ' . . . but to do it within our current social statuses" (94). While Russell's resistance to structural engagement is not uniform among Asbury's faculty, it does give voice to a clear, if implicit, assumption shared by many students. The book promotes a tenuous balance between genderblindness and gendered awareness.

This tension is also evident in institutional discourse. All students learn to use gender-inclusive language. The gender-exclusive "mankind" or "brothers," several students told me, would be unacceptable in written work and in class. "They're not going to let us write papers that say mankind," Andy emphasized. "They're going to say 'humanity.'" I asked how he learned about this rule. "It's their general policy. You will get grade deductions if you do it. They train it out of you . . . it's a way of being egalitarian and saying that these things apply to more than just men, and not being gender-biased." This imperative, however, does not always extend beyond classroom assignments. In formal contexts of public prayer and preaching, men and women alike occasionally slipped into androcentric language. I heard more than one administrator refer to "man" or "mankind" from the chapel pulpit. The inconsistency was even more striking at an evening event when a young woman led worshipers in several songs. One thanked God for "redeeming grace to Adam's race." Another referenced humanity as the "sons" of God. As I looked around me, women sang with confidence. Some closed their eyes as they reflected on the words they sang. Others raised their arms toward the heavens. The event climaxed with a communion service presided over by a woman administrator who broke the bread and offered the elements with graceful authority. No one seemed to question the incongruity.

Linguistic inconsistencies linger in written form as well. Near the end of my fieldwork, Asbury announced production of its own hymnal. On a later visit to the seminary, I stopped in the lobby of the on-campus hotel to page through one of the newly minted books. The crisp, new pages fell open to a favorite, "Be Thou My Vision." The hymn's traditional English wording, penned in 1912, includes the line "Thou my great Father, I Thy true son." Because Asbury does not apply gender-inclusive language to God, I was unsurprised to see retention of the word "Father." I was, however, more interested in the hymnal's preservation of the androcentric "son." While some Christian communities have adapted this particular wording (e.g., "Thou my great Father; thine own may I be"), and others, including the United Methodist Hymnal, simply eliminate this particular verse, Asbury's new hymnal retains it, along with its androcentric lyrics. In small print at the bottom of the page, a line of explanation reads: "The biblical language of the son's inheritance applies to men and women alike, just like the imagery of the bride applies to all."

It is not that the institution categorically opposes changing hymn lyrics. When including the song "In Christ Alone" in their worship sets, for example, Asbury's liturgists have sometimes altered the Calvinist vocabulary of "on the cross as Jesus died, the wrath of God was satisfied" to the following: "the love of God was magnified." This lyrical tweak, which better reflects Wesleyan theology, functions as a welcome reminder that Asbury is unified in its Wesleyanism *against* Calvinist doctrine. Offending the neo-Calvinists, already one of Asbury's favorite out-groups, is less of a problem. In contrast, the new hymnal's compromise on "Be Thou My Vision" minimizes potential for disunity *within* the community. A lyrical shift toward gender inclusivity might run the risk of exposing internal fault lines. Because of the footnote, those who may be uncomfortable with the gender-exclusive language of "sons" have the quiet assurance that women too are included, even as the familiar, traditional wording is preserved. Whatever the reasoning behind this editorial choice, the end result is a curious combination of rhetorical signals.

———

As a matter of institutional practice, the question of women in leadership is not up for debate. Asbury is *Wesleyan*, and Wesleyans let women preach. In striking contrast with Southern's discourse of male headship, Asbury's students tell a compelling story of genderblind equality that extends even to highly symbolic roles of religious authority and, indeed, preaching. Beyond this symbolism, however, are limits. This institutional discourse, explored most thoroughly in considerations of biblical context, encourages only a cursory gendered awareness, bounded by genderblind individualism and impulses to preserve unity. As one Bible professor explained, the question of how Asbury's Wesleyan heritage should inform conversations about gender rarely came up among his colleagues. "At this point," he said, "it's kind of taken for granted. . . . The philosophical debate is not a debate anymore." Most students also take this posture. While they celebrate the radical and antipatriarchal actions of the early Church, their attention to these impulses remains largely confined to the first-century context, giving way in contemporary practice to expectations of unity. Rigorous academic work, much of it emerging from Asbury's own scholars, has yielded robust biblical support for women in ministry. Official policy ensures that contemporary practice can follow suit. Women can be, and indeed are, ordained, hired, and promoted. All that needs to be done, according to Asbury's genderblindness advocates, is to proceed with the business of genderblind unity.

"Not a Big Fan of Extremes": Constructing an Antifeminist Egalitarianism

In addition to my interest in students' beliefs about the Bible and churchly practice, I was curious whether and how feminism informed their egalitarianism. While feminism encompasses a vast array of ideologies and movements including radical feminism, standpoint feminism, womanism, and third-wave feminism, Asbury's brand of egalitarianism most closely resembles liberal feminist impulses. In addition to a common language of equality, the two share a focus on the public (in Asbury's case, churchly) realm and women's access to positions of leadership. Students' initial reactions, in fact, suggested a degree of support for the movement. They often mentioned women's right to vote, for example, as a positive contribution.

Quick and emphatic qualifications, however, nearly always followed. In fact, many expressed overt hostility. Leaning on anticollectivism and individualism,

Students often rejected both feminist ideals and those who espoused them. Against standpoint feminism's emphasis on women's shared experiences and the more general feminist concern for women's collective interests, they argued instead that people should be judged only by their individual merits. According to Jesse, the less that gender factored into a leader's identity, the clearer their focus on things that really matter: "It shouldn't be that I'm a *female pastor*. It has to be that I'm a *pastor*. You see, we've assigned a gender to something that doesn't need a gender . . . if God has called you to ministry, I don't think you need to go out and flaunt the fact that you're a woman, I don't think that matters." A similar individualism colored students' understandings of feminism itself. While some did reflect awareness of the variation within the term, they often pivoted away from "feminism" to tell me instead what they thought of "feminists," that is, individual people. Jeff explicitly situated feminist activism against Christian obedience, naming not a group or a movement but a hypothetical person, "you": "I'm fully in agreement with bringing women to the equal position of men, but when you become radical in a way that is rebellious to the church that you're in and you start caring about your personal agenda and your personal beliefs above and beyond the authority of those who are above you, then you become rebellious. You become disobedient to the authority that God's placed above you." Hannah, more reluctant than Jeff to completely reject feminism, nevertheless illustrates how easily students revert to individualistic approaches:

> What I'm scared of is people taking it way far and being very militant. You know, "we have to make sure on all bases that women are completely included no matter what." I want women to be included, but I don't know. . . . To tell a little girl who is four years old, you know, whatever God calls you to, whatever God has gifted you to, I want you to be able to fulfill that—and that's not just as a wife and mother but that's as a human being, as a woman. I would call that godly feminism . . . but going to an extreme of, "We want to make sure men are in their place." . . . I feel like it becomes exploitative again. That's where I feel that it becomes too much.

In her attempt to salvage the language of feminism, Hannah recast its impulses in individualistic terms. Her suggestion of a "godly feminism" not only resists critiques of patriarchal power but engages only the individual, in this case a hypothetical four-year-old.

Prescriptions of Christian unity further limit feminism's appeal. As this chapter has already demonstrated, students worried that too much focus on gender could result in misplaced loyalties, damaging the harmony of Christian community. "Feminism seemed to put women above God," Alison explained gravely. "The whole point was about a gender, rather than all of us striving to be more Christlike. It took the focus off of Christ and made it more about gender." Alison even used the grammatical construction of her sentences to distance herself from feminism. Her choice of the past tense suggests that feminism is—or perhaps should be—a relic of the past. There may have been a moment when the Church and feminism could have converged, but for Alison at least, that moment had passed. As the Equality Story chronicles, the *imago Dei* draws people together to be a unified Church. But gender points to difference, and difference, worry students like Allison, can divide.

Students also condemned feminism for its activist impulses. They repeatedly denounced "extreme" or "radical" tendencies, frowning suspiciously at the idea of feminists agitating for structural change. Many expressed special wariness of activism on one's own behalf, offering sharp criticism of leaders with "a chip on their shoulder" or who "have something to prove." Individuals invested in equality, they contended, should resist behaviors that betray ambition or self-promotion. They should not become radical or self-serving or try to shake things up. Appealing to the virtue of humility, Will, for example, argued that women should not pursue churchly leadership to make a point: "I think the motivation should be because you feel called. Because you want further communion with God. Not [because you're] doing this for yourself. Not for political reasons. Not because you're a female. When you do it that way then it becomes about *me*, and it damages relationships. . . . People are going to see that [you're] just doing this to prove a point. And [you're] not genuine. I've seen that in female pastors." In contrast, Will also recounted the story, which he had heard from a professor, of a woman who took a more "humble" approach to her new ministry assignment: "She went knowing they didn't want a female pastor. She was genuine. She was humble. She had a good spirit. And within two or three weeks, people were coming to her saying, 'I'm glad that you're here.'" Will commended this "humble" woman because her actions fostered harmony with her congregants. In contrast, the hypothetical woman in his first example "damaged relationships" and marred Christian unity. Students like Will know that women in ministry often face opposition, but they do not view activism as appropriate recourse. They expect women to invest relationally within existing structures, not to seek change in the structures themselves.

Men especially insisted on this point. Josh, for example, explained that advocating for one demographic group over another, whether women or racial minorities, can create unholy division: "There's extreme feminism, and I think that's really damaging. It's not really helpful. To see men as the devil or, you know, kind of like African Americans [who see] white men as the devil. . . . I'm just not a big fan of extremes. I think it's damaging in the sense that it really puts the perspective into an either/or. Either men or women rather than a both/and." With a wry chuckle, Josh punctuated his point by concluding that "the extreme form of feminism, carried to its own end, will end in the death of humanity." Even aside from its hyperbole, not uncommon among the men I interviewed, Josh's statement firmly situates "extremes" outside the Church's mission.

He and others seemed to understand them as distractions, or worse, the enemies of human flourishing. Importantly, Josh's argument also situates feminist
activism alongside struggles for racial justice, suggesting that he expects not only
women but also other marginalized groups to seek equity only through means
that promote, rather than dismantle, unity.

Women too articulated a version of this logic.[3] After lauding Asbury's Equality Story, many clarified that their own churchly ambitions did not stem from
feminist identities or impulses. Grace, for example, feared that being perceived
as a feminist would bring her commitment to the ethics of the community into
question. "I mean, we don't want to talk about it too much," she said, "to where
there is a glaring difference between how we should treat men and women. Of
course, we don't want to come off as feminists, like that kind of thing." Hannah,
likewise, explained her own motives: "It's not like I'm a raving feminist. I mean,
I just want to have an opportunity to do what God calls me to do." Even Nadia, who
most pointedly identified the harmful effects of patriarchal power structures,
rejected feminism.

> NADIA: I think [feminists] have gone to the extreme.
> LWS: And that's not helpful for the Church?
> NADIA: No. Not in my estimation.
> LWS: Do you think that the Church has other tools that can empower women
> in more positive ways?
> NADIA: The Bible! They don't need any other tools! All of us are called. Each
> one of us is the Christian that the Bible is talking about. [We are] the people
> of God. We are each called to align our lives with the will of God for what
> God created us to be and do.

Feminism, according to Nadia, detracts from a biblical vision of equality.

Other students partially embraced feminism, separating it into "acceptable"
and "unacceptable" categories. Owen, one of several men who expressed qualified appreciation for feminism, credited his wife. "I hate to use the word 'feminist' because it has so many bad connotations," he said, "but she's the *good* kind
of feminist." Explaining the difference, he continued, "There are two kinds of
women in ministry. The first is the kind that really shouldn't be in ministry
because they have an axe to grind. They have a stone to throw. They have something to prove—and it makes them bitter, self-oriented, career-oriented." In contrast, Owen described his experience working with a humble, selfless pastor, the
kind of woman who, he believed, *should* be in leadership: "Everything she did
was what she believed the Holy Spirit was leading her to do in the best interest of
her constituency." Owen's genderblind individualism led him to judge women's
fitness for authoritative roles on the basis of motive. He was willing to accept
women's leadership, and even feminism itself, as long as a woman's motives were

oriented toward service of others. Rejecting some forms of feminism allowed him to embrace others.

Dan also carefully scrutinized women's ambitions. "I've come to the place where I don't see a difference in terms of the giftings," he said thoughtfully of his incipient egalitarian beliefs. He was not willing, however, to accept *all* women leaders: "I will say this: I find that I am more turned off when women try to assert themselves into positions of leadership than if they just performed the duties that are appropriate for them. . . . We should be working towards something better than simply trying to affirm one's authority and power. . . . Have your women in ministry conferences all you want, I don't care. But the minute you try to run through these lists of things and say, 'We need to carve out this space for us,' I think you've really missed who the church is to be." This formulation of gen-derblind Christian unity both eliminates the restrictions of complementarian gender roles and precludes egalitarian activism which, in Dan's mind, violates "who the church is to be." To be fair, both Owen and Dan, if asked, likely would have applied the same assessments to men. But neither they nor their peers seemed particularly concerned with policing men's motives for seeking leader-ship. Dan did, however, acknowledge the context: "I know traditionally it's been males who have dominated." He nevertheless failed to engage the enduring legacy this tradition has left in its wake. Instead, he worried about the possibil-ity of what he called "reverse domination" of women over men. Others agreed. Struggles to gain power have no place in a unified Church.

Asbury's community is not completely unified in its antifeminism. Women faculty members occupy a liminal space in this fraught landscape. One, Chris-tine Pohl, coauthored a book titled *Living on the Boundaries: Evangelical Women, Feminism, and the Theological Academy.* The book so markedly deviates from the genderblind language I came to expect from Asbury that I was taken by sur-prise when I began reading it near the end of my fieldwork. The book openly embraces the language of feminism, even in its title. It explicitly recognizes that the theological world is "still largely defined by men's experiences and priori-ties" and that "feminist insights and perspectives are an important part of the larger theological conversation" (Pohl and Creegan 2005, 10). In other women's offices, I noticed occasional feminist theology books including Elisabeth Schussler-Fiorenza's *In Memory of Her: A Feminist Theological Reconstruction of Christian Origins* (1983). Such titles suggest that some faculty may find ways to adopt feminist thought in subtle ways. They do not, however, speak as femi-nists in public. Indeed, Pohl's book, which breaks with genderblindness, appears to be little known among students, none of whom mentioned it to me. Asbury does not hire these women, after all, to be experts in feminist hermeneutics, women's spirituality, or even women's contributions to Wesleyan history. The institution cultivates a genderblind space, not a gender-celebratory one.

The difference might be difficult to recognize, but seasoned faculty women knew it well. As one admitted from the privacy of her office, "I think that's a big step to move from 'I can be as strong as a man' to 'I can be as strong as a woman.'" This is not a step that Asbury, as a whole, encourages.

———

Asbury's Equality Story and its proponents simultaneously uphold gender equality and condemn feminism. Students might argue against male headship. They might ardently defend a woman's right to serve as pastor, evangelist, and bishop. They might acknowledge Wesleyan participation in the nineteenth-century women's rights movement (Dayton 1976). But most actively distance themselves from feminism. Sidestepping the shared ideal of equality—and even a common history—they far more easily situate feminism in opposition to their Christian beliefs. Churchly equality, most believe, is best achieved without emphasizing collective gendered differences or treating any individual differently because of them. Against complementarian divisions of roles as well as against the division feminist collectivism might introduce, students prescribed an anticollectivist unity that precludes both gendered hierarchies and solidarities.

Their discourse bears striking resemblance to the cultural tools white evangelicals have used in their approaches to racial inequality. In *Divided by Faith: Evangelical Religion and the Problem of Race in America*, sociologists Michael Emerson and Christian Smith show how white evangelicals in the 1990s tried to solve racial injustices using accountable freewill individualism, relationalism, and antistructuralism (2000). The first of these tools, accountable freewill individualism, centers individual actors and their choices, emphasizing their freedom from external constraint. Asbury's genderblind individualism represents a variant of this same tool. It assumes gender to be an individual reality isolated from structural forces that affect people as collectives. It supposes that at Asbury, where official policies do not limit individual women from assuming positions of authority and influence, gendered barriers do not exist. While individualism, as Emerson and Smith note, is certainly a broadly American impulse, "the type of individualism and the ferocity with which it is held distinguishes white evangelicals from others" (Emerson and Smith 2000, 76). Genderblind individualism, rooted in the sacred stories of the Bible, features a similar intensity.

Relationalism, the second tool Emerson and Smith identify, also emerged. Like the white Christians who approved of only relational solutions to racism in their interviews, Asbury's students strongly favored interpersonal responses to gender inequality. Recognizing that faithful egalitarian women do sometimes face biases, the Equality Story nevertheless encourages humble, selfless, relational influence as the appropriate Christian response. Paired with prescriptions of personal humility and suspicion of feminist activism, Asbury's relational framework locates Christian ethics primarily in individual relationships. This approach applies both to relationships between individual persons and to relationships between each individual and their larger community. Given the inflexibility of institutions, which tend to evolve very slowly over time (Southern's conservative takeover being one significant exception), the responsibility rests heavily on the individual.

Finally, while the antistructuralism Emerson and Smith found in evangelical race discourse was less pronounced at Asbury, it too threaded student narrations of the Equality Story. Individualistic genderblindness, like colorblindness, has little room for structural activism—particularly when it has feminist overtones. Like colorblind approaches to racism, genderblindness ultimately obscures structural realities. It leaves users to navigate the world only as individuals, seeking right relationship with God and with each other, but largely powerless against structural and cultural inequalities that mark their own contexts. While there are exceptions, especially among faculty, anticollectivist unity and genderblind individualism plainly mark Asbury's dominant ethos. As chapter 4 will illustrate in greater detail, Emerson and Smith's findings in the 1990s remain highly relevant.

Private Gendered Difference

Genderblindness might prevail in Asbury's public spaces, but blindness does not necessarily indicate absence. The same students who argued articulately for genderblind equality in ministerial leadership also expressed commitment to the idea of innate binary gender differences. While somewhat less militant in their insistence on this binary than their counterparts at Southern Seminary, these students too resisted attributing it to social conditioning. Men and women, they explained, are not the same. Along with the genderblind Equality Story, which focuses primarily on public, churchly contexts, students told a parallel story, one that celebrates gendered difference within the private realm of domestic life, especially marriage.

The Difference Story

God created Adam and Eve, students explained, not only as equals, but also with clear and intentional dissimilarities. Kelly, a first-year divinity student wearing a colorful scarf and ornate silver earrings, described just how important the distinction was to her. Connecting the origins of difference to creation, she explained, "Women were created to be women. We were created in a certain way, and men were created in a certain way. We have different strengths, obviously. Right now people are trying to say 'No, everyone's the same, everyone's the same.' But, we're not. Both women and men reflect God in who they are and what they are like." Kelly's conviction that gender differences are important and "obvious" make her typical among her classmates. Also typical was her inability to coherently explain these differences. "Before we move on," I asked her, "can you explain a little more? What are some of the differences? Why do they exist?" In her answer Kelly leaned on cultural explanations, and the longer she talked, the more uncertain—even uncomfortable—she became:

> KELLY: One common thing is that women are very emotional, which obviously can be a bad thing sometimes, but I think it can also be a really good thing. I think we're really strong at empathy, and relating to other people, and being very nurturing and hospitable, and making people feel welcome. Men can do that too, but I think men have more of a very structured—in a sense that—that's not exactly what I'm trying to say—more analytical and thoughtful and rational. . . . Women can tend to, you know, go off of how they feel. And that's not always a bad thing. Sometimes it is, but sometimes it's not. So there's just those different aspects. And men, obviously, are built differently. Physically they are built to do that manual labor. And women are . . . I mean that's kind of what I'm saying, [but] sort of not. . . . [Laughs]
> LWS: You're struggling with this as you're saying it. I can tell.
> KELLY: Yeah! I'm thinking, "Well . . . I don't know." I mean, I think we just have different things about us. I'm not saying that's a bad thing. But you know women are naturally more nurturing and men are naturally more— what's the word? More [sounds unsure] strong . . . but I don't think that's really what I'm trying to say. I don't know. [Laughs]

The harder Kelly tried to articulate her beliefs, the more incoherent her argument became. Like other students, Kelly expressed commitment to gender complementarity, though noticeably without Southern's strictly gendered roles. This pattern may reflect the extensive influence that broader evangelical subculture has in many students' lives. Christian publishing and broadcasting industries, dominated by complementarian theology, have heavily emphasized themes of marriage and family in the content they have produced since the 1980s. While many of Asbury's students have rejected their hierarchical teachings, they seem to have little to replace them with save the lingering sense that difference, some-how, *matters*.

Even advanced students struggled. "Obviously I think that men and women are different," Mike said, drawing confidence from several years of study at Asbury. But he also confessed, "It'd be hard to put my finger on a way that they would be different." He then turned, as seminary students often do, to theological reflection, which strengthened his conviction, but did not add specificity:

> I have studied Genesis 1, and my understanding at this point in time is that God is triune: Father, Son, and Holy Spirit. In Genesis 1, God created man and woman in his image, together. And so I think, number one, that God is love as it says in 1 John. And to me, love implies a relationship. And, also thinking

of Genesis 1, God is a triune being, already modeling that community in the godhead. Man and woman created together are meant in some way to reflect God in their relationality and the contrast between them. So I as understand it, man and woman are not exactly the same, obviously, but something in their separateness and the contrast between them allows us to reflect God in a meaningful way.

These students' inarticulateness put them in stark contrast to Southern students' detailed articulations of gendered differentiation. While both Kelly and Mike affirmed the importance of differentiation, the practical nature of the difference, and its purpose for human relationships, remained unclear.

Students' defenses of gender difference did share one striking commonality. They were nearly always moderated by the Equality Story's individualistic logic. Students were loath to suggest that gender differences prescribed particular roles. For them, differences between unique individuals with their own personalities, strengths, and passions outweighed general differences between genders. In other words, the dominant Equality Story moderated students' narrations of gender difference and curtailed any specificity. Many seemed satisfied with the vague but firm affirmation that difference is, somehow, vitally important. The heavily theoretical nature of this conviction, however, leaves them with an unsettling task: a sense of deep responsibility for upholding differences they cannot quite identify.

There is one significant exception. The institution of marriage offers an opportunity for practical application. When I asked about gender differences generally, many students instinctively framed their responses around heterosexual marriage and family life. Kelly pointed to the creation of Adam and Eve: "I think [the differences] are intentional. I think as women we have strengths that complement the strengths and weaknesses of men, and I think vice versa. And I think that was intentional. I mean, if God wanted everyone to be exactly the same, He would have not made woman. We are created to be helpers and be each other's complements, I think. And so we've got different strengths and weaknesses that help balance out in each family as a whole." Beyond this biblical precedent of Adam and Eve, most student articulations of the Difference Story did not draw from the specific examples of biblical husbands and wives. Instead, they relied on the metaphorical New Testament relationship between Christ and the Church, his "bride." While Southern's men read this metaphor through the lens of their male headship imperative, the men I interviewed at Asbury found a simple call for relational humility. Jesse repeatedly invoked the bride-of-Christ reference as he described his ambitions to be a caring, sacrificial husband: "The biggest thing is putting her wants, wishes, desires, and well-being over yours. That's what Christ did. He was more concerned about the Church than he was his own [interests], even in the garden of Gethsemane. Three times he prayed, 'Father, let this cup pass.' That shows the humanity. 'Let this cup pass. Not my will but your will.' What was his will? That humanity wouldn't perish, that was his will. So even at the point of death, Christ was looking at what was best for the Church." Similarly, Jon explained his convictions about marriage—and his own attempts to facilitate a healthy relationship with his wife—in these terms: "And that's all rooted in love. . . . By having a greater capacity to love, you're also more like Christ. I want to love my wife more each and every day. As I learn to love God more, my capacity to love increases which then allows me to love her more and die to self." For these men, the metaphorical marriage between Christ and the Church infuses the institution of human marriage with self-sacrifice, love, and empowerment.

It does not, however, preclude hierarchy altogether. A few students threaded a logic of male headship through their interpretations of the Christ-and-the-Church metaphor. After Lindsey, for example, made the case that gender shouldn't confine men and women to particular marital roles, like who does the cooking, she added, "I know that the man is called to be the leader of the household, to be the head, and . . ." she trailed off, then tried again to qualify, "but I don't think . . ." she paused again. "I don't know," she said finally. Dan added some biblical context to his defense of marital headship, saying, "Whether you're in the Old Testament, or the passage we just quoted from in 1 Corinthians, [the Bible] is saying that the man should be the head of the household." He quickly added, however, "I don't see that in a domineering fashion." In fact, he described his beliefs about marriage as "kind of egalitarian," explaining that 1 Corinthians calls for "mutual submission." Unlike Southern's complementarian students, Dan did not seem particularly attached to the idea of male headship. He did not dwell on the tension between this idea and his assumption of "mutual submission." Instead, he moved freely between the two frames. Dan and Lindsey are in the minority at Asbury, but they are not dramatic outliers. Their rhetoric points to the considerable flexibility built into the "bride of Christ" metaphor. It includes just enough specificity to subtly reinforce the assumption of differences between husbands and wives without prescribing (or precluding) hierarchy.

Despite its otherwise flexible construction, Asbury's discourse of marital differentiation does strictly prohibit same-sex unions. Although my interviews with students did not include questions about sexuality, the topic surfaced regularly. In keeping with the community's general conflation of binary gender differences with biological sex and reinforcing its heteronormative expectations, most students stressed that difference itself was intentional—even vital—to marriage. When I asked Sara, a PhD student, if men and women should assume different roles in marriage, she immediately framed her answer around rejection of same-sex marriage. "Yeah," she responded. "I do think that's a godly ideal, otherwise you could say two women could be mothers of a family just as easy as a man and a woman. And I personally am not of the opinion that that's the case. I think you do need a husband and a wife, for children in the best-case scenario." Dan likewise explained that same-sex marriage upsets God's design, threatening the well-being of children: "If it is a married couple who has a family, I really think that the strengths of both sexes must be shown forth for the children's sake. And I think that's been an issue in our culture. Our culture has really tried to say, 'well the man and woman they're interchangeable, [their differences] don't really matter.' That's really prevailing right now in terms of the same-sex issue and everything else. . . . And I don't see that as being a good idea." The same students who championed the logic of genderblindness and rejected gendered role prescriptions simultaneously maintained difference itself as a prerequisite for marriage.

Entering this conversation at all, students knew, placed them in an ecclesiastical minefield. They were acutely aware that painful divisions over human sexuality and same-sex marriage were beginning to divide the denominations, and even the congregations, they called home. While my fieldwork took place in the years before the United Methodist split, the tensions that sparked the contentious debates had long been brewing. Most students did not dwell on these tensions. They most often seemed to expect that I would understand them—and their institution—to be conservative on the issue. Expectations for differentiation in marriage loomed large.

Holiness in the Body: Learning the Difference Story

Asbury's curriculum does not teach gender difference in the same way it teaches gender equality. In contrast with classroom content explicitly focused on women in leadership, and also in contrast with Southern's relentless infusion of complementarianism into its curriculum, Asbury's Difference Story generally takes root through far more subtle processes. In fact, one administrator told me, the institution, "doesn't have a formal position" on gender relations within marriage. "I think within the seminary you will get the whole range from egalitarian to complementarian. I would say that we want to embody relationships of mutual respect, but how that gets lived out is left up to individual couples to decide."

Faculty members themselves varied in their approaches. Most extended egalitarian ethics to marriage, but one professor openly expressed complementarian beliefs in an interview. "My views are egalitarian in terms of society and in terms of church," he explained. "In terms of family I'm complementarian. I have a both/and stance that's more nuanced and complex. So [I believe in] the [male] headship of the family." Though exceptional, this position did not appear to marginalize this faculty member among his colleagues or in the eyes of the administration. After all, his beliefs upheld the community's widely agreed upon, but flexible, standards: genderblind equality in public and difference within marriage.

Like many of its students, Asbury's administration departs from this flexibility on the question of same-sex marriage. Leaders explicitly prescribe heteronormative marriage patterns and opposition to Christians who propose alternative formulations. Indeed, they made this commitment very public following the 2015 *Obergefell v. Hodges* Supreme Court decision that legalized same-sex marriage. In a striking pivot away from the community's general reluctance to publicly prescribe ethics for marriage and family life, the chapel programming during the fall semester of 2015 followed the theme of "Holiness in the Body." President Timothy Tennent himself presented a series of seven messages. The series, also published on his widely read blog, covered a variety of topics including singleness, childbearing, and sexual identity. Two themes, however, dominated: a reinforcement of heterosexuality and a rejection of same-sex marriage.

Drawing directly from the Difference Story, Tennent appealed primarily to the marriage imagery used in biblical texts. Extending the familiar New Testament rhetoric of the Church as the "Bride of Christ," he also reached back in time to God's covenant with the Old Testament People of Israel and forward to the eschatological "marriage supper of the Lamb":

> The picture of the church as bride and God as husband finds its final eschatological expression in the following texts. The marriage supper of the Lamb in Revelation 19:6–9 and the New Jerusalem coming down from heaven in Rev. 21:1–4 like a "bride adorned for her husband" draws upon marriage as the most apt analogy to describe the union of Christ and his church. This amazing mystery of Christ and the Church does not fall out of the sky disconnected from all that has gone before it. Rather, deeply woven into the Old Testament is the idea that Yahweh is Israel's husband. We should not read Rev. 19 and Rev. 21 without recalling to mind, for example, Isaiah 54:5 where Yahweh declares, "your Maker is your husband—the Lord Almighty is His name . . . the Lord will call you back as a wife distressed in spirit."[4]

In addition to Tennent's presentations, the community also heard from a guest speaker, a Catholic expert on Pope John Paul's Theology of the Body, who built on Tennent's basic thrust. During a special sermon series for the seminary's annual "holiness week," the congregation in Estes Chapel rewarded his presentations with choruses of hearty amens. As I circulated through campus the following week, I heard a few whispered concerns about these presentations—mostly from women concerned about the implicit denunciation of contraception. Overall, however, students—at least those who voiced their thoughts in public spaces—seemed inspired, perhaps even relieved, to have been given additional rhetorical tools to defend conservative views on sexuality.

Importantly, the Holiness in the Body series said little about churchly practice. Consistent with student articulations of the Difference Story, speakers emphasized difference within marriage. Their teachings paradoxically under-

Figure 3.2. A row of townhomes in Kalas Village, the residential community near campus where many of Asbury's students live with their families. Photo by the author.

scored the Equality Story's ecclesiastical genderblindness by publicly situating differences between men and women in the private realm, acknowledging them explicitly only in terms of sexual complementarity in heterosexual marriage. This arrangement, of course, does not necessarily preclude more public treatment of gendered differences—or even celebration of women's collective identities. Rather, "Holiness in the Body," a theme that saturated the chapel programming for much of the semester and well beyond, simply affirmed what many Asbury students had already told me: difference matters, and it matters for marriage.

Physical architecture reinforces this formulation. Framing the private realm in the imagery of traditional American family life, a community of tidy brick townhomes near the campus houses married students and their families. Named Kalas Village after a former seminary president, its cozy, white-trimmed homes face each other from either side of winding, manicured streets. Children's toys and sports equipment often crowd their miniature front porches. Just past the last row of townhouses, a community garden sprouts neatly cultivated vegetable plants. Nearer the center of the village, a spacious community building hosts holiday parties, craft fairs, and kids' activities. This spatial arrangement recapitulates a 1950s-style community life centered on nuclear families. Lindsey, a counseling student, remarked of Kalas Village families, "They seem very traditional. A lot of them live in the little apartments over there. The wives are always out walking babies in strollers. . . . It's like the husband is a student and the wife is in those apartments raising two or three kids or so." She laughed at her own

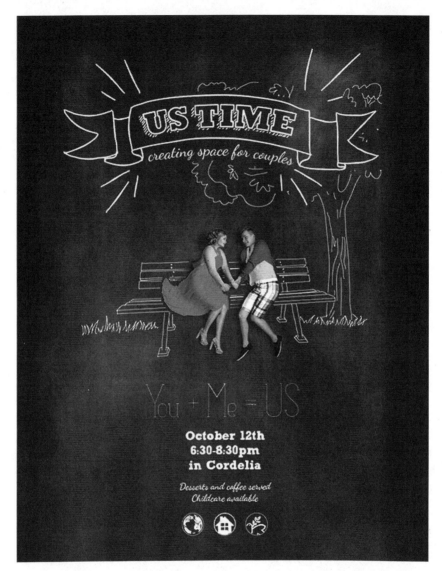

Figure 3.3. Publicity poster for Us Time, a campus event designed to strengthen marriages. Displayed on Asbury Theological Seminary's campus.

description, recognizing that it wasn't entirely representative. Just minutes before, she had expressed delight to participate in classrooms with so many other women. Nevertheless, she shrugged and shook her head. "I've been around a while," she said, and "that's always what I'll see."

Community programming also contributes to this imagery. One new student described a social event, sponsored by the Office of Community Formation, in terms of its orientation around spouses and families:

They had a huge fall festival at the end of October. A big family event. They always have big community formation stuff going on where families are all invited. They have child care and everything that you can possibly imagine so that spouses can come and participate. They seem very supportive of family involvement, of spouses being able to come be part of the community. I think community is one of the biggest things here at Asbury Seminary, so they really, really make an effort to be able to allow spouses to be involved.

The bulletin board that greets students entering the campus center for lunch, intermural basketball, or corporate study sessions regularly advertises these events. Flyers inviting participation in "Us Time," a marriage enrichment series, occupy the same physical space as posters reminding students of the chapel schedule and daily Eucharist. Much like Southern's community-wide gatherings, these events provide opportunities not only for social connection but also for gendered performances and socialization. Unmarried and newly married students watch and learn. This physical proximity suggests that gender—and sexual—differentiation is a necessary component of spiritual and cultural "fit."

Asbury's discursive construction of gender is more complex than Southern's. It spans two theological stories and the twin discourses of public, genderblind equality and privatized gender difference. The combination is not as paradoxical as it first appears. Concentrating the salience of gender differences within individuals' private lives accomplishes dual purposes: it reinforces Asbury's commitment to a firm gender binary while safely removing its salience from public, churchly spaces where it might threaten Christian unity. The stories are mutually reinforcing and powerfully formative.

THE MISSION METANARRATIVE

These two gendered stories are not, however, the only identity narratives at work. On my way to attend one morning chapel service, I noticed something unusual next to the entrance of Estes Chapel. Around the bronze, life-sized statue of early Methodist hymnwriter Charles Wesley that greets worshippers before they enter the building, a sizable number of people gathered. Each carried a brightly colored flag. Curious, I slipped past them through a side entrance and found a seat near the back of the sanctuary where I could immediately tell that this service celebrated something special. More than usual, the wooden pews pulsed with energy as flag bearers filed through the rear doors up the aisles, encircling the congregation with colorful waves of fabric.

Live music added to the energy. A band at the front of the sanctuary led upbeat praise songs at an unusually high volume. Its leader encouraged congregants to clap along with the Latin beat. "In Brazil," he explained with a wide smile, "we consider the congregation part of the band." The congregation complied as participants sang, "Holy Spirit, you are welcome here." A tall middle-aged man a few rows in front of me brushed tears from his eyes. Other worshippers lifted their hands toward the heavens. After a few songs, a young woman from China led the congregation in prayer. She gently invited members of the congregation to pray aloud with her in their own languages. "It's common practice in China," she said, as if anticipating discomfort in the audience, "so don't be embarrassed." To my surprise, and perhaps hers, the congregation followed her lead in an extended time of fervent, multilingual prayer. Someone near the front sobbed loudly through the voices.

The morning's sermon continued this multicultural emphasis. The preacher, an American missiologist, denounced the "othering" of cultural and ethnic minorities. She urged the Church to not simply accept diversity but embrace the great variety of ethnicity, language, and culture within the body of Christ. The sermon drew from several familiar biblical stories including the outpouring of the Holy Spirit on young Jewish believers at Pentecost. "This story," she preached, "is about us. It's our story. Everyone in this room, we all trace our spiritual heritage to this moment at Pentecost." In a final flourish, she reached forward in time to the final chapter of human history:

> We here have a unique opportunity to reflect the future where we will have people from everywhere, every language, every ethnicity worshipping together. We can choose to ignore it. We can choose to accept it. Or we can choose to embrace it and intentionally participate in it. . . . We can embrace and learn from those who are radically different from ourselves. We know that at the end of the story there is no "other." There's only "we." Through the spirit we become one and join together with every people of every tongue and tribe and nation worshipping the Lamb.

This sermon appealed to Asbury's most celebrated story: the Mission Metanarrative. Like the Gospel Story at Southern, this Mission Metanarrative is the most operative articulation of Asbury's group identity. It saturates everything from informal discourse to course catalogs, from worship songs to organizational structures. Unlike Southern's stories, however, the Mission Metanarrative avoids overtly gendered considerations of contemporary context.

Its narrative outlines the biblical story in an elegant, and familiar, shape. Mirroring the Equality Story, it too begins in Eden where Adam and Eve lived in flawless, unified relationship with God. Against this backdrop of harmonious perfection, sin introduces disunity. Christians themselves become the solution to this crisis as they spread the good news of salvation in Jesus—and with it, the restoration of human unity with God and each other—around the globe. Jesus himself commissioned this task, students explained in their own narrations of the story, along with instructions, recorded in the Gospel of Matthew, to "make disciples of all nations," beckoning first-century and twenty-first-century believers alike to take part.

Moreover, the story does not end with the present. It points toward a future eschaton, a glorious gathering at the end of time when all believers will join in perfect unity to worship God. Students spoke of this event with special anticipation. "There's going to be people of all nations, all tongues," said Ethan, "able to worship as a body united." This utopic conclusion promises a restoration of Eden. It recovers all that was lost in Genesis, and it reifies a fully unified Church, free from all division as God intended in the beginning. It will be, finally, the full realization of God's "kingdom." In these final chapters, the Mission Metanarrative intertwines almost seamlessly with the genderblind Equality Story. It lauds the actions of biblical characters like Junia, Paul, John, and Phoebe—men and women working interchangeably on behalf of the Great Commission—as models for contemporary believers. Their genderblind example points to a perfectly unified eschaton, the completion of the Great Commission when gender differences will no longer matter.

Asbury's community rings with enthusiasm for this pan-historical chronicle. The E. Stanley Jones School of World Mission and Evangelism codifies the Mission Metanarrative in academic curriculum. The student body's kaleidoscope of ethnicities embodies it. On Kalas Village's periphery, the Asbury Seminary Garden of the Nations invites these students to practice creation care together in embodied unity. Throughout the campus, visual culture retells the story in vivid, symbolic detail. In the student center, an array of large, colorful flags line the central hallway, representing the student population's twenty-nine home countries. Outside, banners declare, "The Whole Bible for the Whole World." An entire wall in the administrative building boldly proclaims, "The World, Our Parish." Taped to the lectern in the chapel, a small, hand-lettered note reminds all who preached from it to "remember the world."

Students eagerly participate. They revere the memory of the burgeoning New Testament church as if it were their own family history. Aided by the contextual hermeneutics they learn in their classrooms, they pay careful attention to every detail of the pages of their Bibles. They eavesdrop on the Apostle Paul's correspondence with the young congregations in Ephesus, Corinth, and Rome as he guides them through internal strife. They interrogate first-century cultural conventions and political realities. This is more than an intellectual exercise. Envisioning themselves as modern-day Pauls, Junias, and Phoebes, students prepare to join the New Testament Church in its mission to the world. They study homiletics hoping to fill congregational pulpits, missiology in anticipation of careers in international church planting, or counseling in hopes of offering emotional healing to individual souls. One student even tattooed a map of the world across the backs of his calves in an expression of love for the diverse cultures of the globe.

Figure 3.4. A student's tattoos demonstrate his investment in the world. Photo by the author.

Students fluently used "kingdom" language to cite their own investments in this story. God's kingdom, they believe, is both "already" present in the world and "not yet" fully realized. Nevertheless, the Mission Metanarrative's emphasis leans decisively toward the first part of this tension, and students delighted in recognizing the kingdom's "in-breaking" into the contemporary world. One complained that Reformed theology's focus on the "fall" and its effects—the "not

Figure 3.5. A sign marks the Garden of the Nations just beyond Kalas Village. Photo by the author.

Figure 3.6. International flags displayed in the hallway of the Sherman-Thomas Student Center. Photo by the author.

Figure 3.7. A wall in the administration building's hallway. Photo by the author.

yet"—"starts to trickle down to how they approach everything else." In contrast, he explained, "a Wesleyan perspective would say, you know, everybody's equal. Everybody's free. Let's be free from sin!" Toward this goal, the optimistic Mission Metanarrative invites contemporary believers to take preemptive ownership of its grand promise. Why, Asbury's believers may wonder, should the contemporary Church dwell on the messy complexities of gendered social life in the present when it can simply orient itself toward this in-breaking, gender-blind "kingdom"? Like Southern's Gospel Story, the Mission Metanarrative brings together the past, present, and future. It joins the physical and the transcendent. It welcomes contemporary actors to join their work with God's work. Within it, Asbury's egalitarianism is both highly visible and limited by its genderblindness.

———

The same students who chronicled Asbury's stories also subtly suggested inconsistencies within them. Tyler, whose story began this chapter, articulated a robust egalitarian position on both churchly leadership and marriage. In practice, however, Tyler's life was more complicated than his words. Even as he rejected male headship in marriage, for example, he and his wife fit a very traditional pattern. When their oldest son was born, Robin left the workforce to stay at home. "She wanted to," Tyler made sure I understood. The arrangement made sense too because Robin enjoyed being with children and because "she just has a way of communicating at [their] level." He and his wife had made this decision—as well as the decision to come to seminary—as individuals in a partnership. It did not bother Tyler that these choices fit a very distinct pattern at Asbury. Many of the other men I interviewed also came to Asbury with wives—and often children—in tow. As chapter 4 will illustrate, few of them identified the gendered patterns that shaped their worlds.

CHAPTER 4

Men, Churchwomen, and Wives

EMBODIED PRACTICE AT ASBURY SEMINARY

In my undergrad, I would always be a person who would raise my hand in class. . . . I'm just an outspoken person. But here I don't raise my hand in class. And I don't know why that is. —Grace, MDiv student

During my fieldwork, Asbury Theological Seminary made a momentous hire. When the dean of the chapel announced his retirement, the administration mounted a search for a replacement. The position carries a great deal of visibility, and the person who fills it must meet a lengthy list of requirements. Along with planning three chapel services a week, the dean also functions as campus pastor, mentoring students, setting the tone for corporate worship, and walking the community through the rhythms of the church calendar. The individual must be manifestly Wesleyan yet sensitive to those who come to Asbury from other backgrounds, must be pastoral yet also bring technical and administrative skill, must be attentive to detail yet cognizant of the broad institutional vision.

The successful candidate was a daughter of the institution. Jessica LaGrone had graduated in 2002 with an MDiv degree and that year's Stanger Preaching Award. Her installation marked the first time a woman would fill the dean of the chapel position—an egalitarian milestone that the community effusively celebrated. One administrator referred to LaGrone's hiring as a "miracle": "It was just amazing the consensus that emerged. I think there was intentionality and beating the bushes to get male/female/international/minority/whatever in the pool. But there was absolutely unbelievable consensus to hire the first female dean of the chapel in the history of the institution. . . . The way that it shook out was absolutely unanimous support for this individual, and it was a pretty good pool of candidates. This individual had the best characteristics, apart from gender, and then God kind of layered on the blessing of having a female candidate to come in and do that." He made sure I understood: LaGrone was not hired because she was a woman. The committee, he suggested, would have chosen her even if she had been a man.

The hiring process, he wanted me to recognize, had been *blind to gender*. Having a woman in the position was a "blessing," but prioritizing gender was not something the committee felt was their responsibility.[1] They left it, instead, to God.

Women students expressed particular enthusiasm for LaGrone's arrival. Many told me what a gift it was to be at an egalitarian seminary where they could watch women like her lead and learn from their examples. They were, these women told me repeatedly, thankful to be at Asbury. They drank in the academic knowledge that their classes offered. They nurtured warm and fulfilling relationships. They received mentoring, and they learned how to lead. This is no small thing. Evangelical subculture has long upheld the rugged militancy of celebrities like John Wayne and Mel Gibson as its standard for manhood and, consequently, churchly leadership (Du Mez 2020). For women who come to Asbury out of these backgrounds—even softer, subtler varieties—the presence of authoritative women can be profoundly empowering.

———

As this chapter demonstrates, Asbury's community tightly couples all three of its discursive stories—the Equality Story, the Difference Story, and the Mission Metanarrative—with embodied practice. When asked how the community implements its egalitarian discourse, representatives of the faculty and administration almost always gave the same answer: Asbury hires women. The physical presence of women in pulpits, classrooms, and boardrooms provides palpable evidence that Asbury practices what it preaches. Proud of the Wesleyan tradition's history of ordaining women, more than one administrator explained to me that there was no sexism on campus. Here, many said, men and women work, learn, and lead interchangeably as complete equals.

Even the most enthusiastic boosters of genderblind equality, however, often recognized a problem. Some of the same administrators who insisted that Asbury was free from sexism also expressed bewilderment at how difficult it was to attract good women faculty members. They had tried so hard, they assured me, shaking their heads in exasperation. One even asked me if I had any idea why it was so difficult to find good women candidates. They could not explain why men and women, equally called by God, might navigate uneven paths toward answering these calls. Nor could they explain why the women who successfully navigated the institution's genderblind culture continued to experience frustrations. Asbury's talk does not tell the full story. As the sociological notion of "doing gender" anticipates, the individual men and women who work under genderblind policies are not simply passive recipients of institutional narratives. They actively construct gendered meaning as they work, worship, and learn in the daily rhythms of seminary life. Gender is "done" with bodies as well as words.

"Doing gender" also involves power. Gendered biases embed themselves in cultural symbols (Collins 1990), institutional structures (Fenstermaker and West

2002), and identity expectations (Pyke and Johnson 2003; Jones 2010). Inequalities pattern not only individual relationships but also the institutions and communities that birth and sustain them (Smith 1987; Ingersoll 2003). In keeping with this expanded notion of "doing gender" and remaining attentive to Martin Riesebrodt's reminder that religion too is "done" through behavioral liturgies, this chapter explores the ways in which both public genderblindness and privatized gender difference take shape on campus. It affirms Asbury's own contention that its public genderblind posture does offer considerably more opportunities to women as individuals than does Southern's complementarianism. It also reveals a significant limit: egalitarian empowerment is mostly enjoyed by those willing and able to conform to an unarticulated set of gendered expectations. What follows, then, is not a story of unrelenting disempowerment. The same women whose lives testified to the community's inequities also described richly rewarding experiences within a community that most of them experienced as empowering on the whole. Nevertheless, Asbury's women also detailed—sometimes with haunting texture—frustrations and insecurities that men did not. As the patterns in their experiences testify, Asbury's embodied practices neglect—and sometimes even perpetuate—subtle forms of inequity. Women's experiences provide evidence for this book's central contention: that even in its egalitarian expressions, American evangelicalism centers men. Consider the following vignettes:

Both Kelly and her husband came to Asbury in pursuit of degrees and ministerial credentials. When the newly married couple first arrived on campus, Kelly's husband easily found his place, but she struggled. During orientation, the seminary hosted separate events for students and their spouses. Kelly felt torn between the two. Eager to start building relationships with fellow students, she also craved connections with other women at similar stages of life. In the end, she decided to attend an event called "Spouses' Tea." She returned dissatisfied. Looking back, she realized that the event had been a poor fit for her: "It's difficult to relate with the other women, in a sense. Because there aren't as many married women students. Most [women students] are single, which I understand, but it's kind of difficult interacting [with them]. You're a wife, so you've got wife things to do, but you're also a student." As Kelly advanced through her first semester, she ran into more frustrations. Other students sometimes assumed that she had come to the seminary only to support her husband. "Hey," she said in exasperation, "I belong here too! Just because I'm a woman, I'm not just a spouse." Despite her efforts to live into both public and private roles, Kelly reported feeling like a misfit in both.

———

Abbi was the only married woman I interviewed who had moved to the community solely to pursue her own calling. Though she initially struggled to find social support, by the end of her first semester Abbi reported that she was thriving in her classes and that her family was slowly adjusting to small-town life. She especially appreciated the kids' programming that the seminary offered. But the domestic roles Abbi and her husband filled put them in the opposite position of most families—a reversal that she felt acutely. "I don't fit anywhere," she said. "Everybody's so nice, but nobody can identify with me."

———

Sara felt that many of her professors held her at arm's length. She suspected that this was due to fears of sexual impropriety. This frustrated her and made her question her personal style choices. Perhaps, she suggested, these men were not accustomed to women who cared about hair and makeup as she did. Women's physical appearances did seem to be important to Sara; during my interview with her, she even gently critiqued my own makeup application. Nevertheless, given her appearance on the day of her interview, and on the handful of other occasions when I saw her on campus, I would not have identified Sara herself as especially made up, or even particularly feminine. Her hair did not look as though she had spent a great deal of time on it, and her makeup, though carefully applied, appeared natural and understated. Yet Sara was insecure about how her appearance might set her apart from her colleagues.

Asbury might renounce complementarianism's gendered codes, but its students do face similar behavioral expectations. Embodiments of the Difference Story recall Southern's heavily privatized Godly Womanhood script. Asbury's women learn to display a delicate balance of femininity: enough to establish themselves as different from men but not so much as to set themselves apart from the rational, masculine expectations of public Christian ministry. They also learn to cooperate with gendered divisions of labor and navigate all of these expectations largely without the benefit of collective identity. Similarly, while Asbury students largely eschew complementarian notions of male headship, the community nevertheless sustains a more subtle male centering that shapes both men's and women's lives.

Privatizing Womanhood

Held several times each year, Women's Communion services invite all of Asbury's women to a time of fellowship. The first time I attended, I arrived early and watched the room fill with a diverse array of women. A middle-aged Hispanic woman stationed herself near the door and greeted newcomers with warm hugs. Some of the women, who appeared to come directly from work, wore professional clothing with hair carefully styled. Others dressed more casually with hair pulled back into hasty ponytails. A few wore babies in soft fabric carriers strapped to their chests. Several others carried unborn children in rounded bellies. The women slowly filtered into the room, greeting friends and arranging themselves among tables carefully decorated with colorful silk flowers and flickering tea lights. They filled the space with laughter and conversation.

As I scanned the room for a familiar face, I recognized a first-year student named Nicole. She caught my eye, smiled warmly, and crossed the room to greet me. It was her first time at Women's Communion too, she said, and she wasn't sure what to expect. "There are so many women!" she observed happily, gesturing to the room around us. "You know, I go to the cafeteria every day and I think, 'I could sit with those guys, or I could sit with those guys . . . or, well, there are couples over there.'" Nicole was hopeful that she had found a context where a single woman like her truly fit.

As the last of the nearly fifty women arrived, a seminary administrator rose to offer a welcome. Her graceful demeanor testified to her years of pastoral experience. She opened with a carefully scripted prayer: "Thank you for making me a woman in a world that seems to be made for men." She thanked God for bodies that are sacred even when they are "less—or substantially more—than we want them to be." After the chuckles subsided, she noted reverently, "The journey of a woman is different than the journey of a man." After the prayer, we ate. Women took turns filing past a table in the back of the room filled with a bountiful array of salads, vegetables, breads, ham, and smoked chicken—all prepared by the women present. During the meal, the tables filled with warm conversation. Many of the women appeared to be close friends, comfortable in each other's company. The four other women at my table explained that their husbands had been enrolled at the seminary together for the past several years. They were sharing life together.

As we finished eating, the official program began. "Tonight," the moderator said, "we are celebrating that every woman's journey is the same journey. . . . We are the ones who hold onto life." The remainder of the evening told the personal stories of women in the room. One shared memories of life as a refugee with a young son, abandoned by her husband in a war-torn country. As she began, the occupants of the table next to mine passed around a tissue box, exchanging knowing looks. This was definitely going to get emotional. Indeed, as the speaker described the strain of waking up each day wondering what her son would eat and crediting God for His provision, few eyes remained dry. Another woman told her story of fostering several children, recalling their difficult adjustments to middle-class life. When she got to their teenage years, the tissue boxes went around again.

As these stories concluded, the moderator directed everyone's attention to a round table beautifully decorated with colorful textiles. While she gave instructions, one of her associates draped the fabric prayer shawls on the bellies of pregnant women who came forward for special prayer. "If you know what you're having," she directed, "you can choose the color." Turning to the next woman in the line, she said, mostly to herself, but loudly enough for the room to hear, "Amanda's having a boy so we have to give her blue!" As expectant mothers chose their shawls, the leaders encouraged them to value these "precious moments of connection" with their unborn babies. Next, women who were concerned for a child received roses. It could be a child of their own, the moderator instructed, or simply one they cared about. She then directed women who were raising children toward a tall glass vase in the center of the table. "Take a shell for each of your children," she instructed. This part of the program took a considerable amount of time, as the majority of the room's occupants rose to file past the table, carefully selecting their shells. Many were clearly touched by the experience. Deep emotion filled their faces, and several acquiesced to the tears without try-ing to hide them. In prayer for these mothers and their offspring, the moderator implored, "May these children be with us at the great supper feast!" The room erupted with fervently whispered amens of agreement. As the program ended, I looked around for Nicole, curious if the evening had lived up to her expecta-tions. How had she, a single woman barely out of college and pursuing a career in church leadership, experienced this celebration of motherhood? Had she found the kind of kinship and solidarity she had hoped for? But Nicole was already gone.

Churchwomen and Wives

At first glance, Women's Communion appeared to defy Asbury's commitment to genderblindness in its public spaces. Like a scene from Southern's Seminary Wives Institute, the evening was all about women: telling their stories, commem-orating their experiences, and building solidarity. In both its content and its demographics, it highlighted rather than downplayed gender. I left Asbury's campus that night perplexed. Perhaps, I considered as I drove away, the event was an outlier, a deviation from the community's genderblind norm.

But Women's Communion, I realized later, was not a deviation. In fact, it was not part of genderblind public space at all. Instead, it animated Asbury's Differ-ence Story, celebrating binary gendered differences within the context of hetero-sexual marriage and visions of traditional family life. The overwhelming majority of the evening's enthusiastic participants were, in fact, not students. They were *wives* of students. Very much like their counterparts in Southern's Seminary Wives Institute, these women enjoyed rich solidarity forged through their common experience of supporting husbands through the academic rigors, financial difficulties, and vocational insecurities of seminary education—intensified, for many, by the common bond of motherhood. This event, planned with their lives in mind, powerfully symbolizes the construction of women's gen-der identity at Asbury. Along with gendered difference itself, it is largely restricted to individuals' private lives. For women, it is celebrated primarily through familial roles as wives and, especially, mothers.

Even the logistics of the event mirrored these expectations. Its location, a back room tucked cozily behind the large cafeteria, the presence of food, the candles and decorations, and the fact that it was held in the evening after the rhythms of public life had slowed all situated it in the private realm of traditional domesticity. Though nongendered events are sometimes held in this room as well, even its name—Cordelia—evokes a sense of femininity: a softer, gentler corner of the larger Sherman Thomas Student Center where students gather during the day over lunch and between classes. Despite Nicole's hope to find solidarity in this space, it offered little to women like her who inhabit Asbury's public churchly sphere. Even if they wish for solidarity and celebrations of femininity, they are unlikely to find kinship among women whose lives are so different from theirs.

Cultural pressures also nudge students away from Women's Communion. Among the students I interviewed, I found very little support for, or even interest in, the event. Claire, who was nearing graduation, told me that she had never attended a Woman's Communion service, even though they were offered several times each semester. She also airily shared a friend's impressions: "The last time it happened, one of my guy friends was like, 'It's so sexist. They're having it just for women.'" Lauren reported a similar disregard for the event. She and her friends even had an alternative name for it. "We call it 'Kalas Village Moms' Night Out.'" While some women students do attempt to navigate the world of Women's Communion, most—like Claire and Lauren—realize that developing respectability as a church leader does not easily mix with the pursuit of feminine identity or the bonds of women's solidarity.

As women like Nicole quickly learn, there are two kinds of women at Asbury: churchwomen and wives. Student demographics testify to this divide. While women remain a clear minority in Asbury's academic spaces, especially in programs associated with credentialing for churchly authority, they maintain a notable presence within the student body and enjoy greater representation in doctoral and ministerial training programs than do their Southern Baptist counterparts. Meanwhile, even though Asbury lacks a programmatic equivalent to Southern's "Seminary Wives Institute," students' wives maintain just as visible of a presence. This visibility, magnified by the patterns of small-town life and events like Women's Communion, reinforces Asbury's discursive priority on traditionally patterned heterosexual marriage. I did not originally intend to include these wives in my analysis of the seminary's institutional culture, assuming that their presence would be tangential at best to the cultural processes and power dynamics that I was most interested in. I learned quickly, however, that Asbury's education is designed to be holistic. Its formation processes target individuals' public *and* private lives. The wives who bonded over food and conversation at Women's Communion are no less a part of Asbury's residential community—and no less symbolic in their roles—than the women who enroll as divinity students. While not all wives fit easily into the culture that Women's Communion creates, those who do find warm social support and resources for the intensive domestic life that evangelical subculture—both complementarian and egalitarian—has long expected of women.

This subculture especially celebrates motherhood. In alignment with American society's demanding expectations, Asbury's mothers often take an intensive approach to their parental duties (Hays 1996; Newman and Henderson 2014). As the community watches, they push cute babies in jogging strollers, shuffle toddlers between play dates in each other's tastefully decorated homes, and plan themed birthday parties for their children. Unlike their 1950s progenitors, many of these women also manage demanding jobs. Nevertheless, within the seminary's tight residential community, motherhood is their most visible role. The community embraces these women as it does their spouses, with programming and relational spaces tailored to suit their lives. Aided by these supports, Asbury's wives bring intensive motherhood into public view, reaffirming the Difference Story's fundamental message to women: celebrations of womanhood belong in marriage and private, domestic life.

Femininity in Balance

This privatization of womanhood presents a paradox. While femininity—embodied evidence of cooperation with the Difference Story's gender binary—is no less important for women students than it is for their classmates' wives, they exhibit it very carefully in public spaces. In their roles as students and aspiring churchwomen, they learn to look, dress, and act differently—but not too differently—from men. The first part of this equation often yields elements of what R. W. Connell calls emphasized femininity, or "the pattern of femininity which is given most cultural and ideological support" (1987, 24). Neglecting this pattern, women learn, risks disapproval from men. Spencer, for example, openly criticized women who looked or acted too much like men. He described some of his classmates' failures to comply with his expectation of difference: "I'm trying to think how to say this in a nice way. Sometimes I've seen it in terms of women almost seeking to act like they were men. And what I mean by that is, how they carry themselves . . . holding a certain posture at times . . . it's really almost to the point of taking themselves and pulling themselves out of who they really are. Almost giving this demeanor of 'I'm playing this part so that I can be here.'" Ian, likewise, criticized women who downplayed femininity, including even more detail than Spencer:

IAN: I've had so many good relationships here with women in positive ways. Girls in my classes. I didn't feel threatened, and I didn't feel like they looked down on me, but I also felt that with some of the women here . . . it was kind of like that whole thing with those ladies driving tractors when I was out West. It's almost like [they're saying] "We get to do this," but they weren't really comfortable with their feminine side.

LWS: What did that look like?

IAN: This is going to sound ridiculous to you, but . . . real short haircuts. Dress that was nothing feminine at all.

Ian's disapproval extended beyond attitudes and demeanor to physical dress and hairstyles. This critique suggests an assumption that women's appearances can, and in fact do, communicate something about the holiness of inner lives.

Single women can face extra scrutiny. Without husbands and children to physically affirm their cooperation with the Difference Story, unmarried women sometimes felt that their fit for Christian leadership was under especially close inspection. One woman expressed surprise when the denominational committee overseeing her candidacy process for ordination began an interview by asking, "How's celibacy going for you?"[2] While this question in theory also could have been asked of men, she felt that it directly targeted her sexuality as a single woman. The small circle of women gathered around her at the lunch table where she shared the story agreed. They, at least, had never heard of any such thing being asked of a man. As they looked ahead to their own ordinations, these women—many of them also single—prepared for the possibility that they too would need to explain their private lives.

In other cases, single women themselves reflected the assumption that Christian women should be married. Meghan, for example, defended herself in an unrelated argument with a classmate by affirming her desire for marriage. When she told me about the lunchtime spat a few days later, she still seemed upset. Her classmate, a man who was a casual friend, had accused her of being a "radical feminist," an obvious insult, when she had questioned whether John Wesley would have been taken seriously if he had been a woman. She shot back across the table that she was *not* a radical feminist. She wanted, after all, to get married and have a family. Meghan was uncomfortable with her response, she confessed to me later, but couldn't quite explain why. Grace remembered responding to similar challenges, protesting, "I've had to hear my voice say . . . 'I don't believe that I'm better than you.' Even silly things like, 'I *do* want children someday! I *do* want to be married someday!'" She laughed, exasperated. "Why do I need to say that if I have a strong voice about how women should be treated?" Without realizing it, both Grace and Meghan instinctively defended themselves and their fit for the community by upholding the Difference Story's assumption: womanhood makes most sense in the context of marriage.

Femininity might be an obligation, but too much—or the wrong kind— becomes a liability. A heightened feminine affect can convey too much investment in a woman's own gendered identity, signaling a departure from genderblindness and Christian unity. By contrast, muting feminine expression can communicate a better fit for churchly leadership. After all, church work is not an especially girly vocation. Egalitarian theology notwithstanding, the practice of ministerial leadership has been embodied mostly by men. Deemphasizing femininity might also protect a woman against implicit assumptions that women who are feminine are also emotional, irrational, and flighty.

Asbury's women mostly accommodated these unwritten standards. They generally clothed themselves in an identifiable, but muted, femininity, avoiding short, conventionally masculine hair styles and androgynous clothing. They displayed much more subtle nods to emphasized femininity than I saw among Southern's women. Most applied makeup in understated ways and arranged their hair in practical, low-maintenance styles. They opted for casual, conservative clothing that signaled wholesome virtue and modesty. Some added colorful scarves and others costume jewelry, but I saw very little lace, lipstick, or curled hair. They would never have been mistaken for men, but they did not especially stand out from the men around them either. Women themselves occasionally recognized these patterns. "There's this 'I have to be tough enough to roll with the boys' kind of attitude," one counseling student said of her MDiv colleagues. Another confessed that she enjoyed people watching at new student orientation events. She could always identify the MDiv women, she confided, by their mannerisms and clothes. These women, training for careers in the male-dominated field of pastoral ministry, likely receive closer scrutiny of their appearance than their peers in other programs.

Women also guard against sexualization. When Lauren arrived on Asbury's campus several years before I met her, she preferred to wear what she described as cute clothes and a trendy haircut. During her first year as an MDiv student, Lauren struggled to find her place. Rarely, she told me, would a man start a conversation with her in, or even outside of, class. Despite her obvious intellect, engaging personality, and passion for ministry, men seemed reluctant to interact with her. Looking back, Lauren, a conventionally attractive woman, believed her fashion choices identified her as a temptation to be avoided, rather than a colleague. She remembered feeling like a "devil in a red dress." In the end, Lauren accommodated the gendered expectations around her. She revamped her wardrobe, adopted a more conservative look, and changed her hair to a dramatically less feminine style. She also married a bearded classmate named Jake. Lauren now made more sense to the community. By institutional standards, Lauren's is a success story. By the time she graduated, she had not only passed Asbury's official curriculum of homiletics, theology, and biblical interpretation but also mastered its unofficial cultural curriculum. She departed campus nicely positioned to meet genderblind ministry expectations of churches and parachurch organizations in Asbury's ecclesial networks.

Lauren is not alone. Nor is her experience limited to Asbury. Describing ideals for Christian womanhood dating as far back as the late nineteenth century, Leah Payne notes that "a truly womanly woman knew that her modern powers were best exercised within the home" (2015). In more recent decades, evangelical women have often attained what Kate Bowler calls "precarious power" by publicly prioritizing home and family and cultivating wholesome feminine beauty (2019). Bowler carefully illustrates these themes through the careers of famous evangelical women like Phyllis Schlafly, who campaigned against the equal rights amendment in the early 1970s on the grounds that it "deliberately degrades homemakers," and Heather Whitestone, who entered the evangelical spotlight as Miss America 1995 (Klatch 1987, 134; Bowler 2019). In the digital age of the twenty-first century, Bowler also notes, entrepreneurial women like Ann Voskamp and Jen Hatmaker, fused "the commercialization of homespun beauty" with evangelical spirituality, crafting enormous social media brands from the raw materials of domesticity (2019, 204). While Asbury's cultural expectations allow for women to also hold positions of institutional power, expectations of heterosexual marriage and modest femininity remain.

This is not always an easy set of rules to negotiate. While women know, for example, that evangelical culture is often suspicious of unmarried women, they are also aware that pastoral search committees worry about women candidates being encumbered by husbands and children who will compete for their time and energy. These competing external pressures often also accompany women's own desires for husbands and children. The women students I met did not want to choose between being a "wife and mother" or being a "church leader." They wanted to be both. They coveted their professors' churchly voices, but they also wanted the kinds of families that their colleagues and their wives enjoyed. These women have much to navigate but very few models to follow. During the years of my fieldwork, only one woman faculty member was raising a child. Students admired the accomplishments of the others, many of whom remained single, and often deeply valued the relational connections they provided, but these women only partially modeled the lives students themselves wanted to live. While men's private roles flow much more seamlessly toward their churchly ambitions, as the next section shows, women can easily feel torn between their vocational paths and their personal lives.

Nevertheless, most of Asbury's women students embrace their community and its expectations. They know that other parts of the evangelical subculture do not extend opportunities for leadership, preaching, and ordination to women, and they are grateful to be in a space that does. Along with men, they celebrate a largely degendered global mission and absorb as much biblical knowledge as they can. They participate in Kingdom Conference services waving the flags of the world's many nations. They enroll in preaching, theology, and ethics classes, eager to hone the knowledge and skills required for service to the Church. For many of these women, balancing femininity, even when it is a dizzying task, is a small price to pay for these opportunities to serve God and the Church.

Second Shifts

Several hours before the lunch crowd gathered in the student center one morning, I noticed two young men hurry through the lobby, accompanied by three preschool-aged children. As they walked, one man patiently engaged the small boy at his feet in a serious conversation about the emotions that accompany popped balloons. The other man carried the youngest girl comfortably in his left arm, a diaper bag slung over his right shoulder. A few minutes later, as I opened my laptop and began my work for the day, one of the men returned through the front entrance, all three kids in tow. A staff member at the front desk asked curiously, "Do you guys do some kind of trade?" He nodded as the kids bounced happily toward the gym. "Yeah," he said, "Tom has class at nine forty-five, so I'm on duty now."

Scenes like this are not unusual. In interviews, married men often cited their contributions to parental duties as evidence that egalitarian ethics extended to their private lives. Indeed, I regularly saw men like Tom and his friend wrangle toddlers in the common area of the student center and attend chapel services with infants strapped to their chests. The rhythms of seminary life, in fact, encourage flexibility in arrangements of child care and domestic labor. While men—the majority of married students at Asbury—take classes, practice homiletics, and learn ancient languages, their wives often find jobs to make ends meet. This arrangement effectively removes these women from the domestic realm, making them de facto breadwinners. At the same time, their husbands enjoy flexible student schedules that leave more time for familial responsibilities. Asbury might emphasize motherhood, but these men, even more than Southern's family men, expect to pull their weight at home.

Women initially explained their marriages in these terms too. With their husbands, they often said, they tried to delegate each household task to the partner who was better at it or had more interest or experience. When I pressed for details, however, some caveats emerged. Allison, for example, first described her and her husband's roles as complementary: "There are strengths that I have, and there are strengths that my husband has . . . as far as doing things around the house. Or roles, like trash and scooping the cat litter. You know, things that are practical he can do. Whereas I feel like I have strengths in multitasking and running the household, so I'll work on our finances, and bill planning, and groceries and those kinds of things. We do a lot of the grocery shopping together, but preparation comes from my end. So we just fit together." Later, however, Allison clarified: "I run the household," she said, "I keep everything going." The household was her responsibility. While Allison did not reflect on this arrangement, Rachel suspected a broader tendency to assign domestic labor to women, even when equality is the goal: "It seems like ideally we would both be equally in leadership and God would be the head of our home. That would be the ideal thing. But I think realistically [in] the day-to-day, we just kind of take turns sort of being at the helm, keeping things together, keeping things going. And, I think if we're honest, most of the times it's me." Nadia, slightly older and more experienced than many of her colleagues, described her marriage's division of labor like this: "Even though my husband would like to think he's egalitarian and all, he's just not there. He still just wants me to do the traditional stuff, which makes ministry very challenging. At home he still expects me to cook, clean. He loves to iron so I don't have to do that. Well, not all of it. And I don't bother with it. I mean, I do the best I can." Kelly and her husband both worked part-time concurrent with their enrollment as students. Her comparison of their arrangement against other families in the community describes it best: "[The other wives] have no idea what I'm doing because I'm [also] a full-time student. So it's like 'Okay, everything your husband does, I do, and then everything you do, I do.'" The double burden Kelly identifies is what sociologist Arlie Hochschild and Anne Machung call the "second shift" (1989). Kelly and other married women shoulder extra weight: after-hours household labor. Theoretical expectations of equity among Asbury's couples likely make their domestic divisions of labor less unequal than they would be in more patriarchal marriage arrangements. Nevertheless, even these egalitarian husbands' contributions, it seems, might still be better described as "helping" with domestic burdens than "carrying" them, a distinction even the most intentional of egalitarians can struggle to discern (Coltrane 1989). Despite near uniform agreement that household burdens should be shared between spouses, the domestic responsibilities of being a "wife" appear to often outstrip those of being a "husband," even when wives also shoulder the responsibility of an academic workload.

The expectations of intensive motherhood deepen this divide. Abbi, one of only a few mothers in my sample of students, confessed that she struggled to leave her daughter in child care so she could attend classes. "I kind of had a little breakdown with sending my two-year-old to a preschool / day care facility, because I've always stayed home and done that work, but it's not possible here." Abbi also expressed frustration with the lack of good, flexible child care services in the area.[3] "It's a lot to balance," she sighed. I witnessed this balancing act while scheduling and conducting interviews. One woman requested that I come to her apartment so she could care for her young daughter while we talked. Another apologized when she arrived late to her interview with a preschooler in tow. Something had come up, she said, and she was juggling a bit more than expected that afternoon. In contrast, none of the many fathers whom I interviewed brought children with them or reported any concern about leaving them elsewhere. While many fathers do invest regularly in child care, men overall appeared to be less burdened by it.

The institution itself features a subtle second shift. Mirroring patterns of gender segregation in the broader American workplace, Asbury's women employees often fill maternal, nurturing roles, both paid and unpaid (Reskin 1993; England 2005). The Office of Community Formation provides much of the community's paid caregiving. During my fieldwork, women filled all but one of its eleven staff positions. In addition to organizing events like Women's Communion and marriage enrichment "Us Times," these staff members offered mentoring and facilitated counseling and "renewal retreats," offering spiritual, emotional, and sometimes even physical nurture. They created pseudo-domestic space within an institution whose public face is largely rational and academic.

These women are the community's mothers. One, frustrated when an event intended to address tensions between unmarried men and women students went awry, described her own response in maternal terms: "And so I sort of closed it down and said, 'You know, we all create community. So if you hate this community, you have to look and say, "How am I creating it?" and decide you aren't going to participate in that way.' And then everything got silent. What I did was I mothered, and they shut up. . . . I knew what I was doing. I was choosing it. . . . You know when you tell the kids, 'There are starving children, so eat your pie.' That's what I felt like." Students agreed. Hannah was touched by this same administrator's role in welcoming her cohort to campus the previous fall: "When we came to the new student orientation, [one of the Community Formation leaders] spoke to us. [She] just shared some very powerful things with us and seemed to be kind of a wise mama to us, you know?" Faculty women often fill maternal roles too. One, Dr. McGee, told me that students—both women and men—regularly seek her out for mentoring and advice.:

DR. MCGEE: I can think of maybe three or four men every semester that find me to talk about pastoral things.

LWS: What kind of questions would they ask?

DR. MCGEE: Oh my gosh! I'm thinking about Caleb. He asks me, "What do you think about wearing a robe or a collar?" And, "When you do hospital calls, how does that work?" And I'm thinking about Jason, who asks me how to lead and greet people in worship. In some ways I kinda feel like *the mom*.

Dr. McGee continued, describing how often students seek her out:

I'm just sort of the general resource person, and all the time there are students knocking on my door saying, "Can I talk to you about. . . ." I have a woman who is preparing to officiate at her first wedding, but she hasn't yet had a worship class. . . . I don't think I've ever even had her in class, but she came and we spent time just walking through the service and you know, I was just able to kind of coach her along. I guess I do a lot of that. I think the word is sort of out that I'm available, and they find me.

While men dominate the rational spaces of classrooms and administrative boardrooms, women seem to more easily find authoritative space in the kind of relational work that mimics traditional domesticity. Their symbolic motherhood enhances these women's legitimacy as leaders.

This arrangement offers real, but limited, power. Women who occupy maternal roles within the seminary do exercise agency, but they do so in service of an institutional mission largely defined by men. The vice president of formation, for example, sits on the president's cabinet. Her staff oversees events that contribute to the visual, material, and discursive culture of campus life. These cultural forms, as the case of Southern Seminary illustrates, can carry a great deal of influence. Moreover, practices of nurture and emotional caregiving themselves can be profoundly humanizing, even empowering. But the scope of this empowerment is limited. Few of these women hold the authority to change the seminary's organizational processes or direct its cultural priorities. Mothers, after all, soothe battered emotions and tend relational wounds. They listen. They support and encourage. In comparison with the positions of vision and ambition filled almost exclusively by men, women who exercise leadership from midlevel institutional locations occupy modest positions of power.

There are exceptions to this bifurcation of roles. The men on faculty do a great deal of mentoring and nurturing, and a number of women occupy more rational spaces in faculty and administrative roles. But the patterns are stark. During my fieldwork, men outnumbered women on faculty rosters by a count of fifty-three to ten.[4] Quite a few of these women also taught in fields or subjects closely associated with nurture or traditionally feminine roles. One is a professor of counseling, another teaches education and aging, and another is a professor emerita who has published extensively on the ethics of hospitality. Meanwhile, faculty positions devoted to philosophy, leadership, and theology, fields that have historically been filled by men, remain largely masculine territory. There are structural and cultural reasons for this persistent imbalance, some them beyond Asbury's control. Nevertheless, these patterns shape student experience, and Asbury's genderblind discourse does not name them.

The privatization of womanhood, then, extends into Asbury's ostensibly genderblind public spaces. Hidden inequalities accompany them. The expectations of institutional motherhood, not unlike traditional constructions of familial motherhood, cost time and resources, often without commensurate compensation. Churchwomen might craft and deliver powerful sermons, speak authoritatively about biblical texts, administrate academic programs, and participate in presidential cabinet meetings, but even these authoritative roles are subject to gendered constraints. Whether they join the community through genderblind hiring practices or in support of their husbands' calls to ministry, Asbury's women navigate the demands of a second shift that expects maternal nurture in both the private and public arenas.

Genderblind Tensions

Managing public and private expectations in a genderblind culture can lead to personal unease. I met several women who came to Asbury single and remained lonely, agonizingly so, over the desire for a spouse. Even women who are wives and mothers can feel isolated. Kristen confessed that she had a hard time finding other women who resonated with her experience as both a mother and a student. She knew lots of "really nice community wives," but their experiences and circumstances felt distant from her own: "I don't really know many mothers that are pursuing this. There's a lot of single students and there's a lot of older women but there's not a lot of my age, my lifestyle. I joined a woman's group last semester, before I even started seminary, but it was almost like you can either be a woman and a mother or you can be like a woman and a student. There's not many [women who are] wives, mothers, *and* students." Another woman, Rachel, tearfully recounted her journey with infertility and miscarriage as an MDiv student. She recalled the pain of loss compounded by suggestions that "if I don't have a child, I can't be a real woman." At the end of her story, Rachel gratefully remembered the only person, a professor, who offered the empathy she needed: "He said, 'I'm just so sorry for what you've gone through. I just don't feel that we have a good theology for this.' And he's like 'so I would love it if we could sort of talk about that.' I guess just having a person who's in authority that way who was open to listening to me and my ideas . . . he has no idea I don't think, but he's been instrumental in that healing." Although several years removed from the experience when she told me the story, Rachel's demeanor still reflected the pain of that journey. Her wounds illustrate the deep and lonely divide between the Equality Story's genderblind churchly world and the Difference Story's expectations of privatized womanhood. The professor's words touched her so deeply because they defied this divide. As a faculty member, he occupied Asbury's academic, public realm, which is typically blind to women's experiences. By recognizing that the institution, despite its egalitarian theology, lacked tools that fit her journey, he acknowledged the limits of genderblindness. His words resituated her infertility and miscarriage, placing her embodied experiences in the center of a theological pursuit rather than sidelining them (and her). Rachel felt acknowledged, not as a divinity student or as a woman, but as *both*. It was a profound and empowering gift, one that few students reported receiving.

Genderblindness also limits women's understandings of their own lived experiences. Even the women who most plainly illustrated Asbury's structural and cultural inequalities often failed to recognize them. For example, none of the women I interviewed identified the gendered demands of the "second shift." Even Kelly, who so aptly described it, mentioned it only in relation to her difficulty finding friends: "I think [being a student as well as a wife of a student] made it a little bit harder to relate to the spouses. . . . They have no idea what I'm doing because I'm a full-time student [too]. So it's like 'Okay, everything your husband does, I do, and then everything you do, I do.'" While Kelly compared her life to other women's, Mattie compared herself to the men in her classes, especially those training to become pastors: "Where I struggle the most is probably more like a sense of direction. Most of the men I meet are very sure of their direction. They know they're called to be a pastor. They know they want to do this. And they just know the path will be open to them. It's not that they don't respect the women. It's just that there's frequently more ambiguity. I mean, there certainly has been for me." Although Mattie, unlike many of her peers, recognized that gender can influence experience and opportunity, she stopped short of naming systemic inequalities or cumulative cultural biases. Instead, her last sentence pivoted back to her own, individualized experience: "There certainly has been for me." Lacking awareness that others shared their frustrations, women like Kelly and Mattie most often applied individualized explanations for their challenges. Kelly wondered, "It could just be my insecurities." Mattie said, "That could also be a personality thing."

While Kelly and Mattie seemed vaguely unsettled, other women struggled more intensely. One faculty member recalled a student's reaction to a guest preacher whom the professor described as "a large, powerful man who had a large, powerful sermon": "After chapel, a really wonderful, mature, godly, *called* woman came tearing into my office and just wept. She just said, 'I think I should leave.' I asked, 'Why,' and she said, 'I could never do that. I just sat in the service and felt like I didn't belong.'" Clear policies and biblical teachings might support a woman's *right* to pursue churchly leadership, but she must also overcome cultural forces that normalize men's perspectives, leadership styles, and bodily mannerisms. Unaware of these forces, even as she experienced their weight, this woman too assumed that she was the problem. "I could never do that," she said, emphasizing her own responsibility, "I didn't belong."

Genderblindness, after all, does not emphasize collective categories. It identifies individual women teaching, administrating, learning, leading, and serving, just like men. It does not, however, recognize the structural processes and cultural expectations that guide women collectively toward certain roles, practices, and postures and away from others. Nor does it critically engage its own cultural and historical context—one that has long centered men, normalizing their voices, experiences, and mannerisms, and smoothing their paths to leadership. The same genderblind individualism that offers women opportunity also obscures the challenges that they face collectively. Women like the student in this story often have little idea that others share their insecurities—or that these experiences might stem from structural and cultural, not just personal, sources.

Women do, nevertheless, intuitively sense that their journeys differ categorically from men's. No one wonders what it means to be a "man pastor," but women wonder every day what it means to be a "woman pastor." Will she be taken seriously by congregations and bishops? Can she expect to be treated fairly by denominational leaders who assign jobs, facilitate mentoring, and determine pay scales? How will she work with men who follow the "Billy Graham rule" by refusing to be alone with a woman who is not their wife? Does she wear lipstick when she preaches? Does she cross her legs while sitting onstage? The privatization of womanhood notwithstanding, the women who walk Asbury's halls, enroll in coursework, and prepare for leadership face gendered questions and concerns that have little to do with domesticity and motherhood. A student might quietly voice these questions to her friends, but she would be unlikely to broadcast them into the broader community for fear of transgressing genderblind norms. These questions hang in the air, present and pressing to women themselves, but rarely addressed in public.

The privatization of womanhood, however, does affect the entire community. It downplays the positive value of women's standpoint in public spaces and conversations, limiting their contributions. Feminist scholars who advance the concept of standpoint assert that women's voices are valuable not because they are interchangeable with men's, as genderblindness insists, but *because* they are different from men's (Smith 1987). Differences in their upbringing and experiences lead women to see the world in different ways. They might offer insight, for example, derived from the caregiving and maternal responsibilities they disproportionately carry. Without sociological and feminist lenses developed to illuminate these gendered realities and equip women to speak from their own experiences, however, Asbury's women learn instead to speak the language of genderblindness. They find inspiration in the contextualized stories of their New Testament predecessors who worked within the system, and they sideline gendered considerations in their articulations of global mission. While successful at facilitating the seminary's vision of Christian unity, the tension between public genderblind equality and privatized difference also curtails women's contributions to the community.

Why do Asbury's women not challenge inconsistencies that so clearly put them at a disadvantage? So many of the women I met were ambitious, confident, well-read, and intellectually curious. Why did they not mobilize around the experiences and challenges they clearly shared in an effort to raise feminist consciousness and solidarity? A woman might feel slightly irritated when old hymn lyrics praise God for faithfulness to His "sons." She may recognize the lack of women mentors or the underrepresentation of women in the president's cabinet. She might struggle more than the men in her classes to resonate with yet another leadership book written by a successful white man and wonder if she really is cut out for the work of ministry. She may even recognize her need for guidance as she navigates these challenges, but the institution offers a limited set of cultural tools. Among them, the specter of Christian unity haunts the women who navigate this maze of gendered expectations. The community does not consider "unity" something to be built, rather it is something to be maintained. Asbury is *already* unified around its various commitments to historically contextualized hermeneutics, genderblind institutional policies, and degendered global mission. The campus rings with confidence in these commitments. The result is a warm, celebratory atmosphere that most community members, including women, prize. But it comes at a cost: the curbing of voices that might call for change—even change toward an end the community might endorse, like women's empowerment. While a few women did, in fact, attempt to bring gendered awareness, and even feminist ideas, into public conversation, they made little headway. Even the most determined dissenter cannot easily overcome the power of a well-told story. When dissidents graduate and move on, taking their divergent ideas with them, the dominant institutional patterns of individualism, antifeminism, and unity, chronicled every day in material and discursive culture, remain.

The most successful churchwomen adapt. They learn to display just the right amount of femininity in public, navigate the demands of the second shift, and resist developing structural critiques or feminist consciousnesses. Indeed, this formula may, to some degree, prepare women for service in congregational and denominational spaces that, like Asbury itself, assume some version of genderblindness. But it also leaves the next generation of aspiring churchwomen with a litany of unanswered questions: Can they flourish in denominational hierarchies dominated by powerful men? How will they balance the demands of ministry with the cultural expectations of intensive motherhood? To whom will they turn for solidarity and advice?

———

Given the tightrope of gendered expectations they walk, it is no surprise that so many of Asbury's women greeted Jessica LaGrone's arrival with such enthusiasm. In addition to her new post as dean of the chapel, LaGrone also comfortably—and publicly—embodied her role as the mother of two young children. She often included stories about the children in sermons and escorted them to campus family events. Once, to the obvious delight of the congregation, LaGrone used the chapel announcement time to apologize to a student whose car had been doused by her son's water gun. Recalling the women who found legitimacy in nineteenth-century pulpits by framing themselves as mothers to their congregational flocks, LaGrone infused her new public role with displays of motherhood—both familial and pastoral (Payne 2015).

None of this defied the community's genderblindness. In fact, LaGrone accommodated its expectations flawlessly. She carefully inserted stories of her own experiences into churchly spaces in ways that did not compete with the primacy of global mission and Christian unity. She delivered sermons in a voice that was always rational and measured. One student told me later in the year that LaGrone was the only woman preacher whom she could stand to listen to.

Others, she complained, either overplayed their femininity using "Valley Girl" mannerisms or tried too hard to copy men's preaching styles. LaGrone's polished self-presentation, together with her careful references to motherhood, situated her as a legitimate churchwoman in compliance not only with genderblind ministry in public but also with the sacralization of marriage and motherhood in private. She successfully embodied all of Asbury's scripts. She walked a fine line, to be sure, but she did so with such poise that it would be easy for an observer to overlook just how precarious the line itself is.

CENTERING MEN

Peter eagerly confirmed his egalitarian convictions. The Church, the energetic first-year MDiv student insisted, must allow gifted women to serve as leaders. Peter nevertheless resisted certain strategies toward these ends. Dismissing the feminist theology he had read as an undergraduate, he complained about women and minorities who assume postures of activism. "'Well, I'm a woman,'" he paraphrased, "'so I've been [oppressed]' or, 'I'm Black' or 'I'm Indian' or something like that." Peter frowned and shook his head in irritation. "You're going a little too far with some of these things," he said. Feminism could be helpful, he acknowledged, as long as it aimed for genderblindness. Anything more, he feared, might elevate women at the expense of men. He elaborated:

> Feminism is helpful in the fact that there are women that are standing up for women's rights and not letting women just be satisfied with being [in the] backseat—because I don't believe they should be. Where it goes off the deep end is when women are saying, "Down with men." And it becomes the opposite. I actually had a conversation with two girls in one of my [undergraduate theology] classes. We were talking about how there's a women's history month and there's a Black history month and on our campus there was a Asian / Pacific / Middle Eastern / Islander, or Pacific Islander month or something, and then there was like another week for somebody else, and I'm like, "I want a day for white, middle-class American man month. Just give me a day." And then they said, "Well, you've had the past century." And I was just like, "No, not really, because I'm always getting told how I can't do this, I can't do this, I can't do this. I can't get this scholarship. I can't do all of these things." There are so many limitations now to try and keep me from doing a lot of things. I love all the scholarships that are out there for people who are minorities, but I get annoyed when you have to be a minority to even *get* a scholarship. I'm probably smarter than a lot of minorities who get into a lot of the programs and schools, and I get upset with things like that. You're giving them preference just because of their skin color. Why can't we be just be colorblind? Why can't we be genderblind? . . . I wish everything was done blind.

In an unusual acknowledgment of the unmarked categories that Asbury shares with broader American society, Peter named his own demographic realities as a "white, middle-class American man." He wasn't opposed to recognizing other groups, or even elevating women to positions of authority, but he nonetheless longed for a churchly world where gender, along with race and ethnicity, no longer mattered.

Other men generally agreed. Many even described Asbury as a success story. "There's no real difference in how [students] are treated, no difference in expectations," Jack told me, reflecting on several years of experience on campus. "I mean, across the board. Man or woman, a student's a student." As this chapter has already shown, Jack's assertion belies many women's experiences. It also suggests a blindness to the advantages that men—especially white American men—enjoy. While individualism, unity, and genderblindness constrain women, they simultaneously free these men from having to reckon with their intersectional advantages.

Centered in Space

As the lunch crowd slowly thinned from Asbury's student center, I settled into a soft leather chair near the corner fireplace. Students filled nearby tables, finishing packed lunches, studying for classes, and socializing with friends. A small group of men on the opposite side of the large room laughed loudly, seemingly oblivious to the other meetings and activities in progress around them. I could easily hear every word of their conversation over the music playing through my headphones. Finally, after a lengthy discussion, the men decided to disperse. As one gathered his books and headed toward the front door, he raised his voice even louder to greet a friend at a different table. Another cracked a parting joke about a soccer game and comically mimed a drop kick as he crossed the wide room. As the group went their separate ways, laughing loudly, they left the space in near silence. Returning to my own work, I noticed a woman who had been reading nearby rise silently, careful to slide her chair back under the table. She approached the front desk just a few feet away to strike up a quiet conversation with the student working there. In striking contrast with the group of men who had just exited, this woman limited her voice and carefully managed her engagement with the physical space around her.

Versions of these scenes persisted throughout my fieldwork. Although women were present and active, men were far more often the ones who spoke with volume and filled physical spaces with confident bodies. They also filled intellectual space with stimulating discussions of biblical exegesis and bold prescriptions for the Church. Embodying confidence and masculine agency, their actions conveyed a clear sense of belonging. Along with their brothers at Southern Seminary, these assertive men reflect the idealized masculine standards of bravery, relational dominance, and aggression that modern society implicitly expects of men (Connell 1987). In implied support of this construct, one faculty member's institutional web page does not list his academic credentials, as is typical, but indicates his hobbies to include "tree houses, axe throwing, and small business incubation." There was, to be sure, considerable variation in men's behavior. My field notes also contain mentions of quieter men reading unobtrusively in public spaces and listening intently to both men's and women's voices in classrooms and casual conversation. But I never saw women openly disregard the volume of their voices or command informal public space the way men often did. While displays of hegemonic masculinity at Asbury are relatively muted, gendered patterns are hard to miss.

Even the variation in masculine expression underscores men's cultural advantages. "*Look* at that jacket!" a woman playfully teased a friend as he emerged from the campus post office. The owner of the perfectly tailored plaid jacket also wore neatly pressed trousers and polished brown shoes. Another man, sporting a full beard, football jersey, and jogging pants, also noticed the stylish attire as he passed and dramatically looked his friend up and down. "Dude, you are looking *good*!" he said playfully. The trio had a short conversation about men's fashion, which the plaid jacket owner apparently took much more seriously than his peers. The conversation was casual and congenial. The athletically attired student seemed not at all concerned that his peer's wardrobe definitively outclassed his own. His smartly dressed friend—who appeared to have chosen the day's ensemble for its own sake and not because a meeting or interview required it—displayed no sign of self-consciousness about his appearance or its sharp contrast with those around him.

Just as broader society sustains multiple masculinities, Asbury's culture also supports various ways of being a man (Connell 1987, 1995). Some men grow full beards, ride motorcycles, and brew their own beer. These are legitimate Asbury men. But others write poetry, wear religious jewelry, and assume effeminate postures with their bodies. These are also legitimate Asbury men. Those who prefer a more artsy, thoughtful style can find inspiration in Charles Wesley, who was a poet and a musician. Even more individualized fashion choices like body jewelry, creative hairstyles, and sleeve tattoos, though uncommon, are unlikely to be frowned upon as they might be at Southern. This flexibility facilitates masculine agency. In contrast with the feminine tightrope that women walk, men at Asbury can choose a mode of masculinity that suits them. While men may have been more reluctant than women to express their insecurities to me—a reluctance that would also indicate the influence of hegemonic masculinity—they generally did not seem to fear that their style choices or mannerisms would bring their fit for the community into question.

Masculine confidence extends to academics. Many of Asbury's aspiring pastors choose the master of divinity program, which can take five years or more to complete. The degree serves as a prerequisite for denominational ordination.

Figure 4.1. A life-sized statue of Charles Wesley, an early Methodist leader known for his prolific hymn writing, just outside the front entrance to Estes Chapel. Photo by the author.

It also carries overtones of scholarly authority. Students graduate expecting not only to teach the Bible and plant churches but also to speak confidently on cultural trends and to write authoritatively about leadership and social ethics. They expect to be taken seriously.

Women, of course, build intellectual confidence and achieve credentials alongside men. They too learn from professors, conquer impressive reading lists, and receive preaching and theological awards. But they feel their minority status. Grace, a first-year MDiv student, told me that she experienced an unfamiliar intimidation in Asbury's classrooms, even though she was used to being in spaces dominated by men: "In my undergrad, I would always be a person who would raise my hand in class . . . I'm just an outspoken person. But here I don't raise my hand in class. And I don't know why that is. I don't know if it's just a personal fear that I have, or if I feel like because I'm a woman that people won't take me seriously? . . . I'm not sure. I'm working through that." Grace's classes certainly had more men than women in them, she reported, but men dominated the space in more than just numbers. "Women participate," she clarified, "but I'd say it's a mostly male discussion." She continued, "A lot of the guys just want to show off their knowledge. . . . I know that women do it too, but it seems that men more times are the ones that are just showing off how much they know or showing off the big words that they know." Grace shrugged and shook her head in mild irritation at her classmates' oblivious self-importance.

"Oh, you're just auditing, right?" Kelly mimicked a classmate's reaction to her presence in a classroom, rolling her eyes. "Have you been asked that?" I wondered. "Oh, yeah, all the time," she replied and described her frustration with a fellow classmate and personal friend: "We were having dinner with them, and he happened to look at my husband. He was like, 'What classes are you going to take next semester?' and never once acknowledged that I was a student. He knows I'm a student but never once acknowledged, like 'Are you going to do the same?' Or 'What are you going to take?' Never once. It's always right to my husband. So that can be challenging because I'm like, 'Hey, wait a minute! I'm a student too!'" While these experiences clearly annoyed her, Kelly did not interpret the men's oversight as spiteful. Nor did she seem to consider the pattern something that needed to be addressed. Instead, she simply swallowed her frustration and moved on. Meanwhile, men like her friend and like those that dominated the student center as I worked likely remained unaware of how women like Grace and Kelly experienced their actions. They simply filled intellectual and ecclesial spaces in ways that women did not.

Centered through Marriage

Asbury's construction of masculinity does demand one thing of men. They must embody commitment to heterosexual marriage. Unlike complementarian groups like Southern, which also rejects same-sex unions, Asbury cannot lean on rigid gender role expectations as rationale. If gendered roles and divisions of labor are unimportant in a "Christian marriage," as Asbury's official discourse maintains, what makes a marriage distinctively "Christian"? As it scrambles to answer this question in a cultural moment rife with denominational splits over gender and sexuality, Asbury's leadership draws on heteronormative standards embedded in the Difference Story's interpretation of the Genesis creation narrative and amplified in broader evangelical subculture.

Students recognize the weight these cultural tensions carry. It seems likely that some even choose Asbury over other seminaries in part for its explicitly conservative commitments on questions of human sexuality. Eager to establish themselves as guardians of Christian tradition, many prime themselves to join President Tennent in an effort to preserve orthodox Christianity. In addition to voicing their agreement in words, students also embody it by entering heterosexual marriages. When he marries a woman, a man enacts his own affirmation of Asbury's theological stance. Wedding bands worn on fingers, children carried on shoulders, and phone calls that end in "Love you, babe" all powerfully symbolize these commitments. Men who display them are, in this one crucial sense at least, fit for evangelical ministry.

Indeed, congregations, more than one person reminded me, prefer pastoral candidates who are married. Even though Chad had been a student at Asbury for only a few months, he had already participated in several informal conversations that reinforced this expectation. These conversations, he reported to me, emphasized "the importance of women supporting their husbands in ministry. And same goes for male spouses of females . . . in terms of them being really the backbone of our ministry and so forth." Chad was committed to Asbury's egalitarian framework and so was careful to mention the possibility of male spouses. But in practical reality, churches and those who work within them most easily assume the first half of Chad's thought: women supporting their husbands in ministry. Many students themselves come to Asbury from congregations where pastors' wives teach Sunday School, organize holiday events, and lead women's Bible studies. Even students from egalitarian denominations know the expectations. When men marry, they get one step closer to meeting them and to receiving the authority infused into the role of pastor.

Married men also benefit from the same second shift that burdens women. Lessened domestic responsibility allows them more time and emotional energy to devote to academic work, professional networking, ministry opportunities, and social media presences. Moreover, they are also the recipients of the nurture women provide. The products of feminine domesticity—seasonal decorations, hand-lettered birthday cards, scented candles, and dinner parties—nourish their bodies and souls. While women struggle to imagine how they will combine the responsibilities of marriage and parenthood with ministry and church leadership, men know that family life likely will facilitate, rather than compete with, their vocational aspirations.

Unmarried students are not far removed from these expectations. These men and women often live in separate on-campus apartments that offer a more grown-up version of college dorm life. Resident assistants provide mentoring and personal advice. They organize small Bible study groups, carry-in meals, and "fireside chats" that bring men and women together for conversation in semiprivate spaces. As single students watch their married colleagues build relationships with spouses and raise young children, they prepare for a similar path. For many, the transition happens sooner rather than later. It is not uncommon for students who join the community as single adults to marry each other. The pull toward marriage is strong.

Even in this, Asbury's expectations for men are flexible. Unmarried men move toward marital legitimacy by pursuing romantic relationships with women. One student described the response when a classmate announced a new romance on social media. Despite the fact that no one at Asbury had met the girlfriend, who lived outside the community, the young man's Facebook page quickly filled with messages of approval and congratulations. The student who recounted the story to me articulated his own concern that the quality of the relationship seemed to matter not at all. Instead, he noted, his community applauded the fact of the new relationship itself. Another student reported his own initial struggles to navigate Asbury's social scene. When this man started dating a woman, invitations to parties and social gatherings seemed to magically materialize—only to vanish again when the couple broke up.

Men who are not in romantic relationships can embody heterosexuality by pursuing "sexual wholeness." While the community often resists gender-specific groups, one of its most notable exceptions is the Band of Brothers, a small group that meets monthly to offer accountability focused on sexual behavior, including pornography. Though pornography is decisively condemned as unholy, identifying it as a temptation symbolically affirms a man's heterosexuality, which offers social legitimacy. One student, whom I encountered in various contexts throughout my fieldwork at Asbury, told me his story of battling, and eventually overcoming, a pornography addiction on three different occasions. While his eagerness to recount the story seemed unusual, his explanation clearly fit the cultural mores, which valorized heterosexual identity and the transformative power of the Spirit. Now married to a woman, he was ready to defend traditional sexual standards, armed with his own story of masculine victory over temptation. Promotional posters for the Band of Brothers, which featured the rippling arms of two men linked in a strong grasp, affirmed this student's orientation. Their bodies remain hidden from view, far enough apart to accommodate the words underneath and to avoid the suggestion that their physical

Figure 4.2. A promotional poster advertises the Band of Brothers men's groups. Displayed on Asbury Theological Seminary's campus.

interaction is sexual. Beneath their handshake, the graphic depicts an artistic rendition of the earth, giving the announcement a sense of something big, important, and universal. This decisive condemnation of pornography accomplishes a dual purpose. It simultaneously upholds sexual purity and reinforces the importance of heterosexuality.

Despite the strength of its heteronormativity, the institution's flexible composition of masculinity does tenuously allow for the possibility of identification as a gay man. Although this obvious deviation from the heterosexual imperative remains uncommon, a few students have openly identified as gay. Without the opportunity to embody a romantic heterosexual relationship, these men must, even more than their straight colleagues, outspokenly affirm commitments to heterosexual marriage. That is, they must personally and repeatedly and publicly commit to celibacy.

Centered by Calling

Students do not arrive on campus as blank slates. Families, home communities, mentors, and personal life experiences all guide their decisions to attend Asbury and continue to influence their subsequent experiences. The students I interviewed were eager to tell me about their spiritual journeys. Many admitted continuing uncertainties about where their journeys would lead, but they overwhelmingly expressed confidence that they had made the right choice. Many sensed that they were, in fact, called to attend Asbury.

As I listened to their stories, I quickly began to recognize gendered patterns. Some students, nearly always men, had little trouble discerning the Spirit's call to ministry. They typically grew up in supportive churchly communities and received mentoring from pastors or campus ministry leaders. Peter, for example, felt a stirring in his soul as a teenager but was not confident of his call until a leader at summer camp told him in no uncertain terms that "You have the call of God upon you." Peter was not surprised. "I just sat there and I said, 'I know.'" While still a teenager, he entered the candidacy process for ordination into his home denomination. Others, also typically men, framed their stories as struggles with God. A few of these came to faith out of difficult, unchurched backgrounds. More commonly they were raised within the church—even as children of ministers—and did not want to be called to ministry themselves. Chad, for example, never struggled with his commitment to Christianity, but he resisted the idea of ministry as his vocation: "When I was about seventeen years old I started to really feel a potential call to ministry, and it was literally the last thing on my list. I did not want to have anything to do with becoming a pastor or anything like that. It ended up being about a year-long fight with God about [whether] I could serve Him other ways outside of being a pastor of a church." When Chad's mother asked him what he wanted to do with his life, he finally decided to broach the subject:

I just started to name drop different things like engineering, law, possibly medicine, and then I dropped in the word pastor. . . . I shared with her that maybe I felt called into ministry. Then she told me that she and my dad had felt a calling on my life at the same time I had been kind of battling with this and keeping it to myself. When we went home, she showed me magazine articles that she had cut out about the need for young clergy. So that was really where it kind of culminated, and I really felt affirmed in that after about a year of fighting with it.

In these men's stories, family members, pastors, mentors, and friends very often guided them on their journeys, nudging them toward vocational ministry, even when the path was rocky.

In comparison, women's stories often included more ambiguity—and sometimes external resistance. While Abbi, for example, expressed a great deal of confidence in her decision to pursue a ministerial vocation, she described a discouraging exchange with a former pastor that gave her pause: "She [the pastor] asked me what I was doing. I said, 'Well, I'm going to go back to school. I'm going to go to seminary.' She said, 'Are you going to have any more children?' and I said . . . 'Yeah, my husband and I want a larger family.' She said, 'Well, you can't be a pastor and do that.' She said, 'The church is your family, and you're married to this church.' . . . So that was a little disheartening." Abbi, however, was determined. She enrolled at Asbury anyway.

Others who lacked her confidence continued to struggle. "I grew up in the church," Kelly reflected, "and I knew that ministry would play a role somehow in my life, but I never thought it would be full-time ministry." During college, Kelly sought counsel from a campus minister who encouraged her to pursue pastoral training. "When I came [to Asbury], I still had no idea what that was supposed to look like, and I still am not a hundred percent sure. I know that I'm supposed to be getting my degree." Hannah, another divinity student, confessed deep internal struggle over her call, even after a semester of enrollment at Asbury. What exactly was the Holy Spirit calling her to, she wondered. Where did she fit in the Church? She also confessed her inability to articulate a robust theological argument for the full inclusion of women in church leadership—something that bothered her:

It's hard for me as a person who does very much want to take every Scripture seriously and believes the Bible for what it is. . . . I mean if I was going to sit down here with someone from Southern Baptist [Seminary] who was completely sure that women should not be in these certain roles, I don't know if I could give him a great theological argument for how I feel. I couldn't necessarily back it up. So that's concerning, you know? Maybe after three years here I'll be able to. Right now I couldn't. I could just say, "This is my experience and I know God. I know that I know Him, and I know what He has said to me and how He has used me. I know that He doesn't want me to be silent."

She remained committed to both her egalitarian convictions and to her own call. The reason: she had felt the Spirit.

Indeed, the Spirit pervaded nearly all stories of calling. For those who struggled with their sense of call as much as for those who never questioned it, the Spirit was a comforting and empowering personal guide. While both men and women valued this guidance, it seemed especially important to women who, like Hannah, did not come from churchly and family backgrounds that provided them with intensive mentoring and opportunities to develop leadership skills. Both men and women, however, also mentioned the influence of at least one authority figure who, very often, had attended Asbury themselves. Together, these patterns underscore the heavily social nature of calling. While the Spirit might call from the realm of the transcendent, the practice of answering that call by pursuing seminary education is heavily mediated by social ties and opportunities. Virtually no one enrolled at Asbury without them.

Cultural assumptions about vocational ministry might also contribute. Men often framed their calling stories in terms of service or sacrifice. Chad, for example, specifically mentioned choosing ministry over a career in lucrative, high-status fields like engineering, medicine, or law. Tyler explained that he left a good job to come to seminary. Women, in contrast, often seemed concerned that their decision to attend seminary might make them look too ambitious. They just wanted to follow the Spirit and serve the Church, they said. Stereotypes of self-interested women preachers linger, compounding expectations of an evangelical context in which men are most often leaders and women are most often supportive wives. Overall, women's stories of calling included more barriers to be overcome and fewer supports along the way.

Asbury's genderblindness obscures these disparities. While the community overflows with men whose wives followed them to Asbury, I encountered only one woman among the dozens of students I interacted with whose husband and family moved to the community for *her* to attend seminary. Men typically remained untroubled by these patterns because, theoretically at least, they were open to alternative arrangements. If their wives had chosen to pursue demanding ministerial careers, several told me, clearly eager that I recognize the depth of their egalitarianism, they would have happily accommodated. But these men saw only their individual circumstances. They failed to recognize the cultural patterns and economic structures that fast-tracked their own careers while holding women—perhaps even their own wives—back.

Centered by History

Like most American institutions, Asbury has always centered men. Bronze statues around its campus memorialize John Wesley, Charles Wesley, and Francis Asbury. Buildings bear masculine names like "Beeson," "McPheeters," "Frank Bateman Stanger," and "McKenna." The walls of its administrative board room

Figure 4.3. Portraits of Asbury's eight presidents line a meeting room in the administration building. Photo by the author.

chronicle the institution's past with vivid oil portraits depicting the eight presidents who have led the institution since its birth in 1923. The seminary's website profiles these leaders in words. "All have proved to be strong, godly leaders," it says, "well suited for the time and life of the seminary during which they were appointed." All eight have also been white American men.

Faculty rosters have a similar history. In her book on women in theological education, professor emeritus Christine Pohl recalls the disconnect between the institution's openness to women and its actual hiring of them. "From the 1960s to 1987," she writes, "there were no women on the faculty in tenured positions (except the librarian), and when I came in 1989, I became the second woman to be on the faculty in a full-time, tenure-track position." As Pohl also notes, the numbers of women on faculty rosters have fluctuated over the decades, increasing especially in the years that followed her arrival in 1989. Yet in the larger picture of the seminary's history, mirroring the patterns of broader society, women have been a distinct minority in both faculty and administrative positions. Outside a few notable exceptions, like Pohl herself, men have largely constructed the parameters of theology, assessed modes of mission, and interpreted biblical texts. Like the Methodist women preachers of the nineteenth century, when the pioneering women of Asbury's past were granted access to spaces and roles already defined by men, they did not necessarily gain the right to make structural adjustments to accommodate their own lives, or to forge new paths toward leadership that would be more accessible to more women (Hassey 2008; Dayton 1988). They undoubtedly found creative ways to bring their own sensibilities to their work and to derive meaning and empowerment from it, as other enterprising women have done throughout American religious history, but theirs are not the contributions that have publicly driven the institution forward (Brekus 2007; Payne 2015; Bowler 2019).

The institution, like so many others, sustains its male-centered processes without much reflection. The white middle-class men who have defined American evangelical culture, theology, and systemic processes over time have not marked their work with their own labels. Most on campus, accordingly, do not think of the biblical scholarship the institution produces and consumes as "white men's hermeneutics," even when it has been written by white men. Instead, the campus thinks simply of "hermeneutics," centering these men and their ideas as normative, ahistorical, and neutral. At the same time, it decenters other standpoints with labels such as "Black hermeneutics," "feminist theology," "postcolonial perspectives," "mujerista theology," or "women's interpretations." These are *other*. Although some occasionally arise in various classrooms at the discretion of faculty members, they remain largely tangential to the institution's dominant narratives, at least as articulated by students.[5] The official curriculum socializes students into an evangelical Wesleyan paradigm that is predominantly white and masculine. Students who recognized that their demographic realities differed from these unmarked norms described the weight of the campus's expectation of unity. They felt pressure to coalesce around a status quo, even if it did not represent their experience and knowledge.

This is not to suggest that the institution is inattentive to global diversity. The School of World Mission and Evangelism in particular attracts students and visiting scholars from all over the world. The school's faculty members themselves embody a wealth of international experience. Together, they represent missionary service and study in Southeast Asia, East and West Africa, and Latin America, making theirs easily the corner of the seminary most mindful of global diversity. Nevertheless, with one key exception, all of the School of World Mission and Evangelism's full-time, tenure-track faculty are white, and only one is a woman. Even when these faculty members push against sexism and ethnocentrism with their words, they embody a cultural context that centers the same kinds of people it always has. Cultural legacies are hard to displace.

These cultural legacies also carry liabilities for the men they center. Graduates might emerge with a passion for the global church, a respectable knowledge of Greek, and a commitment to egalitarian theology, but the white American men I interviewed remained largely unprepared to problematize their own standpoints. Even those who stood out among their peers for their thoughtful treatments of gender inequalities largely failed to consider the forces of hegemonic masculinity, whiteness, and colonialism that framed their own social—and religious—contexts. There were few exceptions. The outliers I met were almost always motivated to push beyond Asbury's framework because their own experiences as members of minoritized groups placed them on the community's margins. In contrast, the white American men I interviewed, who were the students most firmly centered in Asbury's genderblind egalitarianism, largely overlooked or sidelined standpoints beyond their own. And the language of power, applied often to God, remained all but absent from their considerations of social dynamics.

Not surprisingly, few recognized these limits. In most cases, especially among the MDiv students preparing for pastoral vocations, the educational experience appeared to be accomplishing exactly what it intended. It was empowering these men, giving them confidence to act as authoritative leaders. These students revel in the challenges of their coursework. Doctrine is complex. Hebrew is hard. The American church, they lament, is faltering and urgently needs them to bring it back to life. Cheered by classmates and encouraged by mentors to confront these challenges, their confidence grows. While some graduate with lingering doubts and insecurities about their vocational paths, the vast majority of the men I encountered were eager, if nervous, to enter the celebrated role of pastor and appeared to feel equipped for the task. Even those who embodied more reflective postures spoke confidently, almost without exception, about their community's gender successes. They had, after all, seen egalitarianism at work. They attended homiletics classes taught by women, received communion elements blessed by women, learned in classrooms alongside women. Why, after all, should anyone talk about gender differences or power dynamics if Asbury's genderblindness has allowed the community to rise above them? These men might not object to women's leadership, but they have no particular need for it either.

Women sounded very different. When Grace described the distinctly masculine accent of her classroom conversations, for example, she was in the middle of a course called "The Theology of John Wesley." It was a good class, she reported, but the course's namesake was not the character who captured her enthusiasm. Instead, Grace identified with another member of the Wesley family: John's mother, Susanna. "I *love* Susanna Wesley!" Grace told me, her voice thick with conviction. "She's great. I want to be parts of her so badly." Unlike her sons, whom the community memorializes in sermons, required coursework, and bronze statues throughout campus, Susanna Wesley does not occupy a position of particular importance at Asbury. Indeed, she did not write the books, contribute to the confessions of faith, or establish the institutions that male-centered religion recognizes. Instead, Asbury honors her—as it does other women—as a mother. But Grace described her as "a very strong woman," an inspiring leader, and an ambitious religious educator. Certainly the seeds for this characterization emerged from her coursework, but Grace's enthusiasm for Susanna Wesley came from a different source than the enthusiasm men displayed when they showcased their budding knowledge. While Asbury hands these men models, stories, and tools that naturally match and reinforce their experience, Grace owned the work of discovery herself. This extra work is not entirely to her disadvantage. There is tremendous value in discovery and personal investment. Perhaps it is formative processes like Grace's identification with Susanna Wesley that standpoint feminism has in mind when it insists that women's experiences are distinct and valuable to the public realm. But to take ownership of this gift, women like Grace must master yet another "second shift." That is, they must seek out women-centered stories, books, and models on their own, in addition to mastering the male-centered curriculum that will earn them credentials, legitimacy, and jobs. Although my sample included very few women of color, the few I did interact with reinforced my suspicion that these women face an even more daunting task. They navigate what Patricia Hill Collins calls a "matrix of domination," the intersection of male-centering and whiteness (1990).

These realities persist. Though the board of trustees has taken more diverse shape in recent years, white men maintain a clear majority.[6] They also heavily populate the president's cabinet, which since 2015 has included one woman among six to eight men. The pattern is just as striking among the faculty.[7] The ten women included in the entire 2015 Wilmore campus faculty list were dramatically outnumbered by sixty men. The seminary's founding charge, "The Whole Bible for the Whole World," did not exclude women from its project, but the charge has not belonged to them in the way it belonged to men. Asbury may not employ its past as usable history in quite the same way that Southern invokes the Conservative Resurgence, but the institutional patterns are clear. Even subtle histories leave powerful legacies.

Genderblindness in a Patriarchal World

Despite their limitations, genderblind stories have delivered on their individualized promises. They have yielded a robust tradition that insists on the full churchly equality of women and men. While the women on Asbury's faculty remain in the minority, they stand in stark contrast to the near-complete absence of women on Southern's roster. One directs the doctor of ministry program, one of the seminary's fastest-growing initiatives. Another, a widely respected professor of ethics, served for a time as associate provost. Others research, preside over classrooms, and mentor students. Dean of the Chapel Jessica LaGrone constructs formative community liturgies and delivers masterfully crafted sermons. For these women, genderblindness means not only a job but a seat at the table where conversations about Christian ethics, Wesleyan identity, and the future of the Church happen. They exercise significant agency. Women students also benefit. Genderblindness allows them to pursue ordination and vocational ministry as their life's work. They learn the nuances of biblical texts and hone skills of preaching and counseling. Eventually, many achieve ordination, land pastoral jobs, publish scholarly articles, and write devotional materials. Many of their grandmothers—and even their mothers—would not have easily accomplished these things. Nor are such opportunities available to women in complementarian denominations like the Southern Baptist Convention. Aware of this broader context, few take Asbury's opportunities for granted, even when the institution's stories fall short of their promises.

Hannah, an Asbury student who grew up complementarian and had considered enrolling at Southern, demonstrated this ambivalence. Early in her MDiv work, Hannah was already glad that she had chosen Asbury. When I asked her to describe her experience within the community, she expressed gratitude for three institutional processes. First, she identified the possibilities embedded within the Equality Story's individualism. If a woman was gifted, Asbury offered opportunities. Hannah observed, "I feel like [the community] wants everybody to be able to be able to use their gifts and to be able to serve the Body of Christ, and if this woman is wonderful at this, then we want to give her opportunity to do that. I've seen a lot of grace here. There are always women up doing things at the chapel. I know that they are intentional about that." Second, Hannah herself had benefitted from this intentionality: "I've felt comfortable to share my ideas and my thoughts, to share my call, or whatever it is, to share my passion, and to be me. I felt like that has been respected." Finally, Hannah had also begun forging her own empowering relationships with other women: "I have some amazing, wonderful roommates. They all have their own specific callings and reasons for being here. We've been support systems for each other. It's just a blessing." Asbury's genderblindness was working. It was providing the practical training, credentials, and confidence she would need to enter vocational ministry. It also yielded a small circle of friends, women with whom she nurtured the warm solidarity of shared experience, even if their solidarity was largely confined to private spaces. Almost without exception, the other women I interviewed echoed Hannah's gratitude. They too benefited from the genderblind practices that facilitate journeys toward church leadership and from warm personal friendships that enhanced their private lives. Within the parameters this chapter has already outlined, public genderblindness and privatized difference work.

But Hannah also expressed considerable frustration. She had had other experiences that Asbury's stories could not—or would not—explain. When I reconnected with her near the end of her time on campus, Hannah reiterated these frustrations with renewed discontent. While she still valued Asbury's contributions to her journey and cherished the friendships she had forged, these things offered her little opportunity to bring her gendered questions into the public space where she worked out her vocational calling. In growing recognition of these limits, Hannah, along with her husband, had begun retreating from her Asbury identity and seeking a more diverse network of Christian voices and ideas. While Hannah may be somewhat unusual in how acutely she felt the tension, she illustrates the complexity of many women's experiences at Asbury. She emerged from several formative years within the community both empowered and disillusioned.

Jessica LaGrone also embodies the contradictions of genderblindness. On one hand, her presence in the community, a fusion of churchly authority and maternal nurture, testifies to the possibilities of genderblindness. On the other hand, that so few Wesleyan women share her story and that frustrated hiring committees still complain about the lack of "good women" candidates speak to the constraints that still bind egalitarian communities like Asbury.[8] Women might sometimes occupy positions with deep influence, but the institution's reluctance to explore the structural and cultural sources of its persistent gender imbalance all but ensures that their voices will remain outnumbered—not only in classrooms but on hiring committees and ethics boards, with decisions on faculty policy, and even regarding the ongoing construction of theology. That LaGrone has navigated this male-centered world with such grace speaks volumes about her own fortitude, cultural insight, and commitment to the Church. The fact that her story is so exceptional also points to the many barriers egalitarian women face. She is the exception that proves the rule.

One of the great entitlements of being an egalitarian man is to declare, "I support women in ministry." This affirmation is not, of course, disempowering to women. In fact, within the evangelical subculture it powerfully signals rejection of complementarianism. Without it, Hannah would not have a vocational path within the Church, and Jessica LaGrone would lose her job. But the declaration's clarity is deceptive. By itself, it fails to acknowledge the constraints that frame women's lives. Nor does it suggest that women's knowledge and experience should actively shape biblical interpretation, leadership structures, and liturgies of worship. It can uphold a genderblindness that, as this chapter has shown, structurally and culturally centers men. Whether this genderblindness is a cover for white masculine hegemony or simply the consequence of good-hearted Christians limited by history and cultural toolkits, the result is the same. In the end, Asbury's genderblind empowerment comes with the same caveat as Southern's promises of complementarian flourishing: it is available to women to the degree that they are willing and able to cooperate with the constraints of stories that center men.

This, after all, is how structural and cultural inequalities work. They are not predicated on individuals' beliefs or desires. Rather, they exist beyond individuals, embedded in institutional systems, upheld by behavioral practices, and normalized through cultural processes. Asbury's leaders do not consciously seek to constrain women. In fact, I suspect that the men—and perhaps some of the women—described in these pages will feel unfairly represented by my suggestions of egalitarian complicity in women's disempowerment. And I will believe them when they say that they really do believe in gender equality and truly want to live and work alongside women as equals. But this is exactly the point. Men's intentions are not all that matters.

These intentions are circumscribed by a much broader patriarchal context not of Asbury's making. Indeed, the inequities that this chapter exposes are less indictments of the seminary itself than indictments of its context. American society sustains structural and cultural inequalities that include intensive motherhood expectations, oppressive beauty standards, hegemonic masculinity, and the second shift. Broader white evangelical culture too often upholds, rather than subverts, them. The problem, then, is not that the seminary innovated these disempowering patterns. It is that students were largely unprepared to recognize them. The same students who waxed eloquent about the equality in the Trinity and New Testament women's countercultural agency had little to say about the social patterns and vulnerabilities of their own context. During my fieldwork, considerations of gendered gaps in pay, institutional voice, and cultural resources, painfully obvious to many churchwomen themselves, including some of Asbury's own, were virtually absent from the campus's public discourse. Likewise, conversations about the damaging effects of hegemonic masculinity on Western culture, churchly leadership structures, the history and practice of international mission, and Christian men themselves were rare. Leaning on the Equality Story and its genderblind tools, students largely confined the problem of patriarchy to first-century household codes and cultural beliefs, neglecting the wounds it continues to inflict on the Church and the world in the twenty-first century.

———

As students walked from their cars toward their classrooms during my fieldwork, they passed colorful banners encouraging them in their efforts. One, hanging from a light post, entreated them to "Attempt something so big, that unless God intervenes, it is bound to fail." Empowered by the Spirit, it seems, no dream is too audacious, no task too grand. Messages like this might not deny the influence of social forces, but they can shut down conversations about the cultural biases, structural priorities, and power dynamics that shape individuals' experiences in any community. Indeed, many dreams will not come true. Personal finances will dictate who can afford a seminary education—and the credentials that come with it—and who cannot. Cultural capital, family connections, and social networks will allow some to become "strong and godly leaders" through generous scholarships and extensive mentoring. Others will navigate vocational callings on their own. Institutions are bound too. Economic realities tie churches and seminaries to donors who influence which theological and cultural markers will become litmus tests for institutional fit. Like Southern and every other institution—whether evangelical or Catholic or mainline, whether religious or secular—Asbury is constrained by its own Western context, one marked by a long legacy of patriarchy. Unacknowledged social forces persist within its own walls—and in the world it claims as its parish.

Conclusion

Leaving women to pursue domestic piety through Bible reading is like forbidding a restive population to carry weapons while giving them unrestricted access to gasoline and matches.
                                                                    —Philip Jenkins

Ira Glass has built an impressive journalistic career around the power of story. His soothing voice and inquisitive empathy have earned him a devoted following among public radio listeners weary of the culture wars. In an interview videotaped in 2012, Glass divulges a bit of his own story, including his religious journey. He recalls his formal Jewish education, his existential questioning in adolescence, and his ultimate rejection of belief in favor of what he calls straight-up atheism. "At some point," Glass says matter-of-factly, "when I was in junior high school, I just found I didn't believe." Yet throughout his story, which features his own Jewish family as well as evangelical Christian proselytizers with whom he plainly disagrees, Glass continues to apply the empathy that defines his journalistic practice. He visibly balks when his interviewer presses, "So what you really think is that they're making all this up. This is just a fantasy in their mind to get through their life." At this, Glass frowns and squirms uncomfortably in his seat. "When you say it that way it sounds so *mean*," he objects. But ultimately he agrees, "Yes, I think it's a reassuring story that they tell themselves." Going on, Glass extends the point to himself. "From my point of view, it's just a made-up story, but . . . the stories I tell myself to get through the day, they're just as unlikely." Then the most compelling point of the interview comes to Glass almost as an afterthought. "Christianity," he says, "is number one for a reason. It is a *great* story."[1] Coming from a master storyteller, this is a powerful statement. It recognizes the potency and beauty of the Christian narrative. The story is concrete enough to hold its shape through two millennia but flexible enough to resonate with faithful believers across centuries, cultures, and continents. It is indeed a great story.

STORY AS FORMATION

It is this story that binds Asbury and Southern. While their narrations of the Christian gospel lead students to very different conclusions about gender, both are powerfully formative—and are so in similar ways. Each appeals to human emotions. Each taps deep desires for meaning and agency. To be sure, students explore the rational logics of systematic theologies, but they are drawn most profoundly to the "beauty of complementarity" and the "freedom of egalitarianism" through appeals to collective memory, meaning, and story. Through these gendered gospels, places like Southern's chapel and Asbury's campus center become *their* places. Venerated leaders—both contemporary and historic—become *their* people. And most importantly, the stories become *their* stories. They bind earth and heaven and make visible the transcendent. "We are makers, tellers, and believers of narrative construals of existence and history," writes Christian Smith, "every bit as much as our forebears at any other time of human history. Furthermore, we are not only animals who make stories, but also animals who are made by our stories. We tell and retell narratives that themselves come fundamentally to constitute and direct our lives" (2010, 151). To be human is to be driven by, even made by, the stories we tell.

In this regard, Southern stands as a remarkable success. Its compelling narratives tightly couple language with embodied practice.[2] Behavioral scripts link everyday actions like hobbies, personal affect, and dietary choices to an authoritative past. The spirit of Conservative Resurgence remains alive within the community, sustained through its enshrinement in the physical spaces of the campus itself. Each time students enter the chapel, they pass the cornerstone containing the Abstract of Principles. When they look up and see the tower atop Norton Hall, they are reminded that their president, whose office occupies the floor just below, orchestrated a resurrection that made their institution great again. The stories live, and they shape lives.

Stories can be as telling in what they omit as in what they contain. In contrast with Southern's overtly gendered spaces, Asbury's campus rings with a story that is largely genderblind and focused on global mission. Vibrantly colored international flags line the hallway of the student center and, on special occasions, the sacred space of the chapel itself. World maps adorn hallways and public areas, monuments to the seminary's mission statement: "The Whole Gospel for the Whole World." The seminary might not be inattentive to gender, but its attention is largely decoupled—in both discursive and embodied practice—from narrations of the community's dominant story. While mission permeates material culture, community event calendars, official curriculum, and informal conversation, gender equity remains mostly confined to the narrow question of who does what in church. It should be no surprise, then, that the students who throw themselves enthusiastically into celebrations of global mission might view gender equity as a rival, rather than a resource, as they prepare to serve the Church around the world. The power of the Mission Metanarrative often overwhelms gendered concerns and forms students into practitioners of a genderblind discourse.

STORY AS PRESERVATION OF POWER

This book is about men's command over institutional, cultural, and religious power. Following Kristin Du Mez's historical treatment of evangelical hegemonic masculinity, whiteness, and Christian nationalism—and Beth Allison Barr's exploration of how "the subjugation of women became the gospel truth"—these chapters offer a glimpse into the everyday cultural processes that sustain patriarchal power. In both cases, the maintenance of power relies heavily on cultural centering. Both Asbury and Southern tell stories that center white married men and decenter other standpoints, interpretative frameworks, and material interests. At Southern, this centering is overt, justified in terms of male headship and neo-Reformed notions of hierarchical order. Asbury's more subtle genderblindness also reinforces masculine authority even in its commitment to egalitarianism. As Sandra Harding explains, "The assumption or advocacy of gender-neutrality marks positions that cannot avoid advantaging men since the distinctively human (or modern, or Chinese, or moral, or historical, or philosophical, etc.) systematically has been constituted in terms of the manly, and vice versa" (1998, 113–114). Egalitarian institutions cannot easily throw off the shackles of patriarchy using genderblindness. This strategy allows gendered power dynamics to masquerade as neutrality, making them even more difficult to recognize, let alone desituate.

Institutional histories can compound this difficulty. Both Asbury and Southern began with the visions of powerful American churchmen, confident in their ideals and driven by their theological convictions. Both institutions have attempted to preserve their traditions as the sands of American culture shift beneath them. Both have weathered denominational battles and negotiated internal conflicts. Both have crafted identity narratives that ground the present in the past and inspire investment in the future. The two seminaries also share a host context. Along with other societal institutions, American seminaries like Asbury and Southern emerged, grew, and adapted within an American context that has long prioritized men. From voting rights to equal pay to the right to workplaces free from sexual harassment, women's rights, interests, and opportunities have long come second to men's. In some ways, the male centering of these white evangelical spaces simply testifies to the inequalities of their context. That the institutions' collective seventeen presidents have all been white American men, for example, largely reflects the fact that, in the decades of their existence, white American men have been the dominant demographic in political structures, legal systems, and economic institutions. Broader culture has encouraged patriarchal patterns within evangelical institutions.

Stories, in other words, do not emerge from nowhere. The ideologies underlying these varying narrations of the Christian gospel derive definition from broader cultural norms. Stories are fashioned by human actors who have a stake in their tellings. As they take shape, religious stories become vehicles of power as much as meaning. They legitimate hierarchies, both overt and subtle, situating them within frames of transcendent meaning and shielding them from critique. Evangelicalism has no monopoly on masculine hegemony or emphasized femininity, but its stories provide these patterns with definition and augment them with divine authority.

It is no accident that the types of people centered by the stories in this book maintain a firm hold on institutional power. The stories justify the right of leaders to proclaim institutional stances on hot-button issues like critical theory and intersectionality, or on what a Christian marriage should look like. These leaders maintain organizational flowcharts that perpetuate structural inequities. They invite special speakers and request that certain songs be sung in chapel. They hire and fire and promote in ways that privilege alumni and those fluent in insider stories, practices that can sideline candidates who bring diverse ideas and critiques. Certainly, leaders like these also invest in stories for the sake of maintaining institutional coherence and the valuable legacies of their traditions. But this too underscores the point: stories are powerful. Leaders guard them for a reason.

But power is not always expressed overtly. In fact, these seminaries' most effective mechanisms of inequality are never articulated out loud. They rely instead on the everyday practices of community life that subtly encourage particular actions and sanction others. Such power functions outside the decisions of high-profile leaders like Mohler and Tennent. It spills out of administrative buildings and occupies the informal spaces of Asbury's cafeteria and the unscripted (but still, paradoxically, very scripted) minutes before a Seminary Wives Institute class begins. It gently nudges Asbury's women away from the red lipstick at the makeup counter and normalizes androcentric language in beloved hymns. It might have deep roots in ivory towers and administrative suites, but beyond them it takes on a life of its own.

Within this maze of power dynamics and cultural reflexes, evangelical women—particularly in egalitarian institutions—live in liminality. They are simultaneously empowered and marginalized. Their voices are both celebrated and constrained. Southern's complementarian women enjoy spaces and resources explicitly centering their journeys and encouraging them to develop their own spirituality and standpoint as women, but they are largely prohibited from applying that standpoint in broader churchly conversations. Asbury's women, in contrast, are welcomed into broader conversations and even churchly power structures, but their voices are often muted and their agency curtailed by unacknowledged limitations. They experience lingering frustrations that they struggle to articulate.

These women are, however, neither passive nor powerless. My emphasis on the disempowering structural and cultural realities that their subcultures impose should in no way detract from women's own creativity and resiliency. Historian Kate Bowler has masterfully explored the many spaces that evangelical women have carved out for themselves within institutions that center men. The women of Asbury and Southern beautifully illustrate many of Bowler's archetypes. The campuses are filled with "homemakers," "preachers," and "counselors" who find agency—and sometimes even authority—in cooperation with the expectations of these roles. The patterns in these women's collective journeys, however, and the insecurities that tug at even the most impressive and successful among them, suggest that their individual flourishing is not the whole story. Evangelical women lack ownership over the stories that govern their identities and limit their agency, effectively requiring marriage, classical femininity (but not too much, at least at Asbury), and domesticity in exchange for legitimacy and voice. If, as Christian Smith argues, to be human is to tell stories, this is an unusually disconcerting kind of dehumanization: to have one's own life bound to a story constructed by others, but with no control over its telling. To live on the edges of the dominant story and to be told that this position is one of "equality" and "empowerment" is not, in the end, very empowering.

While this book is about gender, the centering it illuminates does not take only gendered form. It is best understood as an intersection of social factors, including race, social class, and marital status, that prioritize some and marginalize others. To expect Christian women, for example, to build their identities and social postures around the nurture of home and family while rejecting the work of advocacy, prophetic lament, and activism does not only center men; it also centers whiteness. Images of "traditional," that is, white evangelical wives and mothers of the past baking apple pies and sewing curtains (and in the case of Wesleyans, occasionally filling pulpits) neglect the legacies of Black Christian women. No less evangelical in their beliefs, they have long worked both in and outside the home to support their families. They have exercised prophetic voices in advocacy for their communities, and they have been deeply respected figures in Black churches. As Michael Emerson and Christian Smith conclude, Black Christians use very different cultural toolkits.

These toolkits fuse culture and power. Emerson and Smith also argue that "many race issues that white evangelicals want to see solved are generated in part by the way they themselves do religion" (2000, 170). Two decades—and countless racial reconciliation initiatives—after the publication of *Divided by Faith*, observers of battles over #blacklivesmatter and critical race theory might also question how much these white evangelicals really "want to see [these problems] solved," as the authors originally suggested. That very similar cultural tools emerge as operative in these two seminaries' constructions of gender equity also suggests that broader questions of power lie unresolved within evangelical spaces. Human actors prioritize old tools over new ones not only because they are familiar, but because they are effective at maintaining stability. Southern's nostalgic fixation with order, Asbury's imperative of unity, and both communities' individualism have indeed sustained their religious traditions. They have also sustained the advantages of the men they center. In other words, evangelicalism's sacred stories link not only chains of memory, as Danièle Hervieu-Léger puts it, but also chains of power (2000).

Story as Resistance

As I prepared this manuscript throughout 2020, the scandals of #metoo and #churchtoo had temporarily faded. Confronted by a global pandemic, the American social conscience shifted its attention to systemic racism and cultural polarization. Many evangelicals attended to these same concerns. My social media feeds filled almost daily with theological statements denouncing both racism and #blacklivesmatter, advertisements for e-books promising "biblical" approaches to justice, and bold proclamations of God's intentions for human equality—almost always authored by white pastors, men eager to establish themselves as the "good guys." They wanted to be Christians who got it right this time. Among them were some of the aspiring leaders whose voices fill these pages. I have watched them plant churches, rise in denominational ranks, struggle to identify with rural congregations, and land coveted positions at institutions like Asbury and Southern. They will continue to contend with the aftermath of #churchtoo and new waves of racial and sexual violence that will undoubtedly surface. They will attempt to reimagine the rhythms of faith communities and religious authority structures in the wake of COVID-19. They will navigate evangelicalism's newest cultural battle, this time over critical race theory—an analytic lens, it should be noted, that centers those at society's margins. This book provides a window into their formation as leaders. It illuminates the cultural worlds that have shaped their identities and the stories that have made them who they are. My central contention, that evangelicalism in both its complementarian and egalitarian expressions buttresses constructions of meaning and power that center men, raises weighty questions about evangelicals' capacity to embrace the kind of equity and justice they claim to seek. My less-than-celebratory assessment will be especially burdensome for institutions that are more comfortable with boosterism than lament.

But none of the patterns I have described is inevitable. Among this book's primary arguments is that both religion and gender are constructed. They are "lived" in community and "done" through social practices that appeal to human emotion and to our drive for rootedness and transcendent meaning. Buildings are built and named. Faculty members are hired and fired. Cultural tools are employed and passed over. Most important, stories are made and remade to accommodate changing cultural needs. These constant changes underscore the limitations in human understanding. Tradition both constructs and constrains what we can know. Culture influences what questions we ask and the kinds of answers we seek. As evangelicals read in Paul's first letter to the Corinthians, all humans see only in part. They look through a glass darkly. As this sociological examination of evangelical gender practices shows, however, these limitations are not static. In fact, they are constantly changing, driven by stories that are always in flux. In other words, that which is socially constructed can also be reconstructed. Southern's resurgence/takeover of the 1990s presents a striking—if unusually theatrical—case in point. Dramatic change can and does happen. Evangelicals can, if they choose, tell different stories.

What might this look like in practice? Reimagined motherhood might be decoupled from unpaid labor and privatized identity—and paired instead with resources and prophetic authority. Masculinity might be narrated in ways that uphold Jesus's own example of nonviolence and identification with the marginalized. Better stories could inspire employment practices that minimize the burdens of the second shift and differentiate between men who uncritically claim their entitlement and those who recognize the burdens of patriarchy. In an increasingly globalized world that is only beginning to acknowledge the lasting effects of European colonialism and transatlantic slavery, better stories might also recenter conceptions of mission that merely include, rather than prioritize, the experiences of white American men.

Evangelical elites, eager to do better, will be tempted to marshal success stories from their own traditions. Does Southern Baptist history offer tools that might offset the fact that James P. Boyce also owned other human beings—or that many of its other celebrated historic heroes, including Billy Graham, held views on women that even CBMW would now consider misogynistic? Why yes, Baptist leaders will be quick to answer. Baptists have always preached a God of justice and compassion. That Boyce and Graham misunderstood the particulars of that order need not detract from the rest of their legacy. And what about Wesleyans? Does their tradition offer doctrines or cultural tools that might counterbalance the reality that genderblind egalitarianism props up masculine entitlement as much as it empowers women? Yes, Wesley himself contended that experience should help construct theology. Surely, Wesleyan leaders will say, this legacy provides a perfectly adequate point of departure for movements toward more robust gender equity. They may be right. Internal tools are often valuable assets in pursuits of religious change (Van Dyken 2015). Shaping cultural stories around existing frameworks, however, is not likely to yield meaningful change for those on the margins.

Instead, better stories might center the margins themselves. Evangelicals are not without tools for this task. Their sacred book—which is filled with texts that prophesy and narrate Christ's life, death, and resurrection—contains ancient paradoxes that carry an abundance of interpretive possibilities (Smith 2012). Along with the ideal of order that Southern's reformed churchmen draw from its pages, the Bible also celebrates resistance and reordering (Gutierrez 1988; Powery and Sadler 2016). Its pages might embolden powerful Southern Baptist preachers, but they also prioritize the marginalized and empower the oppressed (de la Torre 2002 Nikondeha 2020). The same text that inspires triumphalism also upholds humility, prophetic lament, and repentance for collective sin (Rah 2015). It is not difficult, then, to imagine a retelling of Asbury's Mission Metanarrative, still grounded in biblical authority, that more intentionally foregrounds gendered inequalities and women's experiences around the world. Examined using cultural tools other than individualism and anticollectivism, biblical narratives might expose rather than obscure the structures that continue to perpetuate women's vulnerability to poverty and violence. They might even prioritize women's own knowledge as a mechanism toward restorative justice. Evangelicals, in other words, need not abandon their Bibles in order to pursue social equity. It is not their Bibles but their cultural tools that hold them back.

But biblical truth must also be translated into contemporary ethics. Evangelicals wishing to interrogate their social practices and cultural biases would do well to pair biblical study with the disciplines of history, sociology, philosophy, and social work. These fields offer valuable tools. They might help evangelicals learn to critically engage their own pasts and to free themselves from what Peter Berger calls the "tyranny of the present" (1969). These ties might also motivate churchly collaboration with social scientists, social workers, and policymakers toward subverting the damaging effects of hegemonic masculinity and emphasized femininity, both in broader culture and in the leadership structures and cultural power dynamics of the Church itself.

Telling better stories will not be easy. As this book has shown, religious communities cling tightly to identity narratives—and with good reason. These stories make sense of the past, present, and future. They hold communities together. To be sure, reconsidering long-held stories and telling new ones can be frightening and even painful. But new acts of imaginative story building offer opportunities for renewal—both religious and social. As Martin Riesebrodt suggests, religious practice does indeed connect human actors to the transcendent, but it also powerfully binds them to human communities burdened and empowered by culture and context. It is perhaps easier to imagine such a reformation beginning with Asbury's egalitarian discourse. But even Southern may find inspiration in the historic call of its own Reformed tradition: *ecclesia reformata, semper reformanda*—the Church reformed, always reforming.

Of the two sets of gendered stories this book has explored, Southern's complementarianism appears to be more coherent. It may also be the more precarious. Should they choose to use them, complementarian women, including those trained at Southern, have valuable tools of resistance at their fingertips: awareness of shared experience, established communication and networking channels, a wealth of biblical literacy, and even organizational resources—tools that Asbury's egalitarians largely lack. Whether these resources will be enough to overcome the potency of the Gospel Story and the formidable structures of power that it supports is anyone's guess. But these women are empowered, if not by institutional leadership structures, then certainly by their own investment in their faith's authoritative text: the Bible itself.

Seeds of resistance are already emerging. In 2021, Beth Moore, undeniably the Southern Baptists' most influential Godly Woman, announced her exit from the denomination. For years she had kept her public ministry within complementarian boundaries by insisting that she was not a preacher but a teacher of women. Nevertheless, she increasingly drew controversy, particularly when, during the Donald Trump's presidency, she began to question the rise of Christian nationalism and right-wing political activism among denominational leaders. After Moore mentioned on Twitter that she would be filling a pulpit on Mother's Day 2019, a host of evangelical leaders took to social media to debate the acceptability of women teaching the Bible. Moore later told Religion News Service, "We were in the middle of the biggest sexual abuse scandal that has ever hit our denomination, and suddenly, the most important thing to talk about was whether or not a woman could stand at the pulpit and give a message."[3] She had reached her limit. "I am still a Baptist," she told RNS, "but I can no longer identify with Southern Baptists." Her commitment to serve her denomination ultimately led her away from it.

Moore's defection illustrates both the strength and the precarity of complementarian hegemony. On one hand, pressure from masculine power brokers pushed her out of the denominational fold, a move that cost her both personally and professionally. But the decision did not cost Moore her voice. As a prototypical (perhaps *the* prototypical) Woman of the Word, she had built a powerful platform that does not require male headship. Her Living Proof Ministries remains a formidable force. Her Twitter feed has more than nine hundred thousand followers—over twice as many as Al Mohler and Russell Moore (who is not related to Beth Moore) combined. Nor does she stand alone. Just months prior to his own exit from the SBC, Russell Moore wrote a letter illuminating the "psychological terror" he had been targeted for during his tenure as president of the Southern Baptist Ethics and Religious Liberty Commission. Not coincidentally, the letter reveals that his attempts to advocate for sexual abuse survivors within the SBC drew the most intense resistance. In perhaps the most remarkable part of the document, Moore recalled a conversation with one of his detractors: "One of these figures told me in the middle of the 2017 debacle, 'We know we can't take you down. All our wives and kids are with you.'"[4]

These wives are products of many of the same cultural processes as Southern's Godly Women. They read many of the same books, embody many of the same spaces, and follow similar scripts. Given the tight networks within evangelical complementarianism and the SBC itself, it is likely that some even attended Southern's Seminary Wives Institute or an equivalent program at a sister seminary. Moreover, it is not only likely but also probable that some are among Beth Moore's nine hundred thousand followers. Bibles in hand, they could present a formidable force, wifely submission notwithstanding. As Philip Jenkins observes, "Leaving women to pursue domestic piety through Bible reading is like forbidding a restive population to carry weapons while giving them unrestricted access to gasoline and matches" (2008, 170).

Godly Womanhood's prescriptions have not entirely kept Women of the Word from discovering alternative stories. Indeed, Godly Womanhood itself has paradoxically provided tools for resistance. Whether these women's alternative stories will gain traction within institutional cultures or be relegated to the margins remains to be seen. But the complementarian women who tell them have one key advantage over their egalitarian sisters: they know the power of their shared experiences. In the end, churchmen like Al Mohler and Owen Strachan may overpower women like Beth Moore. They may reinforce stained glass ceilings. But Moore, operating at increasingly porous borders, has her own power. Godly Men cannot out-Bible a restive Woman of the Word. No one knows and loves the Bible like Beth Moore.

Acknowledgments

I have much for which to be grateful:

For the intellectual community, mentoring, and friendships I found within the University of Notre Dame's Department of Sociology, where I first imagined this project, including David Sikkink, Christian Smith, Jason Springs, Kevin Christiano, Sarah Skiles, Ellen Childs, and Meredith Whitnah. I am especially grateful to Mary Ellen Konieczny and wish she could share my celebration at this book's completion. She is so deeply missed.

For the resources that came from the University of Notre Dame's Center for the Study of Religion and Society and from a Joseph H. Fichter research grant, and for all those who advocated for this project at its various stages, especially George Marsden and Mark Noll.

For the many individuals within both seminary communities who granted access, provided resources, made time for conversation, shared ideas, and answered difficult questions to make this project possible. I especially thank the students whose stories are reflected in these chapters. Without their willingness to share their experiences, there would be no story to tell.

For the embodied communities that have encouraged my growth as a scholar to coincide with my journey of faith. Their rhythms of hospitality, humility, and beauty have, indeed, shaped this project as well. Most of all, for the encouragement of teaching colleagues and conversation partners, especially Henry Zonio and Sarah Bellew.

For my parents, Carl and Sharon Weaver, whose own stories nurtured my curiosity about the world.

For my children, Anna, Benjamin, Jonathan, and Andrew, whose childhoods have been marked by parents writing books and who have been mostly patient, occasionally enthusiastic, and always encouraging.

And most important, for David, who has walked with me through every step of this project and the personal journey that birthed it.

Notes

INTRODUCTION

1. Most of the names used throughout this book are pseudonyms. There are, however, several notable exceptions, including Owen Strachan. I include the names of historic figures (the institutions' founders, for example) and of the men who served in the public roles of institutional presidents during my fieldwork: Albert Mohler (Southern), Timothy Tennent (Asbury), and Owen Strachan (CBMW). I also include the names of several high-profile faculty members and churchly figures, when used to identify their published works or public personas.

2. While the Council on Biblical Manhood and Womanhood (CBMW) is not officially under the institutional control of Southern Seminary, a thick web of connections ties the two institutions. In the CBMW's three decades of history, several of its nine presidents have nurtured close ties with the seminary. Both Denny Burk, who holds the position at the time of this writing, and his predecessor Owen Strachan, who filled the post during my fieldwork, concurrently held faculty positions at Southern and its undergraduate wing Boyce College while heading the organization. In a February 2015 news release, CBMW introduced three new positions, each filled by a Southern student. The organization's executive offices are located just down a hallway and up the large, open staircase from where I often worked in Southern's Honeycutt Campus Center.

3. While the word "male" is most accurately applied to biological sex, rather than gender, conservative evangelical discourse regularly conflates the two assuming a clear, innate gender binary to be a direct reflection of biological sex. Although this assumption itself deserves careful analysis, for the sake of simplicity and since this language and its underlying assumptions is key to evangelical paradigms, my analysis follows their lead in using admittedly imprecise terms like "male headship," except where more precision is directly relevant.

4. Ryan Burge, "America Elected a Female Vice President. Now Will It Put Women in the Pulpit?" (Religion News Service, 2020), https://religionnews.com/2020/12/09/congrats-america-you-elected-a-female-vice-president-now-put-a-woman-in-your-pulpit/.

. 5. Council on Biblical Manhood and Womanhood, "Our History" (n.d.), https://cbmw .org/about/history/.

6. These seemingly contradictory arrangements derive from historically situated cultural tools available within the evangelical milieu (Gallagher 2003; Gallagher and Smith 1999), influenced by early twenty-first-century shifts in ideals of masculinity and family life (Wilcox 2004) and the cultural influence of feminist language and principles (Stacey 1990).

7. Many Christian denominations have, in fact, shifted to policies allowing women access to high-level leadership positions (Chaves 1999). Researchers have explored the paths that women take toward these positions (Zikmund, Lummis, and Chang 1998; Nesbitt 1997; Carroll, Hargrove, and Lummis 1983). Others have charted the victories and difficulties of women in their pursuit of these goals (Charlton 1997) and the persistent bias that often faces them (Nason-Clark 1987; Lehman 1985).

8. Jeremy Weber, "'The Nines' Explains Why So Few Women Are among 100-Plus Speakers," *Christianity Today*, November 12, 2013, https://www.christianitytoday.com /news/2013/november/nines-explains-women-speakers-rachel-held-evans-rhoades.html.

9. Beth Moore, "A Letter to My Brothers," *LPM Blog*, May 3, 2018, https://blog.lproof.org /2018/05/a-letter-to-my-brothers.html.

10. Beth Moore, Twitter, May 11, 2019, https://twitter.com/BethMooreLPM/status/1127 214212462383104?ref_src=twsrc%5Etfw.

11. According to the annual data tables of the Association of Theological Schools, in the 2015–2016 academic year, Southern Seminary's head count (2,754) and full-time-equivalent enrollment (1,438) made it the second largest seminary in the United States (second to Fuller Theological Seminary). Asbury was the fourth largest. Association of Theological Schools, "2015–2016 Annual Data Tables" (n.d.), https://www.ats.edu /uploads/resources/institutional-data/annual-data-tables/2015-2016-annual-data -tables.pdf.

12. These numbers, presumably, include all students, including full-time, part-time, residential, and remote. Southern Baptist Theological Seminary, "Year in Review" (2015), https://www.sbts.edu/2015review/.

13. These counts are taken from a spreadsheet of student information, provided to me by the seminary at the beginning of my fieldwork.

14. It is also important to note that not all evangelicals who claim the complementarian label hold the views of Southern and CBMW. Although the hierarchical perspectives that Southern represents appear to be growing in influence, softer, gentler perspectives, as well as more stringently patriarchal versions, exist as well.

15. Asbury Theological Seminary, "Quick Facts: Seminary at a Glance" (n.d.), https:// asburyseminary.edu/wp-content/uploads/quick-facts.pdf.

16. Language can also intertwine with experience and action in causal ways. Mary Jo Neitz (1987) demonstrates that the shift from more authoritarian conceptualizations of God to descriptions of an affectionate "Father" or even "Daddy" impacted the discourse and experience of participants in the Catholic Charismatic Renewal. Similarly, Meredith Whitnah (2015) explores the ways in which South African Christian groups' anti-apartheid rhetoric translated into activism regarding gender-based violence. Both studies highlight not only the situated nature of discourse but also the potential it has to influence other aspects of social life.

17. My initial samples were drawn at random from student lists provided by each institution. From these spreadsheets, I isolated all residential, graduate-level students enrolled full-time in ministerial or theological training programs (with the exception of an oversample of part-time Seminary Wives Institute students at Southern). The samples were also limited to American citizens (i.e., non–international students) who were in either their first or third year of study and were under the age of fifty. I also drew oversamples of women from each list, as well as through snowball sampling among students in my initial sample at Asbury, in order to better attend to their experiences and voices. At Asbury, my formal interview sample included thirty-two students (eighteen men and fourteen women) and six faculty/administrators (four men and two women). At Southern, I also interviewed thirty-two students (twenty-two men and seven women, plus an additional three women enrolled in the Seminary Wives Institute) as well as seven faculty/administrators (four men and three women). The audio recordings of these formal interviews were transcribed, coded for themes, and analyzed.

CHAPTER 1 — MALE AND FEMALE

1. Denny Burk, "Resolute in a Gender-Confused Culture," *Southern Equip*, October 11, 2013, https://equip.sbts.edu/article/resolute-in-a-gender-confused-culture/.

2. The theological view that Alex referenced, the eternal subordination of the Son within the Trinity (ESS), is not universally adhered to at Southern. It has, in fact, been denounced as a deviation from historical orthodox theology by many evangelical theologians and remains controversial, even at Southern. Nevertheless, one of its most vocal proponents, Bruce Ware, is a professor of Christian theology at the seminary, making his teachings accessible to students like Alex.

3. According to the Gospel Coalition's Confessional Statement, "In God's wise purposes, men and women are not simply interchangeable, but rather they complement each other in mutually enriching ways. God ordains that they assume distinctive roles which reflect the loving relationship between Christ and the church, the husband exercising headship in a way that displays the caring, sacrificial love of Christ, and the wife submitting to her husband in a way that models the love of the church for her Lord. . . . The distinctive leadership role within the church given to qualified men is grounded in creation, fall, and redemption and must not be sidelined by appeals to cultural developments." Gospel Coalition, "Confessional Statement" (2022), https://www.thegospelcoalition.org/about/foundation-documents/#confessional-statement.

4. R. Albert Mohler Jr., "A Clear and Present Danger: Religious Liberty, Marriage, and the Family in the Late Modern Age—an Address at Brigham Young University" (October 21, 2013), https://albertmohler.com.

5. Southern's faculty and students do engage with some scholarship written by egalitarians. For example, several students expressed appreciation for N. T. Wright's New Testament scholarship, which they, presumably, had read as part of their coursework at Southern. It was unclear whether or not most of them were aware of Wright's outspoken advocacy for women in ministry.

6. In 2018 Mohler released a seventy-two-page document titled "Report on Slavery and Racism in the History of the Southern Baptist Theological Seminary." In a letter introducing the report, Mohler takes an uncharacteristically repentant tone writing of Southern Baptist history: "We have been guilty of a sinful absence of historical curiosity.

We knew, and we could not fail to know, that slavery and deep racism were in the story." R. Albert Mohler Jr., "Letter from the President" (Southern Baptist Theological Seminary, December 12, 2018), https://www.sbts.edu/southern-project.

7. Dwight McKissic, "An Open Letter to Dr. Al Mohler and the Southern Baptist Theological Seminary Board of Trustees Regarding Honoring the Founding Slaveholders," *SBC Voices*, July 13, 2020, https://sbcvoices.com/an-open-letter-to-dr-al-mohler-and -the-southern-baptist-theological-seminary-board-of-trustees-regarding-honoring-the -founding-slaveholders/.

8. Kyle J. Howard, Twitter, July 6, 2020, https://twitter.com/KyleJamesHoward/status /1280214255158132736.

9. In the June 29, 2020, episode of "The Briefing," Mohler's regular audio commentary on contemporary events, the president said, "As president of this institution, it is certainly not my intention to remove those names from either the buildings or from the school. There would be no school and none of these buildings would matter but for the founding vision of those original faculty members." R. Albert Mohler Jr., "The Briefing," June 29, 2020, https://albertmohler.com/2020/06/29/briefing-6-29-20.

10. Glen Robins, "Gulf Wars Tweak Southern Baptist Thinking," *Ethics Daily*, April 2, 2003, https://web.archive.org/web/20070928135537/http://www.ethicsdaily.com/article _detail.cfm?AID=2375.

11. The Carver School was transferred to Campbellsville (KY) University.

12. An important exception to the male-centered nature of global missions is the dominance of women's missionary unions in the nineteenth century. In *The Preacher's Wife*, Kate Bowler provides important historical context for these groups as well as for women's contributions to the field of social work in the same era. These articulations of women's agency, Bowler demonstrates, eventually faded into the separate-spheres ideology that drew women toward the home (2019, 33–37).

13. Al Mohler was a prominent voice in the revision. His divergence from the Baptist beliefs of "soul competency" and the "priesthood of the believer" is well known. In the introduction to a 1997 reprinting of E. Y. Mullins's *The Axioms of Religion* (published by B&H Group), Mohler denounced the doctrine of soul competency as "an acid dissolving religious authority, congregationalism, confessionalism, and mutual theological accountability," sentiments he later repeated in his 2000 Founders Day address at the seminary. See Russell Dilday, "An Analysis of the Baptist Faith and Message 2000" (Macon, GA: Center for Baptist Studies, 2001), http://www.centerforbaptiststudies .org/hotissues/dildayfm2000.htm.

CHAPTER 2 — BEARD OIL AND FINE CHINA

1. Individual and group identities often converge in agreed-upon behavioral codes (Schwalbe and Mason-Schrock 1996). These codes develop over time through a group's history and repeated social interactions. Claiming an identity as one's own requires both the successful enactment of these codes and the recognition and appreciation of others' use of them. A code that is not practiced loses its meaning.

2. David Platt, "Genesis 1:26-31" (presented at Southern Baptist Theological Seminary, March 20, 2014).

3. Hershael York, "Rahab and the Rule of Nations" (presented at Southern Baptist Theological Seminary, March 17, 2015).

4. This exhibition of protective, loving male headship can look similar to the heavily relational, affective expressions of masculinity found in broader conservative Protestantism, particularly the "soft patriarchy" explored by Bradford Wilcox (2004).

5. Daniel Montgomery, "A Great Communion and a Great Commission" (presented at Southern Baptist Theological Seminary, March 13, 2014).

6. During the 2014–2015 school year, event themes included "Thrive in Louisville," "Thrive in the Home: Hospitality," "Thrive in Stewardship," and "Thrive in Personal Disciplines." One man whom I interviewed mentioned that his wife did not especially care for the events. She did, he remembered, enjoy touring the Mohlers' personal library, but lost her enthusiasm after an event that focused on painting fall pumpkins. This woman's experience demonstrates that participation in Godly Womanhood's idealized scripts, and the cultural mechanisms that sustain them within Southern's community, is somewhat self-selecting. While SWI wives often expressed enthusiasm for Southern's gendered paradigm, there are other wives, like this one, who distance themselves from its idealized expectations. Wives whose attachment to the institution is secondary have this opportunity to a greater degree than their husbands.

7. Kate Brennen Smith, "The Unseen Ministry of Mary Mohler," *Southern Seminary Magazine* 86, no. 2 (2018), https://equip.sbts.edu/publications/magazine/magazine-issue/fall-2018-vol-86-no-2/unseen-ministry-mary-mohler/.

8. George Schroeder, "Seminary Presidents Reaffirm BFM, Declare CRT Incompatible" (Baptist Press, 2020), https://www.baptistpress.com/resource-library/news/seminary-presidents-reaffirm-bfm-declare-crt-incompatible/.

9. R. Albert Mohler Jr., "Report on Slavery and Racism in the History of the Southern Baptist Theological Seminary" (Southern Baptist Theological Seminary, December 12, 2018), https://www.sbts.edu/southern-project/.

CHAPTER 3 — ALL ONE IN CHRIST

1. Similarly, prioritization of the Holy Spirit and the ungendered nature of its work also framed the elevation of Black Baptist women and holiness women preachers in the late nineteenth and early twentieth centuries (Butler 2007; Stanley 2002).

2. Several of Keener's books have received book awards from evangelical magazine *Christianity Today*, and his *IVP Bible Background Commentary: New Testament* alone has sold over half a million copies. Even the neo-Reformed *Gospel Coalition* reviewed the book in glowing terms. "Keener has not simply compiled material," the review acknowledges, "he has mastered it." Edward Adams, 1996. "The Bible Background Commentary: New Testament," *Themelios* 21, no. 2), https://www.thegospelcoalition.org/themelios/review/the-bible-background-commentary-new-testament/.

3. While my interview sample, representative of the broader community, did not include enough women of color to draw any generalized conclusions about their experiences or beliefs, anecdotal evidence from my interactions with some of these women does suggest that their experiences diverge, likely dramatically, from those of their white peers. Though my interactions with these few women were isolated, they were among the most helpful in clarifying my own understandings of the community's social dynamics, underscoring Michael Emerson and Christian Smith's (2000) finding that Black Christians see structural realities that white evangelicals (and, perhaps, white sociologists) very often miss.

4. Timothy Tennent, "Marriage, Human Sexuality, and the Body: The Marriage Supper of the Lamb (Part IX)" (November 6, 2015), https://timothytennent.com/2015/11/06/marriage-human-sexuality-and-the-body-marriage-supper-lamb-part-ix/.

CHAPTER 4 — MEN, CHURCHWOMEN, AND WIVES

1. This account does not entirely represent the community's memory of the hiring process. Others recalled more or less intentional hopes that a woman would rise to the top of the candidate pool. Regardless, this particular administrator's narration of the choice was clearly crafted to highlight for me the role of the Holy Spirit, rather than human intentions.

2. Since Asbury itself does not grant ordination, the committee in question would have been affiliated with this woman's own denomination, not the seminary itself. Nevertheless, this story illustrates the realities that many of Asbury's women will face as they enter the world of vocational ministry.

3. While the seminary itself offers child care during many of its special events, its programming does not include full-time day care options for students like Abbi who parent young children during their enrollment.

4. These numbers represent the faculty roster published in the seminary's catalogue for the 2013–2014 academic year, during which I began my research. The more recent 2020–2021 edition of the catalogue listed forty-nine faculty members, eight of whom (all men) were in residence at the Florida campus. Of the forty-one members remaining at the Wilmore campus, seven were women.

5. The course catalog does include courses titled "Black History, Theology, and Ministry," "Hispanic History, Theology, and Ministry," and "Hispanic Theology and Social Ethics." When I asked about them, however, I was told that they are offered only on the seminary's Orlando extension campus. They are not required for—or easily available to—students on Wilmore's residential campus.

6. In 2015, the board of thirty members included eight women, three international representatives, and one American person of color. By 2020, these numbers rose to include ten women and five American racial minorities out of thirty-four total members. While this movement likely reflects growing institutional awareness of its current disparities, it left eighteen white American men still in a comfortable majority.

7. While the institution now celebrates a multicultural faculty, its Florida extension campus carries much of Asbury's racial and ethnic diversity, leaving the Wilmore residential faculty list heavily white as well as masculine.

8. Christine Pohl's and Nicola Hoggard Creegan's book *Living on the Boundaries* opens with a thoughtful and extensive treatment of the many assumptions and connotations embedded in the question "where are all the good women?"

CONCLUSION

1. "Ira Glass—Atheist," YouTube, October 10, 2012, https://www.youtube.com/watch?v=QYLGc-w1jrM&t=29s.

2. This close relationship also brings into question the ubiquity of the often-cited "loose coupling" of gender policy and practice (Chaves 1999). The experiences of women in both of these seminary communities, in some ways, appear to defy official policy, lending a degree of support to the notion. Nevertheless, the stories that bind discourse

and practice within the communities themselves are much more tightly woven than notions of loose coupling alone would suggest.

3. Bob Smietana, "Bible Teacher Beth Moore, Splitting with Lifeway, Says 'I Am No Longer a Southern Baptist,'" *Religion News Service*, March 9, 2021, https://religionnews .com/2021/03/09/bible-teacher-beth-moore-ends-partnership-with-lifeway-i-am-no -longer-a-southern-baptist/.

4. Russell Moore, "Russell Moore to ERLC Trustees: 'They Want Me to Live in Psy- chological Terror." *Religion News Service*, June 2, 2021, https://religionnews.com/2021 /06/02/russell-moore-to-erlc-trustees-they-want-me-to-live-in-psychological-terror/.

References

Acker, Joan. 1992. "From Sex Roles to Gendered Institutions." *Contemporary Sociology* 21 (5): 565–569.

Ammerman, Nancy. 1990. *Baptist Battles: Social Change and Religious Conflict in the Southern Baptist Convention*. New Brunswick, NJ: Rutgers University Press.

———. 2014. *Sacred Stories, Spiritual Tribes: Finding Religion in Everyday Life*. Oxford: Oxford University Press.

Barr, Beth Allison. 2021. *The Making of Biblical Womanhood: How the Subjugation of Women Became Gospel Truth*. Grand Rapids, MI: Brazos Press.

Bartkowski, John P. 2004. *The Promise Keepers*. New Brunswick, NJ: Rutgers University Press.

Bem, Sandra Lipsitz. 1993. *The Lenses of Gender: Transforming the Debate on Sexual Inequality*. New Haven, CT: Yale University Press.

Berger, Peter. 1967. *The Sacred Canopy: Elements of a Sociological Theory of Religion*. Garden City, NY: Doubleday.

———. 1969. *A Rumor of Angels: Modern Society and the Rediscovery of the Supernatural*. Garden City, NY: Doubleday.

Bowler, Kate. 2019. *The Preacher's Wife: The Precarious Power of Evangelical Women Celebrities*. Princeton, NJ: Princeton University Press.

Brekus, Catherine, ed. 2007. *The Religious History of American Women: Reimagining the Past*. Chapel Hill: University of North Carolina Press.

Butler, Anthea D. 2007. "Unrespectable Saints: Women of the Church of God in Christ." In *The Religious History of American Women: Reimagining the Past*, edited by Catherine Brekus, 161–183. Chapel Hill: University of North Carolina Press.

Carroll, Jackson W., Barbara Hargrove, and Adair T. Lummis. 1983. *Women of the Cloth: A New Opportunity for the Churches*. San Francisco: Harper & Row.

Charlton, Joy 1997. "Clergywomen of the Pioneer Generation: A Longitudinal Study." *Journal for the Scientific Study of Religion* 36 (4): 599–613.

Chaves, Mark. 1999. *Ordaining Women*. Cambridge, MA: Harvard University Press.

Chodorow, Nancy. 1978. *The Reproduction of Mothering: Psychoanalysis and the Sociology of Gender*. Berkeley: University of California Press.

Chong, Kelly H. 2008. *Deliverance and Submission: Evangelical Women and the Negotiation of Patriarchy in South Korea.* Cambridge, MA: Harvard University Press.

Collins, Patricia Hill. 1990. *Black Feminist Thought: Knowledge, Consciousness, and the Politics of Empowerment.* New York: Routledge.

Coltrane, Scott. 1989. "Household Labor and the Routine Production of Gender." *Social Problems* 36 (5): 473–490.

Connell, R. W. 1987. *Gender and Power: Society, the Person, and Sexual Politics.* Stanford, CA: Stanford University Press.

———. 1995. *Masculinities.* Berkeley: University of California Press.

Coontz, Stephanie. 1992. *The Way We Never Were: American Families and the Nostalgia Trap.* New York: Basic Books.

Cothen, Grady. 1993. *What Happened to the Southern Baptist Convention: A Memoir of the Controversy.* Macon, GA: Smyth and Helwis.

Dayton, Donald W. 1976. *Discovering an Evangelical Heritage.* Grand Rapids, MI: Baker Books.

de Beauvoir, Simone. 1953. *The Second Sex.* New York: Knopf.

de la Torre, Miguel A. 2002. *Reading the Bible from the Margins.* Maryknoll, NY: Orbis Books.

Deutsch, Francine M. 2007. "Undoing Gender." *Gender & Society* 21 (1): 106–127.

Dilday, Russell. 2001. "An Analysis of the Baptist Faith and Message 2000." Center for Baptist Studies. http://www.centerforbaptiststudies.org/hotissues/dildayfm2000.htm.

Dowland, Seth. 2018. *Family Values and the Rise of the Christian Right.* Philadelphia: University of Pennsylvania Press.

Du Mez, Kristin Kobes. 2020. *Jesus and John Wayne: How White Evangelicals Corrupted a Faith and Fractured a Nation.* New York: Liveright.

Eldredge, John. 2001. *Wild at Heart: Discovering the Passionate Soul of a Man.* Nashville, TN: T. Nelson.

Emerson, Michael O., and Christian Smith. 2000. *Divided by Faith: Evangelical Religion and the Problem of Race in America.* Oxford: Oxford University Press.

England, Paula. 2005. "Emerging Theories of Care Work." *Annual Review of Sociology* 31:381–399.

Farnsley, Arthur E. 1994. *Southern Baptist Politics: Authority and Power in the Restructuring of an American Denomination.* University Park: Pennsylvania State University Press.

Fenstermaker, Sarah, and Candace West. 2002. *Doing Gender, Doing Difference: Inequality, Power, and Institutional Change.* New York: Routledge.

Flowers, Elizabeth. 2012. *Into the Pulpit: Southern Baptist Women and Power since World War II.* Chapel Hill: University of North Carolina Press.

Gallagher, Sally. 2003. *Evangelicals Identity and Gendered Family Life.* New Brunswick, NJ: Rutgers University Press.

Gallagher, Sally, and Christian Smith. 1999. "Symbolic Traditionalism and Pragmatic Egalitarianism: Contemporary Evangelicals, Families, and Gender." *Gender and Society* 13 (2): 211–233.

Geertz, Clifford. 1973. *The Interpretation of Cultures.* New York: Basic Books.

Gilman, Charlotte Perkins. 1911. *The Man-Made World: or, Our Androcentric Culture.* New York: Charlton.

Griffith, R. Marie. 2000. *God's Daughters: Evangelical Women and the Power of Submission.* Berkeley: University of California Press.

Gutierrez, Gustavo. 1988. *A Theology of Liberation: History, Politics, and Salvation.* Maryknoll, NY: Orbis Books.

Harding, Sandra. 1998. *Is Science Multicultural.* Bloomington: Indiana University Press.

Hartmann, Heidi I. 1979. "The Unhappy Marriage of Marxism and Feminism: Towards a More Progressive Union." *Capital and Class* 3 (2): 1–33.

Hassey, Jeannette. 1986. *No Time for Silence: Evangelical Women in Public Ministry around the Turn of the Century.* Grand Rapids, MI: Academie Books.

Hatch, Nathan O. 1989. *The Democratization of American Christianity.* New Haven, CT: Yale University Press.

Hays, Sharon. 1996. *The Cultural Contradictions of Motherhood.* New Haven, CT: Yale University Press.

Hervieu-Léger, Danièle. 2000. *Religion as a Chain of Memory.* Rutgers, NJ: Rutgers University Press.

Hochschild, Arlie, and Anne Machung. 1989. *The Second Shift.* New York: Avon Books.

Hunt, Susan. 1993. *Spiritual Mothering: The Titus 2 Model for Women Mentoring Women.* Atlanta: Christian Education.

Ingersoll, Julie. 2003. *Evangelical Christian Women: War Stories in the Gender Battles.* New York: New York University Press.

Jenkins, Philip. 2008. *The New Faces of Christianity: Believing the Bible in the Global South.* Oxford: Oxford University Press.

Johnson, Elizabeth. 1992. *She Who Is: The Mystery of God in Feminist Theological Discourse.* New York: Crossroad.

Jones, Nikki. 2010. *Between Good and Ghetto: African American Girls and Inner-City Violence.* New Brunswick, NJ: Rutgers University Press.

Katzenstein, Mary Fainson. 1999. *Faithful and Fearless: Moving Feminist Protest Inside the Church and the Military.* Princeton, NJ: Princeton University Press.

Keener, Craig. 1992. *Paul, Women, and Wives.* Peabody, MA: Hendrickson.

———. 2013. "Why It Is Important to Study the Bible in Context." Bible Background. https://craigkeener.com/why-it-is-important-to-study-the-bible-in-context/.

Klatch, Rebecca. 1987. *Women of the New Right.* Philadelphia: Temple University Press.

Lehman, Edward C. 1985. *Women Clergy: Breaking through Gender Barriers.* New Brunswick, NJ: Transaction.

Mahmood, Saba. 2005. *Politics of Piety: The Islamic Revival and the Feminist Subject.* Princeton, NJ: Princeton University Press.

Majors, Richard, and Janet Mancini Billson. 1992. *Cool Pose: The Dilemmas of Black Manhood in America.* New York: Simon & Schuster.

Mathews, Donald. 1965. *Slavery and Methodism.* Princeton, NJ: Princeton University Press.

McGuire, Meredith B. 2008. *Lived Religion: Faith and Practice in Everyday Life.* New York: Oxford University Press.

Messner, Michael A. 1990. "Boyhood, Organized Sports and the Construction of Masculinities." *Journal of Contemporary Ethnography* 18 (4): 416–444.

Mullins, E. Y. 1997. *The Axioms of Religion.* Nashville: B&H.

Nason-Clark, Nancy. 1987. "Ordaining Women as Priests: Religious vs. Sexist Explanations for Clerical Attitudes." *Sociological Analysis* 48:259–273.

Neitz, Mary Jo. 1987. *Charisma and Community.* New Brunswick, NJ: Transaction.

Nesbitt, Paula D. 1997. *Feminization of the Clergy in America: Occupational and Orga-nizational Perspectives.* New York: Oxford University Press.

Newman, Harmony D., and Angela C. Henderson. 2014. "The Modern Mystique: Insti-tutional Mediation of Hegemonic Motherhood." *Sociological Inquiry* 84:472–491.

Nikondeha, Kelly. 2020. *Defiant: What the Women of Exodus Teach Us about Freedom.* Grand Rapids, MI: Eerdmans.

Noll, Mark A. 1995. *The Scandal of the Evangelical Mind.* Grand Rapids, MI: Eerdmans.

Payne, Leah. 2015. *Gender and Pentecostal Revivalism: Making a Female Ministry in the Early Twentieth Century.* Basingstoke: Palgrave Macmillan.

Pohl, Christine, and Nicola Hoggard Creegan. 2005. *Living on the Boundaries: Evangeli-cal Women, Feminism and the Theological Academy.* Downers Grove, IL: InterVarsity Press.

Powery, Emerson B., and Rodney S. Sadler. 2016. *The Genesis of Liberation: Biblical Inter-pretation in the Antebellum Narratives of the Enslaved.* Louisville, KY: Westminster John Knox Press.

Pyke, Karen D., and Denise L. Johnson. 2003. "Asian American Women and Racialized Femininities: 'Doing' Gender across Cultural Worlds." *Gender & Society* 17 (1): 33–52.

Rah, Soong-Chan. 2015. *Prophetic Lament: A Call for Justice in Troubled Times.* Down-ers Grove, IL: InterVarsity Press.

Reskin, Barbara. 1993. "Sex Segregation in the Workplace." *Annual Review of Sociology* 19:241–270.

Ridgeway, Cecilia L. 2011. *Framed by Gender: How Gender Inequality Persists in the Mod-ern World.* New York: Oxford University Press.

Ridgeway, Cecilia, and Shelley J. Correll. 2004. "Unpacking the Gender System: A The-oretical Perspective on Gender Beliefs and Social Relations." *Gender & Society* 18 (4): 510–531.

Riesebrodt, Martin. 2010. *The Promise of Salvation: A Theory of Religion.* Chicago: Uni-versity of Chicago Press.

Risman, Barbara J. 2004. "Gender as a Social Structure: Theory Wrestling with Activ-ism." *Gender & Society* 18 (4): 429–450.

Russell, A. Sue, and Jackie Roese. 2018. *Relationshift: Changing the Conversation about Men and Women in the Church.* Whittier, CA: Cross Perspectives.

Schussler-Fiorenza, Elisabeth. 1983. *In Memory of Her: A Feminist Theological Reconstruc-tion of Christian Origins.* New York: Crossroad.

Schwalbe, Michael, and Douglas Mason-Schrock. 1996. "Identity Work as Group Process." *Advances in Group Processes* 13:113–147.

Smith, Christian. 1998. *American Evangelicalism: Embattled and Thriving.* Chicago: Uni-versity of Chicago Press.

———. 2010. *What Is a Person? Rethinking Humanity, Social Life, and the Moral Good from the Person Up.* Chicago: University of Chicago Press.

———. 2012. *The Bible Made Impossible: Why Biblicism Is Not a Truly Evangelical Read-ing of Scripture.* Grand Rapids, MI: Brazos Press.

Smith, Dorothy. 1987. *The Everyday World as Problematic: A Feminist Sociology.* Boston: Northeastern University Press.

Smith, Timothy. 1965. *Revivalism and Social Reform: American Protestantism on the Eve of the Civil War.* New York: Harper & Row.

Stacey, Judith. 1990. *Brave New Families.* New York: Basic Books.

Stagg, Evelyn, and Frank Stagg. *Women in the World of Jesus.* Philadelphia: Westminster Press.

Stanley, Suzie Cunningham. 2002. *Holy Boldness: Women Preachers' Autobiographies and the Sanctified Self.* Knoxville: University of Tennessee Press.

Swidler, Ann. 1986. "Culture in Action: Symbols and Strategies." *American Sociological Review* 51:273–286.

Tolbert, Malcolm. 1984. "Frank Stagg: Teaching Prophet." *Perspectives in Religious Studies* 11 (4): 1–16.

Van Dyken, Tamara. 2015. "Always Reforming? Evangelical Feminism and the Committee for Women in the Christian Reformed Church, 1975–1995." *Church History and Religious Culture* 95:495–522.

Weber, Max. 1956. *The Sociology of Religion.* 4th rev. ed. Boston: Beacon.

West, Candace, and Don H. Zimmerman. 1987. "Doing Gender." *Gender & Society* 1 (2): 125–151.

Whitnah, Meredith C. 2015. "Faith and the Fragility of Justice: Religious Responses to Gender Based Violence in South Africa." PhD dissertation, Department of Sociology, University of Notre Dame, Notre Dame, IN.

Wigger, John H. 2009. *American Saint: Francis Asbury and the Methodists.* Oxford: Oxford University Press.

Wilcox, Bradford. 2004. *Soft Patriarchs, New Men.* Chicago: University of Chicago Press.

Wills, Gregory A. 2009. *The Southern Baptist Theological Seminary, 1859–2009.* New York: Oxford University Press.

Witherington, Ben III. 1984. *Women in the Ministry of Jesus: A Study of Women's Attitudes to Women and their Roles as Reflected in His Early Life.* Cambridge: Cambridge University Press.

Wuthnow, Robert. 2011. "Taking Talk Seriously: Religious Discourse as Social Practice." *Journal for the Scientific Study of Religion* 50 (1): 1–21.

Zikmund, Barbara Brown, Adair T. Lummis, and Patricia Mai Yin Chang. 1998. *Clergy Women: An Uphill Calling.* Louisville, KY: Westminster John Knox Press.

Index

About the Author

Lisa Weaver Swartz holds a PhD from the University of Notre Dame. She lives in the bluegrass region of Kentucky, where she teaches sociology and writes about religion and gender.